SOCIOLOGICAL APPROACHES TO HEALTH AND MEDICINE

SOCIAL ANALYSIS
A Series in the Social Sciences
Edited by Richard Scase, University of Kent

Sociological Approaches to Health and Medicine

Myfanwy Morgan, Michael Calnan and Nick Manning

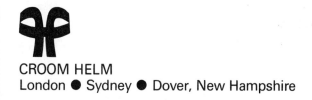

CROOM HELM
London ● Sydney ● Dover, New Hampshire

© 1985 Myfanwy Morgan, Michael Calnan and Nick Manning
Croom Helm Ltd, Provident House, Burrell Row,
Beckenham, Kent BR3 1AT
Croom Helm Australia Pty Ltd, First Floor,
139 King Street, Sydney, NSW 2001, Australia

British Library Cataloguing in Publication Data

Morgan, Myfanwy
    Sociological approaches to health and medicine.
    1. Social medicine
    I. Title   II. Calnan, Michael   III. Manning, Nick
    362.1'042   RA418

    ISBN 0-7099-1705-8
    ISBN 0-7099-3514-5 Pbk

Croom Helm, 51 Washington Street,
Dover, New Hampshire 03820, USA

Library of Congress Cataloging in Publication Data

Morgan, Myfanwy.
    Sociological approaches to health and medicine.
    1. Social medicine. I. Calnan, Michael.
    II. Manning, Nick P. III. Title. (DNLM: 1. Sociology,
    medical. W 322 M847S) 362
    RA418.M67   1985   362.1'042   85-48015

    ISBN 0-7099-1705-8
    ISBN 0-7099-3514-5 Pbk

Phototypeset by Words & Pictures Ltd,
Thornton Heath, Surrey
Printed and bound in Great Britain by
Biddles Ltd, Guildford and King's Lynn

CONTENTS

PREFACE

The sociological study of the determinants of health and responses to illness and the characteristics of medical institutions has grown rapidly over the past three decades and now forms one of the largest specialised areas of sociology. The growth of the specialism has in turn been shaped and promoted by a number of forces, including both the general developments in sociology itself and the interests and concerns of policy-makers and health professionals. Of particular importance has been the increasing emphasis since the early 1960s on the need for research to assist in the planning and provision of health services. Other influences include the widespread recognition of the role of social and psychological factors in determining patterns of service use and responses to treatment, and of the social and psychological dimensions of health itself, together with the increasing number of people surviving into old age, many of whom have chronic conditions posing problems of adjustment and requiring long term management and care.

Although the sociology of health and medicine has now produced a substantial literature, the contributions of different sociological perspectives and methodological approaches often remain rather disparate, posing problems both for the general reader and for the student requiring a broad overview. This book aims to bring together the different approaches which have characterised sociological research in this area and to show how they have contributed to an understanding of selected topics and may result in various prescriptions for health policy.

One important tradition has been research of an empirical, quantative nature, which has tended to focus on problems defined by epidemiologists and policy makers. Initially, sociologists adopting this approach were primarily concerned to identify the characteristics of groups that differed in their incidence of disease, and to establish statistical associations between specific social traits in the population and a number of health behaviours, such as smoking, the taking of self-prescribed medicine and the utilisation of health services. Empirical, survey oriented research continues to provide detailed, quantitative data on a whole array of issues related to the social aspects of medical care. However, an important development in recent years has been the expansion of the scope of this research, reflecting the broadening of approaches to health. Thus, areas of study have included the nature and measurement of disability and handicap, the social and psychological components of health state, the effects of life events and of social ties on health, and the role of self help groups. This new emphasis, together with the increasing recognition that sociological research should not be limited to medical concerns, but instead study the whole range of knowledge, belief, organisation, and institutions associated with health and illness, has been reflected in a change in title of the specialism. Traditionally referred to as medical sociology, it is now commonly described as the sociology of health.

Complementing work of an empirical, quantitative nature has been the development of theoretically based research, which often has as its primary goal the furthering of our understanding of social institutions and social processes. Functionalism originally formed the dominant perspective, and was particularly influential in the development of the concept of the sick role (see Chapter 2), and in analyses of the nature of the professions (see Chapter 4), and the organisation of hospitals (see Chapter 5). During the last decade, research has been characterised by a multiplicity of theoretical perspectives reflecting the developments in mainstream sociology. Of particular importance has been the application of marxist and feminist analyses, which have provided powerful critiques of the dominant approach to health and the organisation of medical practice. This has been reviewed in the discussion of medicine as a form of social control (see Chapter 1), psychiatric hospitals (see Chapter 5), NHS policy options (see Chapter 6), and gender and class inequalities in health (see Chapter 7). The recent application of a social constructionist approach, although involving a different theoretical orientation, has similarly questioned the scientific objectivity of modern medicine and shown how medical knowledge can be viewed as a social product, rather than as technical, asocial, and value-free (see Chapter 1). Complementing these macro level analyses has been the development of micro level studies based on an interpretive approach. This approach puts more emphasis on subjective meanings and the grounding of concepts in the experience of respondents to provide a greater understanding of social inter-actions and responses, and has been particularly influential in the study of the consultation between doctor and patient (see Chapter 4), in the understanding of lay health beliefs and responses to illness (see

Chapter 3), and the hospital as negotiated order (see Chapter 5).

Rather than systematically applying each theoretical approach to every area, the main approaches that have contributed to particular areas of study are presented. Similarly, the topics covered constitute only a few selected areas of sociological research, and were chosen both as representing major issues in the field and for their particular interest to the authors.

The book arose from an undergraduate course in the Sociology of Medicine introduced by MM at the University of Kent and later taught with MC and NM. Although a collective enterprise, individual authors assumed primary responsibility for particular chapters (MC for Chapters 3 and 4; NM for Chapters 5 and 6), while MM (Chapters 1, 2, 7, and 8) acted as coordinator. We owe a debt to a number of people including our secretaries for their efficient typing, and our students for their enthusiasm and questions which encouraged this venture. We would also like to thank our colleagues for their helpful suggestions, and are particularly grateful to David Armstrong, Mick Bloor, Margot Jefferys and Richard Scase for commenting on draft chapters. Naturally, we alone are responsible for the final product.

Myfanwy Morgan
Michael Calnan
Nick Manning

1 HEALTH, DISEASE AND MEDICINE

The role of healers has traditionally been to promote health by ridding the body of disease. Health is thus equated with the absence of disease, which can be viewed in general terms as manifesting itself as disturbances in the structure or functioning of the body. Despite this common approach, differences exist in the dominant theories of disease both among societies and over time. This is reflected in the varying measures taken both to prevent disease and to restore health to the diseased individual, which range from attempts to placate the gods to the diagnosis and therapy characteristic of modern scientific medicine.

This chapter first describes the main theories of disease that have formed the basis of medical practice in different societies and historical periods. It then examines the implications and limitations of the biomedical model, which forms the dominant approach to health in western industrial societies, and considers analyses of the social forces that shape and promote this approach to health provided by the medicalisation thesis, social constructionism, and marxist perspectives. Finally, sociological research concerned with the development of measures of health which emphasise functioning and subjective feelings and which form an alternative to traditional medical indicators is described.

Theories of Disease

The dominant theories of disease causation prior to the rise of modern scientific medicine have been broadly divided into personalistic and naturalistic systems (Forster and Anderson, 1978). A personalistic system is one in which the sick person is viewed as the object of aggression or punishment directed against him, with illness being caused by the active, purposeful intervention of a sensate agent. This agent may be a supernatural being (a deity or God), a non-human being (such as a ghost ancestor or evil spirit), or a human being (a witch or sorcerer). The tendency for simple societies to provide supernatural explanations of illness reflects the dominance of the spirit world in nearly every aspect of life, and serves to explain aspects of the world beyond their limited control. Despite this emphasis on the supernatural, in most societies some natural causes of disease are recognised, such as burns, overeating, and falls. The inhabitants of Papua, New Guinea, for example, distinguish between 'illness without cause', which is never attributed to sorcery or the action of spirits, and 'illness of the settlement', which is more serious and generally caused by sorcery or spirits (Hamnett and Connell, 1981). Ridding a person of disease in personalistic systems, as in modern Western medicine, involves identifying the cause of the disease, with specific forms of treatment being related to etiological beliefs. The causes of disease include the violation of social norms or taboos, the intrusion of a spirit or disease-object invested by evil spirits, or soul loss brought about by the evil magic of a sorcerer. If disease is thought to be caused by a person's violation of tribal norms, thus offending his ancestors or gods, appeasement may be made in ritualistic form or by some kind of social restitution. In contrast, if sickness is seen as a case of malevolent sorcery, counter-sorcery and other spells are employed. In view of this emphasis on the supernatural and on the need for magical divinatory powers to identify the source of ill health, shamans or witchdoctors are generally required to rid people of disease.

In naturalistic systems ill health is explained in impersonal terms as the effect of a lack of balance of the basic body elements. This balance may be upset from without or within by natural forces, such as heat, cold, or sometimes, strong emotions. The three main naturalistic systems are those of humoral pathology, Ayurvedic medicine, and traditional Chinese medicine.

Humoral pathology of Ancient Greece was concerned with the balance between four 'humors': black bile, yellow bile, blood, and phlegm. According to the writings of Hippocrates, these four humors made up the constitution of the human body and caused its pain and health. 'Health is primarily that state in which these constituent substances are in correct proportion to each other, both in strength and quantity, and are well mixed. Pain occurs when one of these substances presents with a deficiency or an excess, or is separated in the body and not mixed with the others' (Chadwick and Mann, 1950). Ayurvedic medicine, found in India and adjacent countries, showed many similarities with humoral pathology. It recognised the existence of three humors or 'dosha' (phlegm, bile, and wind or flatulence), and regarded good health as obtaining when the three doshas are in equilibrium. Traditional Chinese medicine was similarly based on the need to obtain an equilibrium between the yin and yang. The yin represents all negative elements including cold, dampness, and darkness, and the yang all positive elements, including, sun, fire, heat, and light. Excessive yang was thought to cause fever, because of its heat, and excessive yin, because of its coldness, to produce chills.

Rather than requiring the shaman or diviner with magical powers, naturalistic aetiologies require a physician or herbalist who knows the medicine and other treatments that will restore the body's equilibrium. Furthermore, his aid will be sought, not so much to find out what has happened, or the causes of the problem, but rather to relieve the symptoms.

Up to the late eighteenth century European medicine was characterised by a variety of approaches and beliefs about disease, including elements of both personalistic and naturalistic belief systems. Medical knowledge at this time has thus been described by Jewson (1975) as made up of a 'chaotic diversity of schools of thought'. However, it was generally believed that disease resulted from an underlying state of the body, and that each individual had a particular 'pathological career' because of his/her own individual circumstances and situations. As Jewson (1975) states: 'Each man suffered from his own peculiar combination of factors which accounted for his physiological disequlibrium.'

From the early nineteenth century a change in the conceptualisation of disease occurred with the rise of the scientific paradigm and doctrine of specific aetiology. This views diseases as having specific causes which can be identified and treated, as with the tubercule bacillus being the cause of tuberculosis. Diseases thus came to have specific labels. Between 1897 and 1900 the causative agents of at least 22 infections were discovered and increasingly other diseases produced by physiological lesions or which reflected deficiencies in growth or metabolic processes were identified (Dixon, 1978). With the establishment of specific disease categories, the main task of diagnosis became one of approximating the patient's pathology to an established disease category through observation, physical examination, and the study of various biochemical parameters, such as height, weight, haemoglobin and blood pressure, heart rate and so on. Diseases thus came to be regarded as universal, in the sense that disease symptoms and processes are expected to be the same in different historical periods and in different cultures and societies.

The dominance of scientific medicine, with its emphasis on specific disease categories and processes, resulted in the body being considered as the analogue to a machine whose individual parts could be examined and treated without the rest of the body being affected, for the mind and the body were no longer regarded as closely associated. Thus, increased attention was paid to the results of complex diagnostic tests and much less to the patient's feelings, emotions and perception of their problem. This approach to promoting health through identifying and curing specific diseases has also resulted in health and illness being seen in individualistic terms, with the causes of illness and responsibility for health largely residing with the individual. The main emphasis is therefore one of promoting health through medical intervention, which is directed either towards raising an organism's natural resistance to specific agents (frequently through immunisation), or towards restoring to normal an identified or presumed disturbance of the biological system (usually by chemical, surgical or physical intervention). This biomedical interventionist model forms a contrast to what can be regarded as the social model of health, which emphasises the social, economic and environmental causes of illness and has led to a large proportion of health service resources being devoted to high technology medicine, and to the central role played by the hospital in the health care system, whereas the promotion of health through social policies and legislative measures to receive a more healthy environment has tended to receive less emphasis.

Despite the dominance of the biomedical model, some elements of earlier approaches to disease causation are still evident in lay theories of disease (see Chapter 3). There also exist large numbers of healers whose approach to health differs from conventional medical practice, and, in many cases, is derived from different conceptions of disease. In Britain, in 1980, there were estimated to be 7,800 full and part-time professional alternative healers, consisting of acupuncturists, chiropracters, herbalists, homoeopaths, hypnotherapists and osteopaths, as well as about 20,000 men and women who practise spiritual or religious healing (Helman, 1984).

The biomedical model, although forming the cornerstone of modern medicine, is subject to increasing criticisms of both a pragmatic and a more fundamental nature. Writers adopting a pragmatic approach do not question medical definitions of disease, but regard the prevailing medical model as too limited in its approach to disease. In particular they question the assumed effectiveness of Western scientific medicine, and draw attention to the influence of social and psychological factors on the aetiology and distribution of disease. In contrast, writers adopting a more fundamental approach question a basic assumption of the scientific paradigm that medicine is objective and value-free, and draw attention to the social forces influencing approaches to disease and the application of disease labels.

Biomedicine: A Limited Approach

The Effectiveness of Medicine

The dominance of the prevailing interventionist approach to health is generally justified and distinguished from previous approaches in terms of its effectiveness in controlling disease and improving the health of the population. The substantial decline in the death rate, which coincided with the spread of the biomedical model and specific aetiology theory of disease, is generally regarded as evidence of the effectiveness of this approach to health. For example, between 1851 and 1971 the death rate in England and Wales declined from 22.7 per 1,000 population to 12.5 per 1,000 population. It has been estimated that 76 per cent of this decline was due to a reduction in mortality from infectious diseases, such as tuberculosis, cholera, diphtheria, and dysentery (McKeown, 1979).

The beginning of a serious debate on the contribution of medical intervention to this decline in mortality is commonly associated with the work of Talbot Griffiths (1967). After examining certain medical activities associated with the eighteenth century, particularly the growth of the hospital, dispensary, and midwifery services, additions to knowledge of physiology and anatomy, and the introduction of smallpox inoculation, Griffiths concluded that they made important contributions to the observable decline in mortality at that time. Subsequent work has challenged this conclusion. Of particular importance is McKeown's (1979) historical demographic study of the reasons for the decline in mortality in England and Wales, which took the form of a detailed investigation of the rate of decline and possible factors influencing the decline of each of the major causes of death. McKeown, a doctor by training, concluded from his careful historical research that the importance of medical intervention in contributing to the substantial decline in mortality has been overemphasised. To support this conclusion he points out firstly that the number of drugs known to be effective was quite small prior to the development of the sulphonamide drugs in the 1930s. Secondly, most of the decline from infectious disease appears to have occurred before effective immunisation, antibiotics, and chemotherapy became available, with the possible exception of diphtheria and smallpox. For example, the BCG vaccination for respiratory tuberculosis was not available until 1954, by which time the majority of the decline in mortality from TB had already occurred (see Figure 1).

Figure 1.1: Respiratory Tuberculosis: Mean Annual Death Rates (Standardised to 1901 Population), England and Wales

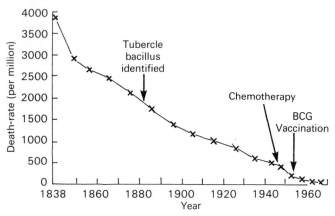

Source: McKeown (1979), p. 92.

McKeown identified the main determinant of the decline in mortality from infectious diseases from the mid nineteenth century as being the improvement in nutrition. This was brought about by an increased food supply, which occurred both as a result of advances in agricultural methods and through increased wheat imports. Improved nutrition not only reduced deaths directly attributable to starvation but also had the effect of increasing the resistance of the population to infectious diseases. Secondly, environmental measures, such as better sanitation and a purer water supply — introduced following Chadwick's Report on the Sanitary Condition of the Labouring Population in 1842 — served to reduce risks of exposure to disease, and especially to typhus, typhoid, and the water-borne diseases. The third major factor identified by McKeown as contributing to the decline in mortality was the limitation in family size. This occurred in the nineteenth century, and was important in ensuring that the growth of population did not outstrip the food supply, and thus in maintaining the effects of improved nutrition in combating infectious disease.

Restraint on reproduction also had a direct effect on mortality through virtually eliminating infanticide, which made a major contribution to the decline in deaths from non-infectious causes.

In contrast to the widely held belief in the effectiveness of medical measures in contributing to the decline in mortality from infectious disease, McKeown's analysis thus identifies social, environmental, and behavioural changes as forming the major influences. As he states:

> If we group together the advances in nutrition and hygiene as environmental measures, the influences responsible for the decline of mortality and increased expectation of life were environmental, behavioural and therapeutic. They became effective from the eighteenth, nineteenth and twentieth centuries respectively, and their order in time was also that of their effectiveness. (p. 78)

McKeown's interpretation is based on the experience of England and Wales, although he has examined its credibility in four European countries: Sweden, France, Ireland, and Hungary. He concludes that a similar pattern holds for these countries, with social and environmental changes forming the predominant cause of the decline in mortality rates (McKeown *et al.*, 1972). This view is shared by the McKinlays (1977) whose analysis of data for this century suggests that medical intervention has had a relatively limited impact on the overall decline in mortality in the United States since 1900.

McKeown extrapolated from his historical analysis to the present day, to suggest that curative medicine can be expected to make only a small contribution to the prevention of sickness and death. This is because the two main causes of death in modern industrial countries now consist of a small number of conditions which are relatively intractable, notably congenital abnormalities, and a large number of potentially preventable conditions for which there is no effective cure, such as heart disease and cancer of various sites. Taking the view that external influences and personal behaviours form the predominant determinants of health, McKeown thus advocates a shift in the balance of interests and resources from curative medicine to caring for the sick and disabled, and to the prevention of disease, to ensure that those born free of congenital disability remain well, apart from minor morbidity, until late life. However, whereas in the past the predominant health problems were associated with poverty in the form of malnutrition, defective hygiene and bad living and working conditions, he suggests the main causes of preventable mortality in modern industrial countries are chiefly those associated with affluence. McKeown thus regards changes in personal behaviours (in relation to diet, exercise, tobacco, alcohol, drugs, etc.) as being more important than non-personal measures (in terms of measures to combat food deficiency and to control hazards, etc.) in preventing disease in modern industrial countries.

McKeown's assessment of the contribution of medical intervention has been criticised by the medical profession for considering its impact solely in terms of mortality rates. This is because mortality rates provide a limited measure of health and take no account of improvements in the quality of life and the reduction in pain and suffering, thus overlooking the primary contribution of much modern medicine, such as hernia repair, hip replacement, and various types of drug therapy. Furthermore, the contribution of medicine is not limited to medical intervention, with doctors often being influential in promoting the environmental reforms which have had a major impact on health. Despite these reservations, many nevertheless agree with McKeown's broad conclusions regarding the need for a change in emphasis from curative medicine to care and prevention.

Although often agreeing that the prevention of illness forms the key to improving the health of the population, there is less consensus regarding the priorities that should be assigned to different forms of prevention. McKeown places particular emphasis on the importance of education and increasing knowledge as a means of preventing disease in modern industrial societies, through changing personal behaviours (e.g. smoking, drinking). In contrast to this essentially individualistic approach is the view that the greater priority should be given to achieving changes in the social environment, and especially in working and living conditions, so as to reduce risks of exposure to physical hazards and mental stress. A second criticism of McKeown's analysis focuses on his lack of attention to the problems of achieving a change in the dominant approach to health. McKeown appears to believe that once the emphasis on curative medicine has been demonstrated to be based on a mistaken assumption of its effectiveness, the medical profession and scientific community will respond by re-orienting approaches to health. However, this overlooks the vested interests built into professional structures and institutional arrangements which serve to maintain the dominance of curative medicine at the expense of a greater emphasis on care and preventive activities. This is clearly illustrated by the way in which the achievement of national targets for the provision for dependency groups is continually frustrated at the local level, as resources continue to be directed to the acute sector (see Chapter 4).

Preventive activities which pose the least threat to prevailing institutional structures and which are most compatible with the biomedical model include the use of preventive services, such as antenatal and screening programmes to detect disease and disorders or risk factors at an early stage, and rehabilitation programmes designed to increase functioning and reduce disability. In addition programmes designed to educate the population to adopt healthy life styles in terms of patterns of consumption and exercise, although going beyond the traditional medical model, share a similar emphasis on individual functioning, behaviour and responsibilities. In contrast, preventive measures which seek to improve the environment and reduce risks of exposure to physical hazards and mental stress reflect an essentially social approach to health. This approach requires changes beyond the health care sector, which may often conflict with other interests and goals (Renaud, 1978). The nature of these conflicts and groups involved is, however, subject to differing interpretations. Pluralist approaches stress the importance of diverse interest groups (including doctors, industry and lay pressure groups) in promoting or resisting legislation and other social, economic and environmental measures which aim to improve the health of the population. For example, the raising of taxes on cigarettes and alcohol, with the aim of reducing consumption of these products, requires people to accept what are often perceived as immediate disbenefits in return for the promise of long-term and uncertain benefits. Similarly, legislation barring certain products or requiring particular behaviours raises questions of individual freedom, as with the recent legislation to make the wearing of seat belts in the front seats of cars compulsory in Britain. Attempts to control the consumption of products harmful to health, and to reduce environmental pollution, or the use of certain toxic substances in manufacturing processes, also place considerable economic costs on governments and industry. In contrast to the view that diverse interest groups shape policies, including the introduction and enforcement of preventive health measures, is the view that a single group or class exerts an overwhelming influence. This approach is most clearly illustrated by marxist analyses, which suggest that the dominance of curative medicine and the failure to control hazards at the workplace can be explained in terms of the interests of the ruling class and the needs of the capitalist economic system (*see* pp. 35–7).

Alternatives to improving health through paying greater attention to the prevention of disease have been put forward by Cochrane (1976) and Illich (1975). Cochrane acknowledges the limited effectiveness of medical intervention. However, unlike McKeown, he maintains a commitment to the primacy of this approach. Relying on scientific knowledge as the key to progress, Cochrane advocates the use of Randomised Control Trials (RCTs) to compare the effects of treatment and non-treatment, or different forms of treatment, in situations where this approach is not ruled out on social, moral, or technical grounds. This reliance on RCTs to assess the effectiveness of medical procedures reflects his belief that the lack of effectiveness of medical intervention stems not so much from the inappropriateness of this approach, as from the application of procedures which have little value, with many procedures resting on habit, custom, tradition, and privilege rather than on rationality.

Illich (1975), like Cochrane, doubts the value of expanding the role of medicine. This reflects his belief that medical intervention may not merely be of little clinical value but may also have harmful effects. These harmful effects are regarded as being not only of a clinical nature but also of extending to the social sphere, through reducing people's autonomy and increasing their dependency on medical care (see pp. 23-4). This reflects Illich's view of health, of which an integral component is the individual's freedom, autonomy, and ability to cope with pain, sickness, and death. He thus believes that better health can only be achieved by a reduction in the activities of organised medicine and returning responsibility for health to individuals. Illich would thus regard a greater emphasis on prevention, at least to the extent that it involves an increase in preventive activities by doctors, as having the adverse effect of extending the medical sphere.

Social Factors and Disease Processes

The specific aetiology or monocausal model of disease, which was associated with the germ theory and the rise of modern scientific medicine, has now been replaced by a multi-causal model. This model, which is compatible with McKeown's analysis, suggests that the physical and biological causes of disease often work in relationship with a variety of other causes, including social and environmental factors, rather than a specific disease being the product of a single risk factor. For example, environmental pollution and poor physical development may interact to produce respiratory disease among children. A third model of disease causation, which complements and supplements the monocausal and multicausal models of disease, is the model of general susceptibility. This model, which has gained increasing prominence over the last ten years, shifts the emphasis away from the identification of the causes of specific diseases to look at why certain groups in the population are more susceptible to disease in general. For example, it focuses on explaining why married people have lower death rates from a wide variety of causes than unmarried people, and why churchgoers have lower mortality rates than non-churchgoers. One approach is to explain differences in susceptibility to disease in psychosomatic terms as arising from differences in exposure to stress. This may in turn increase susceptibility to well recognised pathogens as well as giving rise to a broad range of somatic and psychiatric illness. However, although stress appears to increase risks of morbidity and mortality, many people who experience stressful events do not suffer increased risks of illness. This has led to the incorporation of the notion of the protective effect of support, which appears to mediate the adverse health effects of stressful life events. This stress-support theory of susceptibility to disease is examined in Chapter 8. Another approach is to explain differences in the distribution of disease in sociosomatic terms, as arising from differences in the ways of life (patterns of consumption, etc.) of different groups in the population. This may again give rise to a wide range of conditions and contribute to the inequalities in health experienced by social classes and other social groups which differ in their life styles and behaviour (see Chapter 7).

Recognition of the pervasive effects of social and psychological factors on health has not only influenced the epidemiological study of the causes of disease, but has also resulted in a broadening of definitions of health to encompass social and emotional elements, rather than being restricted to clinical criteria. One of the earliest definitions to acknowledge these broader dimensions of health was contained in the constitution of the World Health Organisation in 1948, which defined health in idealistic terms as 'a complete state of physical, mental and social well-being and not merely the absence of illness'. More recently a large number of health status measures have been developed, which define health in terms of social functioning or emotional states, and thus serve to complement clinical definitions in terms of pathological abnormalities (see pp. 37-41).

Despite the increasing recognition of the social determinants of health, and of its social, psychological and physical dimensions, the dominant approach to health continues to be disease oriented. Thus, although non-health services measures, such as the control of environmental hazards and campaigns to promote a healthy life style, have received increased attention, the main emphasis continues to be on promoting health through medical intervention. Explanations of the continued dominance of the medical model, as it developed in the nineteenth century, must thus focus on the interests of the medical profession and the needs of the wider society in maintaining an interventionist approach to health, and on the forces which shaped and gave rise to the biomedical model.

Biomedicine: A Social Construct

The development of the biomedical model is generally presented in terms of the triumphant progress of science and scientific discoveries. Modern medicine is thus viewed as distinct from previous approaches not only in terms of its effectiveness, but also as being objective and value-free. This is generally associated with the view that the disease entities identified by modern medicine constitute natural objects which exist prior to and independent of their isolation or designation by doctors (Wright and Treacher, 1982). However, this assumption that society and medical knowledge are distinct, since medicine is a product of science which forms an asocial and independent body of knowledge, is questioned by both the medicalisation thesis and by social constructionist and marxist approaches, which offer differing explanations of the forces shaping medical knowledge and approaches to health.

Medicalisation

The expansion of modern medicine into areas which were not previously within the medical sphere, such as the increasing medical intervention in pregnancy and childbirth and the definition of depression and alcoholism as medical problems, has been attacked for increasing medical control through expanding its sphere of influence. However, views differ as to the motive power responsible for such medicalisation. This section considers the way in which both the interests of the medical profession and the functional needs of society can be viewed as giving rise to medicalisation and thus of shaping and promoting definitions of disease. (The role of male professional interests in defining women as sick and in need of medical attention is considered in Chapter 7.)

The sociology of professions emphasises the autonomy enjoyed by professional groups and identifies knowledge as a powerful asset for groups to use to attain and maintain power (see Chapter 4). For example, Freidson (1970) suggests that the medical profession's power to control what constitutes health and illness has been used to extend the medical monopoly over areas of life and behaviour which were not traditionally the concern of the medical profession. The medical profession is thus seen from this perspective as using its ability to create illness to extend its professional dominance, with its authority deriving from its professional status and claims of competence. Such claims are based on appeals to the scientific basis and effectiveness of medicine — claims which have only recently been seriously challenged. However, in recent years the role of the medical profession in defining conditions as requiring medical intervention, and thus as coming within the sphere of medical control has been vigorously challenged, especially in relation to pregnancy and childbirth. For example, Oakley (1980) in her study of childbirth shows how medical criteria and choices regarding place of delivery and the use of various forms of intervention in the delivery process are increasingly replacing personal choices and serve to reduce individual control. Furthermore, although justified on medical grounds, the adverse effects of some forms of intervention in terms, for example, of risks of depression, are often overlooked.

In contrast to the view that doctors act in their own self-interest in extending the sphere of medical intervention is the view that doctors assume a responsive role. This approach is taken by Illich (1976), who regards the increasing medicalisation of life as forming an inevitable product of broader social processes. Illich identifies industrialisation as the motive force that gives rise to the professionalism and bureaucratisation of all major institutions in modern industrial society, including the educational and the medical spheres, and regards this as having adverse consequences for the individual. Although he attributes the medicalisation of life to the characteristics of the industrial system, rather than to the characteristics of the medical profession, the medical profession is nevertheless seen as instrumental in this process. In particular, he believes that the medical profession has not only duped the public into believing it has an effective and valuable body of knowledge and skills but has also created a dependence on doctors and medicine which has taken away people's ability to engage in self care. As a result, 'the medical establishment has become a major threat to health'. Illich termed the process of dependence created by the medical bureaucracy 'iatrogenesis', and saw this occurring on three levels. Firstly, Illich describes 'clinical iatrogenesis' as where the medical profession has hidden the fact that many modern-day medical treatments are ineffective and even dangerous in that they can produce serious side-effects. Secondly, there is 'social iatrogenesis', which has been created by the expansionist activities of the medical profession, who in turn have responded to the needs of increasing industrialisation. This has created a population of consumers who are passive and dependent on the health care system. Examples of the medicalisation of life given by Illich are the increasing dependence on drugs, the medicalisation of the life span where old age has been reinterpreted as a geriatric problem, and the medicalisation of prevention, where consumer dependence on professional medical remedies, such as annual check-ups, has been fostered. Thirdly, the medicalisation of life is so significant that it has produced an even stronger effect, which Illich terms 'structural iatrogenesis', where individuals have been deprived of their ability to cope with pain, sickness, and death in a meaningful way. Illich's solutions to the problems of 'iatrogenesis' emphasise the need to educate the public so as to re-equip them with the knowledge of how to cope with illness and death, and to deprofessionalise medicine through political action.

Whereas Illich regards the medicalisation of life as resulting from the increasing professionalisation and bureaucratisation of medical institutions associated with industrialisation, other writers regard medicalisation as serving particular interests in society. One approach is to regard the medicalisation of life, and the role of doctors in this process, as serving to control disruptive behaviour. This approach is taken by Szasz (1961, 1971) in relation to the use of the label 'mental illness'. Szasz distinguishes between what he terms Contractual Psychiatry, which he describes as a voluntary exchange between doctor and patient in which the patient is free to initiate and terminate the encounter, and Institutional Psychiatry, which he regards as psychiatrists paid by and acting on behalf of the state. Institutional psychiatry, which forms the focus of Szasz's critique, is regarded as creating a collectivist society by applying the label of mental illness to behaviours which do not conform to the norm. Such people are then treated within the medical setting, and often subject to involuntary incarceration in mental hospitals, ostensibly for their own benefit. Szasz argues that the label of mental illness being used in this way serves as a means of coercive social control, or extralegal punishment, and draws a parallel between the use of psychiatric concepts in the modern world and the belief in witchcraft in the Middle Ages. He argues that the change from religious to medical beliefs and forms of control did not take place because of the realisation that persons who were supposed to be heretics were actually mentally sick. Instead, it reflected the wider transformation of a religious ideology into a scientific one. As a result, 'medicine replaced theology, the alienist the inquisitor, and the insane the witch'.

Szasz does not deny that people have what he terms 'problems of living'. His main concern is that problems of human conduct may have a moral and political character, which is masked by medical labels. He thus advocates that 'real' (i.e. biological) illness should be separated from 'mythical' mental illness and that the disease concept should only apply to 'demonstrable bodily illness' and not to mere deviations in behaviour.

Szasz's views concerning the use of psychiatric labels as a form of social control is regarded as particularly applicable to the involuntary hospitalisation of political dissidents. However, Szasz's thesis has been heavily criticised as a general critique of psychiatry and psychiatric concepts.

Szasz places great emphasis on the role of psychiatry in involuntary hospitalisation, although this has always been a minority procedure in Britain and its significance has declined over the last 30 years. It is also argued that Szasz's exaggerates the differences between mental and physical illness. With regard to diagnosis, it is widely accepted by the medical profession that 'symptoms' of schizophrenia are not bodily complaints, but instead are framed as a result of the application of the disease model to people's talk, conduct, beliefs, and communicated experiences. However, the traditional psychiatric view is to regard 'symptoms' of schizophrenia as evidence of some underlying disease process, reflecting some structural imbalance in brain biochemistry, whose specific form and cause are yet to be fully understood,* rather than the terminology of disease being used as a form of social casting and social control.

---

* Psychiatric theories can be broadly divided into biological theories, which emphasise the presence of underlying biological/biochemical causes of psychiatric disorders, and psychological theories, which emphasise the importance of interpersonal relationships and in general reduce mental illness to some problem of maladaptive behaviour. However, most psychological theories acknowledge that biochemical changes do occur and share the belief that psychiatric disorder is fundamentally a problem of the mind. In this chapter the traditional psychiatric approach is taken to refer to all theories which regard mental disorder as having an actual or potential biological/biochemical cause, and as being a problem of the individual mind, although differing in their analysis of the underlying causes of this disturbance. For a detailed discussion of the application of the medical model to mental illness see Wing (1978).

Furthermore, as Ausubel (1962) notes, the diagnoses of physical and mental illness share certain common features. For example, whereas the variability in psychiatric diagnosis is commonly cited as evidence that mental and physical illness are of a different order, the diagnosis and response to physical conditions can also be seen to be surrounded by great cultural variability and influenced by subjective judgements. As he points out, even allegedly objective signs, such as blood pressure and pulse rate, have their subjective aspects, being subject to emotional influence. In addition, there are situations in which ethical norms are invoked in relation to physical illness, including abortion and the preferential saving of the mother's life as against the foetus's life. Ausubel thus argues that Szasz overstates the differences in the diagnoses and interpretation of mental and physical illness, and claims, in contrast to Szasz's contention, that there is no inherent contradiction between using cultural and ethical norms as criteria of mental illness but also of employing medical treatment measures.

A further argument often advanced in support of the traditional psychiatric perspective and as challenging the 'myth' of mental illness is that the efficacy of physical treatments (drugs, ECT, etc.) is a justification of labelling and treating behavioural deviations as mental illness. This, however, poses the question of what we call effective. Can, for example, tranquilisers be regarded as a cure because they enable people to handle emotions by reducing their capability for emotion. Furthermore, to the extent that conditions have a known organic cause, Szasz would regard them as coming into the category of physical illness.

Whereas Szasz's thesis is criticised by psychiatrists for over-emphasising the social nature of the disease category 'mental illness', writers adopting a social constructionist perspective regard Szasz's analysis of the social nature of disease as too limited. This is because whereas Szasz believes that mental illness is socially constructed, he appears to regard physical illness as forming a biological reality which is independent of human construction and interpretation. In contrast, the way in which physical conditions are perceived and interpreted can be viewed as determined by social processes and as reflecting the nature of the prevailing clinical gaze (pp. 28–33).

The question of who exerts control through defining disruptive behaviour as a sign of mental illness is answered by Szasz as being 'society's power holders'. An alternative view is taken by Morgan (1975), who, adopting an interpretive approach, suggests that the labelling of people as mentally ill occurs not because of the exercise of political power but because such people are in fact unintelligible to their own friends and families, as well as to the powerful. He suggests the reason for madness being encapsulated as an illness with the public's approval is that unintelligibility is particularly threatening to the dominant twentieth-century value of rationalism. Unintelligible behaviour thus requires the powerful antidote of medicine, which represents the embodiment of twentieth century scientism.

Another response to the question of why medicalisation occurs and who initiates the medicalisation of behaviour is that taken by Conrad (1981). Like Szasz, he is concerned with the way in which medicine may be used as a form of social control. However, whereas Szasz regards the state as using medicine as a form of social control, Conrad emphasises the variety of interests which may be served by defining disruptive behaviours as coming within the medical sphere, and identifies four basic conditions for medicalisation to occur. These are: (1) the traditional forms of control are inefficient or unacceptable; (2) there exists some medical form of control by, for example, drugs or surgery; (3) the problem must be associated, even if in a rather ambiguous sense, with some underlying organic cause; and (4) the medical profession must accept the deviant behaviour as being within its jurisdiction, while the greater the benefit of medicalisation to established institutions the more likely it is to occur. Conrad illustrates how the development of the medical label of hyperkinesis fulfilled these conditions. Long before this diagnostic label was introduced, restlessness, extreme activity, not paying attention, and not sitting still were defined as deviant behaviour in school classrooms and in the family, and were usually controlled by corporal punishment. As this form of control came to be seen as unacceptable, this 'maladjusted' behaviour became increasingly medicalised. The process of medicalisation was aided, firstly, by the availability of biophysical explanations about the cause of hyperactivity, suggesting that it had some organic base. Secondly, the medical profession (or at least some segments) was willing to accept that hyperactivity was a disease, which might be medically treated and would thus fall within its jurisdiction. Thirdly, according to Conrad, the medicalisation of 'maladjusted' behaviour also served the interests of schools because it provided an effective means of reducing the disruptiveness of such children. In addition, the interests of families were served, for by viewing such behaviour as having an organic origin, parents were relieved from guilt. Other vested interests in this form of treatment for deviance also became increasingly evident as the pharmaceutical industry began to promote drug therapy for hyperkinesis.

Conrad's analysis is important in drawing attention to the multiple interests which may be served by medicalisation, and hence groups involved. Nevertheless, there are questions as to whether other conditions fit so neatly into his general framework. For example, mental handicap is treated as a medical condition, although no effective treatment is available. In addition, whereas children are likely to have little influence on medical labelling, adults whose behaviour is subject to medical labelling may form a powerful force in attempts to resist both individual labelling and the social construction of disease labels (see Chapter 2). An important example of the successful demedicalisation of behaviour is provided by the official demedicalisation of homosexuality by the American Psychiatric Convention, when in December 1973 delegates voted that homosexuality was no longer to be considered an illness. A major factor precipitating this decision is thought to be the politicisation of the issue by the gay liberation movement.

The medicalisation thesis has formed a powerful critique of medicine in its role as an agent of social control, and in reducing the freedom of the individual. However, views are seen to differ on questions of the forces primarily responsible for medicalisation and the scope for individual or collective resistance to medical labelling. In particular, the presentation of the role of the medical profession in this process is seen to range from one of the actively encouraging medicalisation to one of merely facilitating medicalisation. Blaxter (1978) further suggests that even when a condition has been accepted as a medical category, doctors may often be reluctant to use this diagnosis if no effective prescription for action exists, as is currently the case with alcoholism.

Social Constructionism

This approach takes the view that disease labels are social constructs much further than does the medicalisation thesis. Rather than regarding special cases, such as hyperkinesis and mental illness, as socially constructed, it regards all medical categories as social constructs which define and give meaning to certain classes of events. Sedgewick (1982) captures the essence of this approach when he points out that natural events, such as fractures of bones, ruptures of tissues, and tumorous growths, do not constitute illnesses, sicknesses, or diseases prior to the human social meanings we attach to them. As he explains:

The fracture of a septuagenarian's femur has, within the world of nature, no more significance than the snapping of an autumn leaf from its twig: and the invasion of a human organism by cholera germs carries with it no more the stamp of 'illness' than does the souring of milk by other forms of bacteria (p. 30).

Social constructionism does not imply that disease is imaginery but rather that medicine is a form of social practice, which observes, codifies, and understands these sufferings. Concepts of disease thus have no necessary, transhistorical, universal shape, and reflect a particular way of viewing the world.

Foucault (1973) has played a major role in the development of a social constructionist approach to the history of medical knowledge. Through his analysis of the history of medical ideas in France, he shows how the changing medical approach and views of disease can be seen as a product of particular ways of viewing the body, or what he terms the 'clinical gaze'. Foucault identifies a major change in the dominant approach to disease as occurring in France towards the end of the eighteenth century. He describes this change as being promoted by the establishment of a new type of clinic, which formed in response to widespread medical quackery and malpractice following the revolutionary period. The clinic provided a centre for medical training, and was characterised by a new medical approach, which emphasised clinical observation, bedside teaching, and physical examinations. This approach was promoted by the invention of the stethoscope in 1819 and by developments in pathology, which meant that disorders became localisable to a distinct point within the body, rather than being seen as before in terms of more general disturbances of the body. The clinic formed an ideal setting for the development of this new clinical gaze for it provided for the close observation in one place of large numbers of patients. The admission of poor people as patients also meant they were able to show little resistance to what could be construed as an invasion of their privacy associated with the close examination and observation required by this new approach to medicine.

With time the new clinical gaze, with its emphasis on detailed clinical observation and examination of the inner workings of the body, was viewed as giving rise to a belief in the solid invariate reality of the body. As a result, a new anatomical atlas began to emerge which involved a different way of viewing the body. As Armstrong (1983) explains:

The anatomical atlas directs attention to certain structures, certain similarities, certain symptoms and not others, and in so doing forms a set of rules for reading the body and for making it intelligible. In this sense the reality of the body is only established by the observing eye that sees it.

Foucault suggests that the analysis of the way the body is seen, described and constructed, might be called 'political anatomy'. It is political because the changes in the way the body is viewed are not the consequences of some random effect or progressive enlightenment, but are based on certain mechanisms of power. Foucault described the medical view of the body which developed in the eighteenth century as reflecting wider changes in European society. Thus the view of the body as 'something docile that could be surveilled, used, transformed and improved' was increasingly evident not only in the clinical examination in the hospital but also in the test in the school and the military inspection in the barracks. It was also reflected in the changes that occurred in criminal punishment, with criminals being subjected to continuous surveillance behind the high walls of the prison, rather than being subjected to torture, pillorying, and public display.

The modern medical approach with its emphasis on the close scrutiny of the inner workings of the body developed later in Britain than in France. This has been largely attributed to the slower growth of hospitals, and hence of the opportunities available for close observation of large numbers of patients (Waddington, 1973). Ackerknecht (1967) provides an estimate by Bourchardat that Paris hospitals received 37,743 patients in 1807 and 53,000 in 1827, whereas Abel-Smith (1967) estimated that there were only about 3,000 patients in British hospitals in 1800; and in 1851, 7,619 hospital patients were enumerated in the census. As in France, the growth of hospital based medicine in Britain was accompanied by the development of a reductionist gaze which sought to pinpoint pathology within the body. This was consolidated in the twentieth century with the development of more investigative procedures and greater specialisation as different parts of the body were investigated separately.

Armstrong (1983) in *The Political Anatomy of the Body* suggests that the twentieth century has been characterised not only by a consolidation of the reductionist gaze but also by the development of a new clinical gaze. This has involved the extension of the medical gaze beyond the confines of the body to its social sphere. He identifies the Tuberculosis Dispensary as forming a major influence on the development of this extended medical gaze. The dispensaries set up in the early years of this century formed a new way of organising health care, for they provided not only a centre of diagnosis and treatment but also screened people in close contact with TB patients and coordinated home visits, checks, and follow-ups. They thus radiated out into the community, identifying and mapping diseases. As a result, diseases came to be geographically pinpointed in the community, while superimposed on this geographical outline was the map of the social body on which a network of social relationships was plotted through the screening and observation of patients contacts. This approach established the social origins and distribution of tuberculosis and other conditions which until the closing decades of the nineteenth century had been seen as disease of individual bodies and of environmental neglect rather than of social contact and social space. The dispensary also established the social origins and character of new medical problems, such as venereal diseases and infant mortality. The dispensary thus justified its existence by establishing the social basis of disease and itself as the appropriate mechanism to combat it. By its activities the dispensary also served to raise consciousness in the community, which in turn enabled the intrusion of surveillance to be more easily justified. In other words, the activities of dispensaries both reflected and contributed to the new extended way of viewing diseases.

Whereas dispensaries had engaged in a rudimentary form of population surveillance, the scope for community surveillance increased with the emergence of the social survey during the 1940s as a specialised tool with more refined techniques. This enabled detailed information about illness to be collected and analysed for large population groups in relation to environmental factors, age and occupation. Developments in survey techniques were thus prompted by and contributed to the more precise mapping of disease in terms of the social body, and served to distribute the effects of the new disciplinary gaze throughout society. In a similar way, earlier developments in clinical techniques (e.g. the stethoscope and X-rays) had enabled disease to be localised with greater precision to specific anatomical locations and contributed to the development of hospital based medicine.

Armstrong (1983) has traced how this new medical gaze, or way of seeing the nature and source of disease, served to create new specialities, such as geriatrics and paediatrics, by drawing attention to what came to be viewed as particular problems of these groups. For example, the survey drew attention to the extent and nature of chronic health problems among the elderly, and to the way in which illness comes on insiduously with less obvious symptoms in old people. This in turn underlined the importance of organising comprehensive services for old people involving clinical, social, preventive and remedial measures. The survey further suggested that the dichotomy between the normal and the abnormal was less applicable to old people, who instead could be assigned to a point in a conceptual space characterised by a 'continuous distribution curve' of health. This led to the growth of the science of the study of ageing (gerontology), which had the important effect of underpinning geriatrics as a discipline separate from general medicine.

The changed medical gaze, including an increased emphasis on the patient's social context and experiences, is viewed not only as giving rise to new specialities but also as influencing the development of long-established specialities. For example, from the 1950s general practice came to be dominated by an emphasis on the need to understand the patient's psycho-social context. This was associated with an increasing acceptance of the role of the general practitioner as friend, guide and counsellor, and of emotional illness, stress and psychotherapy as integral elements of general practice (Armstrong, 1983). Of particular importance in integrating the social-psychological and physical aspects of illness in general practice was the work of Balint (1967), who argued that an adequate diagnosis could be made only through a consideration of the patient's social and psychological state. He thus viewed the traditional search for a localised pathological lesion as forming only part of clinical practice, and emphasised the importance of identifying the possible social and psychological causes of ill health in terms of the patient's emotions, and personal and family life. This new approach involved greater attention being paid to the patient's marital history and 'social history', or the experiences of personal worries, adjustments and disappointments. As a result:

> The patient's view was no longer a vicarious gaze to the silent pathology within the body but the precise techniques by which the new space of disease could be established; illness was transformed from what was visible to what was heard. (Armstrong, 1984, p. 339)

The greater attention paid to what patients say and feel began to characterise medicine from the mid 1960s and still competes with the traditional more limited role assigned to the patient's view. However, in contrast to the belief that this change forms the product of humanistic enlightenment, Armstrong regards it as a necessary element of the new medical gaze, which required the doctor to understand the patient as a person.

The study of the broad development and changes in medical knowledge and practice from a constructivist perspective has been complemented by the detailed study of specific disease categories. This in turn shows how disease categories can be viewed as a socially generated way of grouping phenomena which endows them with particular significance. For example, Yoxen (1982) contends that genetic disease, although appearing particularly strongly anchored in material reality, incorporates socially derived assumptions about resemblance and dissimilarity. He also demonstrates how the development of genetic diseases as a broad category was closely linked with the advancement of particular professional groups and with changes in the form and availability of medical services.

The permeation of medicine and specific disease categories by social forces is not viewed from a constructionist perspective as meaning that medicine is unscientific, but rather that both medicine and science are essentially social enterprises. Thus the aim is not to search for a timeless medicine unaffected by its social context, but rather to recognise and understand the inherently social nature of medicine. Nevertheless, this approach, like the medicalisation thesis, serves to challenge the claim that modern medicine is technical, asocial and value-free.

Functionalism and Marxism

These approaches both focus at a societal level on the fit between prevailing definitions and approaches to health and the needs of society or its ruling class. However, whereas marxist analyses view the biomedical model as shaped and supported by the economic and political system, functionalism tends to accept the biomedical model as technical and asocial and focuses on its role in reducing the disruptive effects of illness in society.

The functional importance of health for society was recognised by Parsons (1951), who defined health as the 'state of optimum capacity for an individual for the effective performance of the roles and tasks for which he has been socialised'. Since illness constitutes a 'cost' to society it must be kept in check, which leads Parsons to consider the way in which society minimises the amount of illness and its potentially disruptive effects. He saw this as being achieved through the creation of socially defined roles for doctors and patients (see Chapter 4). Although Parsons recognises the importance of health for the smooth functioning of the social system, he does not regard the biomedical model as shaped by the needs of the social system. Instead, he accepts the prevailing medical ideology and definitions of disease as constituting a distinct and separate reality. Nevertheless, in a subsequent essay, Parsons (1958) traces links between the needs of the social system and health values. He argues that the emphasis given to health in American society is connected with other values, such as 'activism' (control over the environment), 'worldliness' (emphasis on secular interests) and 'instrumentation' (belief in indefinite progress). The maintenance of good health is thus seen as functional for the system in that is is congruent with a perspective which encourages individual mastery and achievement.

The societal concern for the health of the population, and especially the link between health and role performance identified by Parsons, becomes more pronounced in times of war and the checking of the fitness of men for the army. How far health is seen as important merely because of the societal need for healthy people is, however, unclear. Nevertheless an implication of the conception of health in Parsons' functionalist terms is that the health needs of and health services for those who do not work or are no longer fit for work, such as the elderly and the chronically ill, may be devalued, and the health services for these groups receive a relatively small share of resources.

Marxist analyses have developed this theme of the relationship between the needs of the economy and health values in terms of the influence of the capitalist economic system in shaping prevailing definitions of health. Kelman (1975), for example, argues that the social conditions which give rise to the acceptance of a functional definition of health may be very different from those which are needed for the acceptance of an experiential definition. Adopting an experiential definition, health can be defined as 'the capacity for human development and self discovery and the transcendence of alienating social circumstances'. Kelman suggests that a functional, as opposed to an experiential, definition of health and illness is more likely to be found within a capitalist society because of the priority assigned to and overriding needs of the economic system. As he points out, maintaining a workforce which is healthy enough to perform essential work roles does not necessitate an approach to health which is more than mechanistic. Health is thus likely to be defined in limited terms in capitalist societies, and to focus on the ability of the population to meet the requirements of the system for capital accumulation. Kelman described this more specifically:

> A population is said to be optimally functionally healthy if the last increment of resources directed towards health contributes as much to overall productivity and accumulations it would if directed towards direct capital investment (accumulation).

With regard to medical knowledge, marxist analyses share some affinities with the social constructionist approach to the extent that medical knowledge is viewed as a product of social forces, rather than being a form of knowledge which is technical, timeless and absolute. However, these approaches differ in terms of the social forces identified as shaping medical knowledge. Marxist analyses identify medical knowledge, like definitions of health, as being shaped by the bourgeois ideology of capitalism. Medicine is regarded as simply forming part of a wider struggle between labour and capital, and as sharing a dominant ideology which appears in all institutions, including the institutions of medicine and science. Navarro (1980), for example, claims that the dominance of the biomedical model, with its emphasis on individual intervention, represents not so much the linear outgrowth of previous knowledge, but rather came to assume its dominant position as a result of the support received from the 'industrial' bourgeoisie. This approach to health was in turn supported, rather than a broader social approach, because it directed attention to individual biological phenomena as the causes of disease and away from its social and environmental determinants. It thus would not threaten the power relations in which it was dominant. This function of the interventionist approach to health is regarded as continuing, with the biomedical model serving to support capitalism through obscuring the importance of the social causes of ill health. Concealment of the social and economic origins of disease and acceptance of an interventionist approach is functional for the capitalist system because elimination of the social factors believed to form causes of disease, such as environmental and occupational hazards, would increase the costs of industrial production. This is regarded as explaining why measures to control industrial pollution and enforce health and safety standards have generally been weak, despite their known health risks, whereas considerable emphasis is placed on health education programmes. These programmes emphasise the need for individuals to become more responsible for their health, to change their life styles, and to adopt health habits, such as to diet, to exercise, to relax, to quit smoking and control drinking. They thus suggest that the individual is responsible for his/her health and is to blame for his/her bad health and hence divert attention from the social and political determinants of disease. McKinlay (1974) describes this view very clearly:

> Individuals are either doing something that they ought not to be doing or they are not doing something that they ought to be doing. If only they would recognise their individual culpability and alter their behaviour in some appropriate fashion they would improve their health status or the likelihood of developing certain pathologies.... To use the upstream-downstream analogy, one could argue that people are blamed (and in a sense even punished) for not being able to swim after they, perhaps against their own volition, have been pushed into the river by manufacturers of illness. (p. 116)

A further function of the medical system for the capitalist economic system is identified by Navarro (1978) as its role in encouraging the demand for consumption, including the demand for medical services. Navarro regards the need for consumption as reflecting a dependency of the individual on something that can be bought, whether a drug, a prescription or a car. According to Navarro, consumption is encouraged by the acquisitive ideology of capitalist society, which has the effect of sustaining the economic system by creating a demand for its goods and services. Consumption also forms a response to the lack of control experienced by workers in the workplace, which leads to a need to look for self realisation in the sphere of consumption. Navarro thus disagrees with Illich that social iatrogenesis, or people's excessive reliance on medical services, is created by the medical bureaucracy. Instead, he regards drug companies and the medical profession as responding to a need which is already there and which is created by the conditions of work. As Navarro explains:

> Illich's focus on the world of consumption and his theories of manipulation ignore the main determinants of people's behaviour, which are not in the sphere of consumption, but in the world of production. (p. 355)

The analysis of the relationship between the political-economic structure of capitalistic societies and approaches to health has been extended by Doyal (1979) who traces ways in which the advanced capitalist countries can be regarded as exporting ill health to the Third World countries. She states that advanced capitalist countries introduce new health hazards to the Third World in their quest for raw materials for industrial processes and cheap food for their populations. This is seen as occurring through the hazards of industrial processes and mining, which are even less regulated than in richer countries, and from the stresses arising from the disruption of traditional cultures and patterns of life. The export of Western scientific medicine is also seen as serving a similar function in Third World countries, as in advanced industrial countries, of detracting attention from the fundamental social and environmental determinants of health. More specifically, Doyal claims:

> while those aspects of curative medicine which have been successful in the metropolitan countries have been predicated on the prior implementation of basic public health measures, in the third world, curative medicine has become a substitute for public health and as a result is inevitably less effective. (p. 256)

Marxist analyses of the forces shaping prevailing definitions and approaches to health have formed a powerful influence in challenging widespread assumptions regarding the nature of medical knowledge as technical and value-free, and have served to bring health care more firmly into the political arena. However, whereas marxist approaches focus on the basic conflict between capital and labour and the needs of the capitalist economic system in determining prevailing approaches to health, other analyses, as we have seen, attribute a primary role to the medical profession or adopt a pluralist approach and see definitions and responses to health as shaped by the power and influence of a variety of interest groups, including doctors, industry, the government and lay pressure groups.

Socio-medical Measures of Health

So far this chapter has focused on the limitations of the biomedical model and the social forces that have been identified as creating and sustaining this approach to health. While sociologists have been active in offering critiques of the dominant approach to health, many are engaged in research on problems defined by the medical profession and policy makers, and thus conduct research cast within the prevailing medical framework.

An important contribution of social scientists adopting this pragmatic approach has been to draw attention to the role of social and psychological factors in the onset, management and outcome of disease, and thus to extend the traditional biomedical model. Another area in which sociologists have increasingly participated is in the development of composite measures of health based on individual functioning and/or feeling states. The expansion of work in this area reflects both the current emphasis on the planning and evaluation of health care, together with the increased importance attached to the social and emotional dimensions of health, which are not reflected in more traditional measures, such as mortality rates, sickness absence rates and rates of service use.

Socio-medical measures of health can be broadly divided into three main groups.

Self Care Measures

These are concerned with identifying the extent to which people are able to perform essential tasks, such as dressing, bathing, etc., and thus allow assessments to be made of the extent and nature of activity restrictions. One example is Katz and Akpom's (1976) Activities of Daily Living Index (ADL), which assesses disability in terms of six socio-biological functions — bathing, dressing, toileting, transfer, continence and feeding. Katz and Akpom's ADL measure was originally developed to assess comprehensive care for chronically ill people. Its use has since been extended to children as well as adults, and to mentally retarded as well as physically disabled people.

A second example of the use of a self care measure to determine the extent and nature of activity restrictions is provided by Harris's (1971) National Survey of handicapped and impaired people living in private households in Great Britain, carried out in 1968-9. Impairment was defined to include both the lack of all or part of a limb or having a defective limb, and the experience of certain activity restrictions or disabilities, namely being able to get about, work, or undertake self-care activities. The scores obtained for nine self-care items, which included feeding, using the toilet, dressing, washing and getting in and out of bed, were assigned to grades of handicap. This assessment of handicap was based on people's difficulty with different numbers and combinations of major and minor items, and aimed to identify people's needs for assistance. The National Survey produced a prevalence of impairment of 7.8 per 100 population aged 16 or over, with arthritis as the greatest single cause of impairment. Of all impaired people, 5.3 per cent were classified as very severely handicapped (157,000 people in Great Britain living in private households), 11.6 per cent as severely handicapped and 20 per cent as appreciably handicapped. Information collected in this study on the number and characteristics of people with different degrees of restriction in their self care capacity has formed the basis for policy making at a national level. Similar surveys have been conducted by local authorities following the 1970 Chronically Ill and Disabled Persons Act, to assist in planning services at a local level (Knight and Warren, 1978).

Function Indices

These measures focus on people's ability to function in their role and their capacity to carry out a variety of activities in their social, domestic, and personal lives. A trend in recent years has been to broaden the definition of disability from one based on self care to one which includes a wide range of functional limitations or activity restrictions consequent on disease or impairment. This has the effect of increasing estimates of the prevalence of disability in the community. For example, on the basis of a 25-item definition of disability, used in a postal survey of 10 per cent sample of households in the London Borough of Lambeth, it was estimated that 17.9 per cent of women and 12.5 per cent of men had some functional limitation or activity restriction. This was double the prevalence obtained when the more restricted National Survey definition was applied to Lambeth (Patrick *et al.*, 1981). Items which significantly increased reported disability in the Lambeth survey were sensory-motor items, such as difficulty in doing job of choice or housework.

Function indices designed to assess the prevalence of disability generally focus on fairly severe restrictions. However, function indices may also be used to provide a more general measure of health status or functioning. An example is the Sickness Impact Profile (SIP) developed at the University of Washington, Seattle (Bergner and Gibson, 1981). The SIP is designed to reflect performance in twelve categories of behaviour, relating to both physical and psychosocial functioning. It is based on responses to 136 statements with which the respondent is required to agree or disagree, and allows a global score to be obtained, as well as scores for the twelve individual categories. The SIP was initially designed for the use on general hospital populations, although recently it has been used more widely. For example, it has been employed in evaluating the impact of trained paramedical and emergency technicians as part of the assessment of an experimental suburban paramedic programme, and in assessing the health status of disabled people living in the community and their changes in physical and psychosocial functioning over time (Patrick and Peach, 1985).

Whereas the SIP consists entirely of behavioural items, Rosser and Kind (1978) have developed a measure of health based on eight states of objective disability (ranging from no disability to unconsciousness) and four states of subjective distress (ranging from no distress to severe distress). As with all such measures, there is the fundamental question of whether a social consensus exists as to the relative desirability of different health states judged on these criteria. Rosser and Kind examined this by asking doctors, nurses, and patients to rate 29 descriptions of illness states which varied in the disability and distress displayed. They concluded that although there were some differences between the groups, the main characteristics associated with scale differences were current experience of illness and neuroticism.

Most of the rating scales developed for use in evaluating psychiatric patients are designed primarily for detecting and recording those psychopathological signs and symptoms assessed by the traditional mental status examination. The Psychiatric Status Schedule (PSS) forms one of the few more general measures of functioning and aims to provide a measure of functioning in four spheres: (a) impairment in formal role functioning; (b) impairment in the efficiency and conduct of leisure activities and daily routines (e.g. travelling and personal hygiene); (c) impairment in interpersonal relationships (e.g. friendship patterns and visiting); and (d) the use of drugs and alcohol, and illegal and other antisocial activity. The PSS has been employed to compare the relative benefits of brief hospitalisation and standard hospitalisation, and is regarded as sensitive to changes in patients' functioning (Hertz, Endicott and Spitzer, 1977).

Subjective Health Indicators

These differ from function indices in that they emphasise the respondents' feelings rather than behaviour. An example is the Nottingham Health Profile (NHP) (Hunt and McEwen, 1980) which is designed as a self-administered questionnaire comprising 38 statements with which the respondent is required to agree or disagree. These statements refer to the person's emotional life, pain, energy levels, social integration, physical mobility and sleep patterns. Responses to each statement are used to provide a series of scores or 'health profile' which is intended to portray the severity of perceived dysfunction in each domain. The NHP has a number of similarities to the SIP, although it contains fewer statements, is self-administered rather than interviewer-administered, and so far its separate dimensions have not been aggregated to provide a global score. A further, more basic difference is that the NHP places greater emphasis on subjective feeling states, although there are plans to add further sections to the profile that will attempt to assess the perceived effect of the respondent's health on task performance.

The NHP is claimed to differentiate well between groups of different clinical health status and life circumstances, to be easy and quick to administer, and sensitive to changes over time. There is, however, the question of the extent to which such a measure, which assigns uniform weightings to indicate the severity of dysfunction, can provide a true reflection of lay people's subjective perceptions and evaluations of health.

Health, Disease and Medical Sociology

This chapter has identified two broad approaches to the study of disease. One approach is characterised by an acceptance of prevailing medical definitions and a concern to contribute to the solution of problems of health and health services within a framework provided by clinicians, epidemiologists, and planners. A second approach involves a questioning of medical definitions and assumptions, which are regarded as problematic and objects of study in their own right. These two approaches broadly correspond to Strauss's (1957) early distinction between the concerns of sociology in medicine, which has as its primary goal the furthering of the medical enterprise, and sociology of medicine, which is primarily concerned to further an understanding of the nature and properties of social relationships, beliefs and organisations, although welcoming the use of such knowledge to inform policy and practice.

The two approaches to health and disease described in this chapter are evident in the study of lay health beliefs and behaviour. Work in this field has traditionally been characterised by an acceptance of medical definitions and of a single value system, and has thus been concerned to identify why people deviate from medically prescribed behaviour. More recently, increasing emphasis has been given to the study of the structure and nature of lay health beliefs, which are regarded as valid concepts in their own right, rather than deviations from a medical norm (see Chapter 3). Similarly, Chapter 7 shows how the differences in rates of recorded morbidity and mortality among social groups have been explained in two ways. One approach is to employ a social causation hypothesis and to seek to identify the social causes, or risk factors, which give rise to medically defined disease. An alternative approach focuses on the social construction of medical labels and the ways in which they may be differentially applied to social groups, thus creating the observed inequalities in health.

Another theme identified in this chapter, and which is also taken up in subsequent chapters (see Chapters 6 and 7), concerns the effectiveness of the prevailing interventionist approach to health and the scope for broadening approaches to health and addressing the structural determinants of disease within the prevailing socio-economic and political structure. These approaches are likely to increasingly form the focus of sociological analysis and of more general debate. The nature of the dominant approach to health necessarily has far-reaching implications for the distribution and use of resources devoted to improving health, and for the position and role of the medical profession, as well as influencing the distribution of health and illness in the population.

References

Abel-Smith, B. (1964) *The Hospital, 1800-1948*, HMSO, London

Ackerknecht, E.H. (1967) *Medicine at the Paris Hospital 1795-1848*, Johns Hopkins Press, Baltimore

Armstrong, D. (1983) *The Political Anatomy of the Body*, Cambridge University Press, Cambridge

Armstrong, D. (1984) 'The patient's view', *Social Science and Medicine*, *18*, 737-44

Ausubel, D. (1961) 'Personality disorder is disease', *American Psychologist*, *16*, 69-74

Balint, M. (1957, 2nd edn. 1980) *The Doctor, His Patient, and the Illness*, Tavistock, London

Bergner, M. and Gibson, B. (1981) 'The sickness impact profile', in L. Eisenberg and A. Kleinman (eds.), *The Relevance of Social Science to Medicine*, Riedel and Co., Dordrecht; Holland

Blaxter, M. (1978) 'Disease as category and process: the case of alcoholism', *Social*

Science and Medicine, *12*, 9-17

Chadwick, J. and Mann, W. (trans. and eds.) (1950) *The Medical Works of Hippocrates*, Blackwell Scientific, Oxford

Cochrane, A. (1976) *Effectiveness and Efficiency*, Oxford University Press, Oxford, for Nuffield Provincial Hospitals Trust

Conrad, P. (1975) 'The discovery of hyperkinesis', *Social Problems*, *23*, 12-23

Dixon, B. (1978) *Beyond the Magic Bullet*, George Allen and Unwin, London

Doyal, L. (1979) *The Political Economy of Health*, Pluto Press, London

Foster, G. and Anderson, B. (1978) *Medical Anthropology*, John Wiley & Sons, London

Foucault, M. (1973) *The Birth of the Clinic*, Tavistock, London

Griffith, T. (1967) *Population Problems in the Age of Malthus*, Frank Cass, London

Hamnett, M. and Connell, J. (1981) 'Diagnosis and cure: the resort to traditional and modern medical practitioners in the North Solomons, Papua, New Guinea', *Social Science and Medicine*, *15B*, 480-98

Harris, A. (1971) *Handicapped and Impaired in Great Britain*. HMSO, London

Helman, C. (1984) *Culture, Health and Illness*, Wright & Sons, London

Hertz, M., Endicott, J. and Spitzer, R. (1977) Brief hospitalisation: a two year follow up', *American Journal of Psychiatry*, *134*, 502-7

Hunt, S.M. and McEwan, J. (1980) 'The development of a subjective health indicator', *Sociology of Health and Illness*, *2*, 231-46

Illich, I. (1975) *Limits to Medicine*, Marion Boyars, London

Jewson, N.D. (1975) 'Medical knowledge and the patronage system in nineteenth century England', *Sociology*, *83*, 309-85

Katz, A. and Akpom, C. (1976) 'A measure of primary sociobiological functions', *International Journal of Health Services*, *6*, 493-508

Kelman, S. (1975) 'The social nature of the definition problem in health', *International Journal of Health Services*, *5*, 625-42

Knight, R. and Warren, M. (1978) *Physically Handicapped People Living at Home: A Study of Numbers and Needs*, HMSO, London

McKeown, T. (1979, 2nd edn.) *The Role of Medicine*, Oxford University Press, Oxford, for Nuffield Provincial Hospitals Trust

McKeown, T., Brown, R. and Record, R. (1972) 'An interpretation of the modern rise of population in Europe', *Population Studies*, *26*, 345-82

McKinlay, J. (1974) 'A case for refocusing upstream: the political economy of illness', unpublished paper quoted in J. Ehrenreich (ed.), *The Cultural Crisis of Modern Medicine*. Montly Review Press, London

McKinlay, J. and McKinlay, S. (1977) 'The questionable contribution of medical measures to the decline in mortality in the United States in the Twentieth Century', *Millbank Memorial Fund Quarterly*, 405-28

Morgan, D. (1975) 'Explaining mental illness', *Archives européenes de Sociologie*, *16*, 262-80

Najman, J.M. (1980) 'Theories of disease causation and the concept of general susceptibility', *Social Science and Medicine*, *14A*, 231-7

Navarro, V. (1978) 'The industrialisation of fetishism or the fetishism of industrialisation: a critique of Ivan Illich', *Social Science and Medicine*, *9*, 351-63

Navarro, V. (1980) 'Work, ideology and science: the case of medicine', *Social Science and Medicine*, *14*, 191-205

Oakley, A. (1980) *Women Confined: Towards a Sociology of Childbirth*, Martin Robertson, Oxford

Parsons, T. (1951) *The Social System*, The Free Press, Glencoe, Ill.

Parsons, T. (1958) 'Definitions of health and illness in the light of American values and social structure', in E.G. Jaco (ed.), *Patients, Physicians and Illness*, The Free Press, Glencoe, Ill.

Patrick, D., Darby, S., Green, S., Horton, G., Locker, D. and Wiggins, R. (1981) 'Screening for disability in the inner city', *Journal of Epidemiology and Community Health*, *35*, 65-7

Patrick, D. and Peach, H. (eds.) (1985) *Disablement in the Community*, Oxford University Press, Oxford

Renaud, M. (1978) 'On the structural constraints to state intervention', in J. Ehrenreich (ed.), *The Cultural Crisis of Modern Medicine*, Monthly Review Press, London

Rosser, R. and Kind, P. (1978), 'A scale of valuations of states of illness: is there a social consensus?', *International Journal of Epidemiology*, *7*, 347-57

Sedgwick, P. (1982) *Psycho Politics*, Pluto Press, London

Strauss, A. (1957) 'The nature and status of medical sociology', *American Sociological Review*, *22*, 200-4

Szasz, T. (1961) *The Myth of Mental Illness*, Free Press, New York

Szasz, T. (1971) *The Manufacture of Madness*, Routledge and Kegan Paul, London

Waddington, I. (1973) 'The role of the hospital in the development of modern medicine: a sociological analysis', *Sociology*, *7*, 211, 224

Wing, J. (1978) *Reasoning About Madness*, Oxford University Press, London

World Health Organisation (1948) *Constitution*, WHO, Geneva

Wright, P. and Treacher, A. (eds.) (1982) *The Problem of Medical Knowledge: Examining the Social Construction of Medicine*, Edinburgh University Press, Edinburgh

Yoxen, E. (1982) 'Constructing genetic disease', in P. Wright and A. Treacher (eds.), *The Problem of Medical Knowledge*, Edinburgh University Press, Edinburgh

2 ILLNESS AS A SOCIAL STATE

This chapter develops some of the notions introduced in Chapter 1 and shows that just as medical definitions of disease can be viewed as socially constructed, so the sick person is also surrounded by social expectations and evaluations which influence his/her self conception and behaviour. This view of illness as a social state originated with Parsons' functionalist analysis of the sick role. It has since been developed by writers adopting what is broadly termed a labelling approach, who have focused particularly on the nature and effects of illnesses which carry a negative social evaluation or stigma, notably mental illness and physical deformities.

Parsons' Sick Role

Theorists of deviant behaviour had traditionally excluded illness from the scope of their enquiry because illness, unlike law violation, represented unmotivated deviance for which the individual could not be held responsible. A major reorientation was provided by Parsons (1951), who described illness as deviant from the point of view of the social system because it interferes with the performance of normal social roles. Parsons thus viewed society as setting up mechanisms for channelling and controlling deviant behaviour, so that it does not place too great a strain on the social system. Sanctions against preventable disruption are developed and institutionalised in the law, and administered by those recruited to administer the law. Behaviour which cannot be prevented, as in the case of illness, must be controlled by assigning approved roles. In the case of illness, this is achieved by the socially prescribed roles for the sick person (examined here) and for the doctor (examined in Chapter 4).

Parsons presented the socially prescribed role of the sick person as an ideal type model consisting of four expectations. In his 1951 formulation he described the two rights as:

(1) The sick person is allowed exemption from the performance of normal social role obligations.

First is the exemption from normal social responsibilities, which of course is relative to the nature and severity of the illness. This exemption requires legitimation and acceptance by the various others involved and the physician often serves as a court of appeal as well as a direct legitimizing agent. It is noteworthy that, like all institutionalized patterns, the legitimation of being sick enough to avoid obligations cannot only be a right to the sick person but an obligation upon him.

(2) The sick person is allowed exemption from responsibility for his own state.

The second closely related aspect is the institutionalized definition that the sick person cannot be expected by 'pulling himself together' to get well by an act of decision or will. In this sense also he is exempted from responsibility — he is in a condition that must 'be taken care of'. Of course, the process of recovery may be spontaneous but while the illness lasts he can't 'help it'.

Secondly, the two main obligations are:

(3) The sick person must be motivated to get well as soon as possible.

The third element is the definition of the state of being ill as itself undesirable with its obligation to want to 'get well'. The first two elements of legitimation of the sick role thus are conditional in a highly important sense. It is a relative legitimation so long as he is in this unfortunate state which both he and others hope he can get out of as expeditiously as possible.

(4) The sick person should seek technically competent help and cooperate with medical experts.

Finally, the fourth closely related element is the obligation — in proportion to the severity of the condition, of course — to seek technically competent help, namely, in the most usual case, that of a physician and to cooperate with him in the process of trying to get well. It is here, of course, that the role of the sick person as the patient becomes articulated with that of the physician in a complementary role structure.

The first two expectations of the sick role are regarded as dependent on the obligations to want to get well and to seek and cooperate with the treatment agent. Failure to fulfil these obligations may lead to a person being defined as responsible for the continuation of his/her illness, and to possible sanctions, including the withdrawal of the rights or privileges of the sick role. Other characteristics of the sick role are that it is regarded as a temporary role, and a contingent role into which anyone, regardless of his/her status, may come. It is also inherently universalistic, in that generalised objective criteria determine whether one is or is not sick, how sick, and with what kind of sickness.

The primary function of the sick role is to control the disruptive effect of illness in society by ensuring that those who do become ill are returned to a state of health as quickly as possible. This objective is achieved through the obligations placed on the patient to cooperate in the medical task, and by preventing the formation of a deviant subculture, with the sick being 'tied up not with other deviants to form a subculture of the sick but each with a group of the non-sick, his personal circle, and, above all, physicians' (Parsons, 1951). Furthermore, the obligations of the sick role are regarded as ensuring that people do not use this role as a means of opting out their normal social responsibilities, and that the role does not become a desirable object of secondary gain. In addition, the doctor is identified as the gatekeeper, controlling access to the sick role, and thus determines the official labelling of conditions as health or sickness. However, it is important to note that for Parsons the social control function of the doctor is seen in purely positive terms, in contrast to Szasz's concern that the doctor uses medical labels on behalf of the state as a form of extra-legal control (Chapter 1).

Parsons focused on the manifest functions of the sick role in contributing to the social stability and health of society. However, Waitzkin (1971) has drawn attention to the latent function of the sick role in reducing social disruption and preserving institutional structures, and thus of maintaining the *status quo*. Following Merton's (1968) analysis, he described the sick role as serving a latent function to the extent that its objective consequences contribute to the system's adjustment or adaptation. This function is neither intended nor consciously recognised by those who adopt the sick role, their prime concern being the secondary gains afforded to the individual rather than to the social system. Waitzkin illustrated the way in which the sick role performs this latent function in relation to six institutional settings — the family, the mental hospital, the totalitarian state, penal institutions, the armed forces and the selective service system (conscription). In each of these institutional settings the sick role, by allowing a limited degree of deviance which can be carefully controlled, can be viewed as preventing potential conflict and opposition being directed against the institutional structure itself, thus fostering institutional stability. For example, the sick role can provide an escape from strains experienced by family members, through providing an opportunity for their release from normal responsibilities. In this way it serves as a temporary safety valve, allowing people to cope with problems that otherwise might result in family break-up. Similarly, the sick role avoids widespread and disruptive opposition to conscription, by establishing a mechanism by which men can deviate from military obligations within controlled limits. If a country provided no alternative role for men who wished not to participate in a given war, the possibility of desertion and revolt — in both military and civilian life — would increase. A regime must therefore establish carefully controlled mechanisms by which individuals can deviate from military obligations without threatening political stability, with the sick role providing one such mechanism. Waitzkin illustrates this in relation to the Vietnam War in the 1960s. As opposition to the war grew, there was an increase in the establishment of organisations to provide medical and psychiatric services for draft-eligible men. This was associated with an increase in the rate of medical disqualifications from army service. The disqualification rate increased both for individuals who had not been examined previously and for those who had had a previous examination. However, the rate of disqualification was highest for those with a high level of education, who also comprised the potentially most vocal critics of the war.

Critiques of the Sick Role

Parsons' sick role, although forming one of the most influential concepts in medical sociology, has nevertheless provoked considerable criticism and debate. Particular attention has been paid to questions of its empirical validity in relation to different types of conditions and different groups in the population.

A large number of conditions have been identified for which the expectations of the sick role to not appear to apply. One group consists of minor illnesses from which the individual is expected to recover without recourse to the sick role (Levine and Kozloff, 1978). Another group consists of conditions which may require medical treatment but are not temporary acute physical illness for which the expectations of the sick role seem most applicable. In the case of alcoholism, Chalfont and Kurtz (1971) showed that most of the social workers they studied did not accept alcoholics as legitimate incumbents of the sick role, and did not view them as seeking help and desiring 'release' from their usual social responsibilities. Patients defined as mentally ill are also often reluctant to accept the sick role, while the willingness of hospital staff to view them as legitimate occupants of the sick role has been shown to depend on whether the patient was a voluntary admission, how long he was in hospital, and the congruence between the perceptions of patient and therapist (Denzin and Spitzer, 1966). Chronic illness is generally regarded as providing a particularly clear case of the non-applicability of Parsons' sick role for, by definition, these conditions are not temporary, and the sick person cannot be expected to get well. In addition, maximum functioning is achieved if patients are encouraged to continue their normal social role in so far as they are able to, rather than being relieved of their responsibilities and put in a dependent patient role (Kassebaum and Baumann, 1965).

The applicability of Parsons' sick role to pregnancy has also formed the subject of much debate. Some writers have drawn attention to the similarities in the expectations surrounding pregnant women and other sick people. These include the exemptions granted from normal social roles and the obligation to seek professional care (Hern, 1975). In contrast, other writers have pointed out that, although pregnant women occupy a special position in society, pregnancy differs in fundamental ways from illness. Whereas illness can be viewed as a departure from some norm, pregnancy is a 'normal' state in the statistical sense that most of the population of possible conceivers are at some time in this state. It is also a necessary biological function for survival of the species, and generally regarded as a desirable state of affairs. Thus, although pregnancy involves a disturbance of a biological state, and at some point a disruption of role obligations, it calls forth a set of responses, both from the woman herself and her significant others, which are in many ways different from those elicited with the onset of illness. As McKinlay (1972) notes, an important characteristic of pregnancy in our society is the fact that the attached role is so ill-defined, with the result that pregnant women are often provided with inadequate, confusing, and often conflicting guidelines for role behaviour.

One of the few empirical studies to examine the expectations of the sick role in relation to different types of conditions was undertaken by Gordon (1966) based on a sample of 1,000 persons residing in New York City during 1957-8. Gordon found that there were at least two distinct statuses and complementary role expectations associated with illness states. One set of expectations, which was similar to Parsons' conception of the sick role, occurred when the prognosis was serious and uncertain. The other set of expectations comprised what he termed the 'impaired roles', and was applied when the prognosis was believed to be known and non-serious. In contrast to the sick role, the expectations of the impaired role, rather than insulating and protecting the ill person, encourage normal behaviour, and serve to aid and maintain normal activities and involvement. Gordon pointed out that there is no inherent sequential relationship between the two roles, and it is possible to occupy either role without occupying the other.

A second major criticism of the validity of Parsons' sick role concerns the extent to which its expectations are accepted by different groups (age, social class, racial, etc.) in society. In a study of patients recently discharged from hospital it was found that variations occurred in acceptance of the four expectations of Parsons' sick role, by income, family size and age. However, the variations were fairly small (Arluke, Kennedy and Kessler, 1979). Similarly, a comparison of Anglo-Saxon Protestant and Jewish housewives who had undergone the same surgical procedure showed that the Anglo-Saxon Protestants tended to perceive the sick role more in terms of the Parsonian ideal type, but the differences were not statistically significant (Segall, 1976). It has been suggested that there is more agreement about sick role behavioural expectations among different sectors of society than there is in actual sickness behaviour. Parsons was aware of variations between individuals in their readiness to adopt the sick role. However, he explained these variations in psychological terms as reflecting individual characteristics, rather than arising from social and cultural factors. This question of the way in which individuals and groups differ in their response to illness and readiness to enter the sick role became the subject of studies of illness behaviour. These studies did not seek to challenge Parsons' formulation of the sick role but rather shifted the focus of attention from the general societal level to the analysis of the behaviours of individuals and groups (see Chapter 3).

Assessment of the value of Parsons' sick role in terms of its empirical validity can be viewed as misdirected. This is because the sick role was presented as an ideal type model towards which behaviour tends to conform. As Parsons (1951) himself has commented, the two main characteristics of ideal types are those of 'abstract generality' and the 'ideal-typical exaggeration of empirical reality'. Parsons employed an ideal type model as an analytical construct as he was interested in the medical process largely as an illustration of his general theory of social systems. Parsons was therefore concerned to provide a macroscopic theoretical perspective, rather than to specify what empirical reality is and document variations in role conceptions and role performance of the sick person and therapist. This emphasis can also be seen in Parsons' (1975) later reconsideration of the sick role. In response to the criticism that the sick role is not applicable to chronic conditions, he pointed out that although the goal of a complete recovery is impractical for such conditions, they can often be 'managed' so that the patient is able to maintain a relatively normal pattern of physiological and social functioning. He thus concludes that because a condition, such as diabetes, is not — as in the sense of pneumonia — 'curable', does not put it in a totally different category from that of acute illness.

Criticisms of Parsons' model in its own terms have focused particularly on the problems introduced by his insistence on the functionality of the medical care sub-system for the wider social system. This led to the presentation of a unimodal doctor-patient relationship and to the definition of the sick role in terms of the medical conception of 'ideal' patient behaviour. This in turn involved an emphasis on the complementarity of the doctor-patient role set and the absence of any conflict creeping into the relationship. Insistence on the functionality of the medical sub-system also led Parsons to make no conceptual distinction between a sick role and a patient's role. Since it is necessary to return the sick to 'normal functioning' as quickly as possible, the obligation to seek technically competent help becomes an element of the sick role. The failure to differentiate between a sick role and a patient's role has, as we have seen, been associated with the criticism that the sick role fails to fit many situations, for in some cases a person may claim a sick role without seeking treatment and in other cases (such as minor illness or non-incapacitating stigmatising conditions) treatment may proceed without the person claiming exemption from normal roles and tasks (Bloor and Horobin, 1975).

Freidson's Sociological Types of Illness

Whereas many writers have criticised Parsons' formulation of the sick role, few have offered viable alternatives in its place. An exception is provided by Freidson's (1970) reformulation of the Parsonian framework using Lemert's (1951) social reaction theory, which was central to the development of what has become known as the labelling approach.

Lemert's social reaction theory involves a distinction between two types of deviance — primary and secondary deviance. Primary deviance is merely symptomatic behaviour, or an undesirable difference from the norm. Such differences are not significant for the individual rule breaker unless they give rise to the assignment of a new social status — that of 'deviant'. Secondary deviance occurs when the individual reorganises his/her self perception to match the new role and socially defined expectations. The mechanism which transforms primary into secondary deviance is a change of identity and acceptance of a deviant social status as a result of other people's responses to the individual rule breaker. Lemert's formulation of primary and secondary deviance thus suggests that significant deviance is a function of others' responses to an individual's characteristics, and an individual's response to himself or herself. The characteristics themselves are thus of less importance in producing and forming a deviant identity and role than are the social responses to them.

Freidson (1970) makes a clear distinction between disease, which he regards as a biophysical phenomenon which exists independently of human evaluation, and the experience of illness, which depends on the social response to disease including that of the medical profession. The difference between disease as a biological process and state of the organism and the experience of illness is illustrated by Freidson in terms of the following example:

> Consider two men in different societies, both with the same debilitating infection: in one case, the man is said to be ill, put to bed, and taken care of by others; in the other case, he is said to be lazy, and he is abused by others. The course and outcome of the disease may be the same biologically in both cases, but the social interplay between the sick man and others is significantly different.

Freidson analysed illness as a social state in terms of a six-fold typology of sociological types of illness. This was derived by applying Lemert's social reaction theory of primary and secondary deviance to two aspects of Parsons' sick role — the notions of responsibility and seriousness — and combining these with a third notion of legitimacy. The three key variables which form the basis of his classification are:

Imputations of Responsibility to the Person Being Labelled

Freidson adopts Parsons' notion of the distinction between illness and crime in terms of individual responsibility. However, he emphasises that the imputation of responsibility is interpreted and defined socially rather than being a direct consequence of medical and legal definitions. Thus, in some instances, conditions which are medically defined as illness are reacted to like crimes, with deviance being imputed to the individual. For example, reactions towards venereal disease are influenced by whether or not the sufferer is viewed as responsible.

Degree of Seriousness Imputed to the Illness

Parsons' notion of the variations in the sick role associated with the seriousness of the condition is similarly presented in terms of the imputed seriousness of an individual's deviation from normality. Using Lemert's concept of primary and secondary deviance, Freidson distinguished between deviance which is reacted to as a minor deviation and is allowed to remain as primary deviance, and deviance which invokes a strong social reaction, and causes the offender to reorganise his/her role.

Imputation of Legitimacy of Illness

Freidson regarded the conditional legitimacy that Parsons assigned to the sick role, involving temporary exemptions from normal obligations, with a few privileges gained on condition that help is sought to return to a normal role, as only appropriate to acute illness with a chance of recovery. Unconditional legitimacy, which involves permanent exemption from normal role obligations and some additional privileges, occurs when illness and impairment are believed to be incurable. Using Goffman's (1963) notion of stigma as a social reaction which 'spoils' normal identity, Freidson identified a third situation of illegitimacy. In this case, exemption from some normal obligations is granted by virtue of the fact that the person is not held technically responsible for his/her condition, but this exemption is not accompanied by any additional privileges and carries with it handicapping new obligations. It is important to note that in each case the legitimacy ascribed to illness is imputed rather than being defined by medical criteria, although medical definitions may be reflected in lay beliefs and responses.

Table 2.1 shows Freidson's six types of illness, with examples of conditions which are likely to be placed in these categories on the basis of contemporary American middle-class social reaction. The first row consists of deviations which remain within the realm of primary deviations, for they do not replace a person's normal social roles. The second row consists of deviations which become special social roles. The sick role, as Parsons defined it, is only to be found in cell 5, stigmatised roles are in cell 4 and chronic sick and dying roles in cell 6.

Table 2.1: Types of Deviance for Which the Individual Is Not Held Responsible, by Imputed Legitimacy and Seriousness (Contemporary American Middle-class Social Reaction)

Imputed seriousness	Illegitimate (stigmatised)	Conditionally legitimate	Unconditionally legitimate
	Cell 1 Stammer	Cell 2 A cold	Cell 3 Pockmarks
Minor deviation	Partial suspension of some ordinary obligations; few or no new privileges; adoption of a few new obligations	Temporary suspension of few ordinary obligations; temporary enhancement of ordinary privileges. Obligations to get well	No special change in obligations or privileges
	Cell 4 Epilepsy	Cell 5 Pneumonia	Cell 6 Cancer
Serious deviation	Suspension of some ordinary obligations; adoption of new obligations; few or no new privileges	Temporary release from ordinary obligations; addition to ordinary privileges. Obligation to cooperate and seek help in treatment	Permanent suspension of many ordinary obligations; marked additions to privileges

Source: Freidson (1970).

Freidson believed that movement through the various categories of deviance, shown in Table 2.1, during the course of disease is quite common. This is because health and illness are dynamic processes. He claims that 'it is appropriate to call the movement a "career" — a conventionally patterned sequence of social events through which people pass'. The concept of career is viewed as organising the various types of deviance in terms of a time dimension, and also as linking individuals and their experience to different lay and professional groups. At the level of primary deviation, the individual is largely in contact with friends and family members. Movement into Parsons' sick role is associated with contact with a professional, usually a doctor (often a general practitioner). Movement across to one of the other roles connected with illness and disability is likely to lead to contacts with a medical specialist and with other professionals.

One important difference between Freidson's and Parsons' approach is that Freidson discards the functionalist notion of a unitary and homogenous social structure where participants accept and respond to a single value system. He substitutes for this plural value systems, and thus accounts for the difference in lay definitions of symptoms and illness between groups within a society. Secondly, Freidson does not consider the doctor as merely the legitimator of one's acting sick but also as the creator of the social possibility of acting sick, for the medical profession labels as illness what was not previously labelled at all (as in the case of alcoholism) or what was labelled in some other fashion under some other institution's jurisdiction (as in the case of homosexuality). He views the medical task as in some cases that of minimising the social reaction to deviance by influencing people's beliefs about the conditions. However, on balance, the prime consequence of medical activity is to increase the total number of conditions treated within the medical sphere and, in the course of so doing, to increase the intensity of the social reactions to such conditions by stressing their seriousness to individual or public health. The medical profession 'is therefore engaged in creating, indeed pressuring for the proliferation of situations that create deviant illness roles'.

Freidson's analysis overcomes a number of the problems of Parsons' approach, for it acknowledges that reactions to illness and the expectations of the sick person may vary between different groups in society and according to the nature of the condition. Nevertheless, there are two questions neglected by Freidson which are central to the labelling approach. First, how do the specific social expectations surrounding illness arise, and why do they differ between societies? For example, why is epilepsy a stigmatised condition, regarded as a serious deviation in terms of American middle-class reaction, whereas in certain segments of the Brazilian population and in some African tribes epileptics qualify for the prestigious position of witch doctor because of their symptoms. Secondly, how do individuals respond to negative evaluations, and in particular to what extent can they be viewed as the passive recipients of social labelling?

Social Creation of Stigma

Conditions which attract a stigma tend to evoke feelings of fear and repulsion and to be associated in people's minds with an array of negative attributes. These may include particular personality traits. For example, blind people are often regarded as loners, sad or depressed. One type of restriction or disvalued attribute is also often generalised to other areas, as shown by the tendency to assume that physically handicapped people are also mentally handicapped. Responses to stigma bearers range from fairly minor forms of avoidance, in terms of a reduction in the frequency or length of social contacts, to the legal exclusion of stigma bearers, as with the exclusion of deaf and dumb people from voting in nineteenth-century America, and the practice of apartheid in South Africa today.

The question of why some conditions are responded to in terms of stigma in some societies, or at particular times in history, has received relatively little attention, probably reflecting the dominance of an interpretive approach to the study of stigma. Sontag (1977), in one of the few historical analyses of stigmatising conditions, suggests that certain diseases are regarded with special fear, dread, and repulsion because their causality is unclear and the treatment ineffectual. In the last century tuberculosis was the disease forming the greatest mystery, and was seen as in insiduous, implacable thief of life. Cancer now fills this role — a role Sontag believes that it will keep until, one day, its aetiology becomes as clear and its treatments as effective as those of TB. As Sontag explains:

> Any disease that is treated as a mystery and acutely enough feared will be felt to be morally, if not literally, contagious. Thus, a surprisingly large number of people with cancer find themselves being shunned by relatives and friends and are object of practices of decontamination by members of their household, as if cancer, like TB, were an infectious disease.

Whereas Sontag emphasises the stigma surrounding cancer in contemporary society, Freidson classified cancer as an unconditionally legitimate condition in terms of contemporary American middle-class social reaction (see Table 2.1). Whether cancer sufferers fall into cells 4 or 6 in Freidson's typology may however vary between social groups, and according to the type of cancer and stage of disease.

Just as negative evaluations may come to be attached to medically defined diseases if these conditions are surrounded with fear, so negative evaluations may also come to be attached to racial or religious groups, or to groups displaying certain types of behaviours (e.g. drug addicts, homosexuals, political activists) regarded as a threat to the dominant social institutions and values, or to the holders of power. In defining such conditions as deviant, attention is generally drawn to what are perceived as the undesirable aspects of these groups or behaviours, such as violence, a low educational level, untrustworthiness, etc., which in turn serves to justify discrimination, avoidance and exclusion, and may result in medical or legal control, if the conditions for such control are met (see Chapter 1 on medicalisation).

An example of the way in which groups who are seen as posing a threat may come to be stigmatised is provided by Waxler's (1981) study of the moral definition of leprosy in Hawaii. During the 1860s a flood of Chinese immigrants arrived in Hawaii and at the same time leprosy apparently reappeared in the country. The Hawaiians attributed the outbreak of leprosy to the Chinese immigrants and used this to blame, stigmatise and exclude the Chinese population. Waxler maintains that it is not clear from the records that the Chinese actually brought leprosy into the country, and it is more likely that it was brought by the whaling ships with their mixed crews of Negroes and black and white Portuguese who came from countries where leprosy was still prevalent. However, the association between the Chinese immigration and the occurrence of leprosy on the island can be seen as providing a rationale for rejection that had other basic causes. Belief in the introduction of leprosy by the Chinese may have formed a convenient excuse for excluding Chinese workers who posed an economic threat. It may also have served to confirm the nineteenth-century belief in the superiority of white people. Furthermore, as Waxler notes, if the Chinese were stigmatised ostensibly because they brought leprosy, then the association could also work the other way, with leprosy becoming stigmatised because it was common among the Chinese.

Factors accounting for differences between societies in whether particular attributes or behaviours are viewed as undesirable include their general social values and tolerance of differentness, as well as particular economic, historical and social circumstances, which result in certain groups (particularly those with little power) being regarded as a threat. Stigma labels, once established, are most likely to be maintained if they are sustained by social and organisational forces. This is illustrated by the difference in the socially defined role and response accorded to leprosy sufferers in India and Sri Lanka, despite the fear of leprosy among the general population in both societies (Waxler, 1981). In India lepers are removed from the family, isolated, shunned and treated as outcasts. In contrast, leprosy sufferers in Sri Lanka remain in their own homes after diagnosis and carry on their usual occupations. Although the patients themselves sometimes withdraw into their families and avoid unnecessary non-family contact, the general pattern relative to the Indian one is of acceptance, or at least of tolerance. Such differences have been explained in terms of the caste structure. In India rejection is made possible by the existence of a clear and elaborate hierarchical caste structure — justified by the ideology of impurity and sin — into which a threatening person may be placed. Caste beliefs and practices therefore serve to handle society's fear of the leper, with it being fairly normal to equate leprosy with the punishment of sins and to treat lepers as outcasts. In contrast, in Sri Lanka the caste structure is less hierarchical and there is less experience with low caste and especially outcaste groups. In addition, the majority of the population is Buddhist, not Hindu. This is thought to be significant because Buddhism places greater stress on the toleration of differences and compassion for others, which in turn may contribute to the greater acceptance of the leprosy patient by family and neighbours in Sri Lanka.

In Western industrial society, the medical profession is regarded as playing a central role not only in determining whether conditions defined as deviant are treated within the medical sphere (and thus medicalised) but also in shaping and promoting images of stigma bearers. An example of the role of medical professionals in promoting particular images of stigma bearers is provided by Scott's (1969) comparative study of professional theories of blindness and the goals of organisations for blind people in the United States, Sweden and England. He describes professional theories about blindness held by workers in the United States as being cast in psychological terms.

These theories focus on the impact which blindness is thought to have on people's personality and psychological adjustment. A basic goal of rehabilitation in the USA is therefore to achieve adjustment to blindness, with considerable emphasis being placed on psychological counselling. In contrast, in Sweden, blindness tends to be viewed as a technical handicap, which can be compensated for by the mastery of new techniques and the use of technical aids. As a result, rehabilitation is viewed as a process of learning how to use techniques and technical aids most effectively, and relatively little attention is given to psychological counselling. Scott describes professional ideologies about blindness among leading workers for the blind in England as being cast in terms of 'mood states', with blind people being viewed as especially vulnerable to depression and despair. Thus, one of the chief goals of work with the blind is to 'buoy up their spirits,' through music and diversional social and recreational activities.

Scott describes the images of blind people conveyed by professional theories, and which underpin rehabilitation programmes, as being the product of four sets of forces. These are: (1) the prevailing cultural values, attitudes and beliefs, and the need for organisations to work within this framework in order to receive public funding and support; (2) the views and expertise of the various professionals involved, who have a vested interest in ensuring their own skills are employed; (3) the need to construct 'legal' or 'administrative' definitions for various kinds of stigmatising conditions, which results in people with sight often being put into the formal category of 'blind'; and (4) the power of the clientele to force experts to respond to their own needs and wishes. In many cases this power is fairly limited in view of the low status of the clientele.

Acquiring a Deviant Identity

The labelling approach has not only drawn attention to the construction of illness as a social state, but has also identified the processes through which people come to be formally labelled (or diagnosed) and to accept a deviant identity and life style. However, within what is broadly defined as a labelling approach views differ as to the extent to which labelling is seen as challenging the traditional medical model. Some accept medical definitions and view disease and diagnosis in purely technical terms, and are thus concerned solely with the nature of the social expectations surrounding illness. Others regard the diagnostic process and application of medical labels to be a product of social forces, and may also view disease labels as social constructs following Conrad's approach (see pp. 27-8). Similarly, views differ as to whether people are regarded as passively accepting the labels applied to them, or as actively resisting negative labels. These differences in views regarding the nature of and responses to social labelling reflect the wide variety of theoretical perspectives which are now associated with a labelling approach. Whereas Lemert's theory is based on an interactionist perspective, the 'labelling approach' now tends to be a term employed to encompass all those who are united by a concern with common substantive problems regarding the nature, emergence, application and consequences of social labels but not by common theories (Plummer, 1979).

Formal Labelling

In many cases (e.g. mental illness, epilepsy, multiple sclerosis) the identification of a stigmatising illness depends on medical diagnosis. The medical model views diagnosis as a neutral scientific process which seeks to identify the nature and cause of disease and disorder through examining its signs and symptoms. This model has however been challenged in two ways. Firstly, medical diagnosis can be regarded in some cases as not merely identifying but also as creating a deviant condition. This view has been advanced most frequently in relation to mental illness. However, there is also some evidence to suggest that a formal diagnosis of hypertension can itself produce symptoms of this condition, as well as causing changes in the individual's role and self conception (Eichorn and Anderson, 1962). Secondly, attention has been drawn to the way in which doctors may differentially apply disease labels, with the diagnostic process being influenced by the characteristics of the patient (age, sex, social class, race, etc.), and by the particular circumstances in which the diagnosis is made. For example, the readiness of doctors to diagnose alcoholism has been shown to be influenced by the opportunities that exist for formal referral to non-medical agencies that deal with the problem and by the patient's associated condition. In one study based on a review of hospital case notes, patients who had sustained injuries after they had been drinking and patients who had added some alcohol to an overdose of drugs were more likely to have 'alcoholism' recorded as the primary diagnosis in their case notes than patients who presented with an ulcer or bronchitis coexisting with alcoholism.

Among the latter group there was also often no reference made to the alcohol problem in the patient's treatment notes or in the summary sent to general practitioners (Blaxter, 1978).

Scheff's (1966) analysis of the labelling of mental illness is important in that it incorporates these two critiques of the medical model and draws attention to the social forces which influence both the formal application of the label 'mentally ill' and the way in which the social meanings and responses attached to this label produce a change in the individual's self concept and behaviour, thus causing secondary deviance. Scheff describes behaviour which may come to be classified as a sign of mental illness as consisting of activities which break the residual rules of society. Residual rules refer to the unspecified rules of conduct which are expected to be followed in a social situation and are thus themselves social constructions. For example, everyone knows that during a conversation one looks at the other's eyes or mouth, but not the ear. Such rules are residual in the sense that they deal with areas of life that are not formally controlled by legal, religious and moral constraints, and take the form of expectations which are regarded as the norm. Acts of residual-rule breaking are described by Scheff as frequent and committed by a very wide segment of the 'normal' population. He regards the breaking of residual rules as leading to a person being labelled and responded to as mentally ill if the act of residual-rule breaking becomes public knowledge and the person is referred to the police, a psychiatrist or other official. If this does not occur and the residual-rule breaking is ignored or explained away, it has only transitory significance and remains within the realm of primary deviance. Thus, for Scheff, the nature of residual-rule breaking is of less importance than the reaction of others to the act of residual-rule breaking.

The likelihood of residual-rule breaking being referred to an official agency and processed through the system is viewed by Scheff as depending on four factors:

(1) The perceived seriousness of the act of residual-rule breaking.
(2) The level of tolerance of residual-rule breaking in the community.
(3) The social distance between the rule-breaker and the control agents; the chances of being referred for treatment are regarded as greater if the rule-breaker is of a lower status than the control agent than if they are of a higher status.

(4) The marginality of the patient; those on the margins of society with little power and few resources are most likely to be dealt with by the official system.

Of these four factors Scheff regards the marginality of the rule-breaker as the most important determinant of their chances of being referred to an official agency. Referral to an official agency forms the crucial step in determining whether residual-rule breaking leads to secondary deviation and a change in an individual's self-image. This is because once a person has been referred, there is a high chance he/she will be channelled through the system and officially labelled as mentally ill. Scheff gives three reasons for the likelihood that official labelling will occur: (1) psychiatrists are more sensitive to signs of mental illness than are the general public; (2) when the question of whether or not a person is ill has been raised, there is a tendency to assume that illness exists in the belief that it is safer to treat someone who may not be ill than to release someone who may be ill; and (3) there are a number of features built into the commitment process, such as established routines, and the payment schedule for examiners, etc., which make it difficult to reverse the process once begun. Scheff's investigation of commitment procedures led him to conclude that 'the official societal reaction . . . exaggerates both the amount and degree of deviance', and once the official process is initiated the person is almost invariably routed to the mental hospital. The experience of hospitalisation is in turn regarded as central in confirming a deviant identity, and thus contributing to a changed self conception and secondary deviance. Furthermore, after discharge the patient carries the label of 'ex-mental patient', which, if known about, is likely to give rise to various forms of avoidance and exclusion, thus further confirming the deviant identity. As a result of these pressures, the initial diagnosis is regarded by Scheff as having a self-fulfilling prophecy, leading to self conceptions and behaviour which conform to this role. For Scheff, mental illness is therefore primarily an ascribed status, entry into which is primarily dependent on conditions external to the individual.

Scheff's approach to mental illness has been criticised by writers adopting a traditional psychiatric perspective, who argue that people formally labelled as mentally ill 'really' are mentally ill. Gove (1975), who is one of the foremost critics of Scheff's thesis from a psychiatric perspective, has assembled a large number of empirical studies which he believes cast doubt on the validity of the central tenets of Scheff's thesis. For example, he challenges Scheff's assumption of professionals' readiness to identify illness and have people hospitalised and cites a study by Bittner (1967) to support his argument. Bittner's study suggests that except in the case of suicides the decision by the police to have people hospitalised is based on 'overwhelmingly conclusive evidence of illness'. In contrast, the police regularly assist people in the community whom they and other people recognise as having a serious mental disturbance, while making no effort to have them hospitalised. Other aspects of Scheff's thesis challenged by Gove include his belief that people with the fewest resources are most likely to be labelled as mentally ill, and his description of the ritualistic nature of the commitment process which he views as leading almost inevitably to formal labelling and hospitalisation. Gove also claims that Scheff overlooks the positive consequences of formal labelling, which may in some cases involve entitlement to financial benefits, as well as the benefits to the individual of a short period of hospitalisation.

Gove in criticising Scheff's thesis tends to present the labelling approach to mental illness as a challenge and alternative to the traditional medical model. Scheff's stand on this point however appears to vary. Occasionally he seems to regard his formulation as a sufficient explanation of mental illness (Scheff, 1970). However, he also acknowledges that residual-rule breaking may have diverse causes and that some residual-rule violations are expressions of underlying physiological processes, as with the hallucinations associated with toxic psychosis and the delusions associated with general paresis, while future research may identify further physiological processes that lead to violations of residual rules. However, he suggests that for the present the key attributes of the medical model have yet to be established and verified for the major mental illnesses (Scheff, 1975). In view of the uncertainties surrounding the medical model Scheff argues that the labelling approach may serve an important function in alerting us to its untested assumptions. Adopting this stance, he describes his formulation as probably exaggerating the processes of social reaction, with the aim of sensitising people to these processes. He thus describes the purpose of his theory as not to reject psychiatric and psychological formulations in their entirety:

The ... purpose, rather, is to develop a model which will complement the individual system models by providing a complete and explicit contrast . . . By allowing for explicit consideration of these antithetical models, the way may be cleared for a synthesis. (Scheff, 1966, p. 27)

Institutional Pressures and Responses

Writers adopting a labelling approach generally assign a central position to institutional pressures in the development of a deviant identity. Thus, institutions such as hospitals and specialist centres for the blind, deaf, etc., whose ostensible purpose is to treat and assist sick people, are seen as exerting a powerful influence not only in shaping general social attitudes and beliefs surrounding illness but also in directly determining their patients' (or clients') self conceptions. However, views differ as to whether the acceptance of a deviant identity is seen as an almost irresistible product of hospitalisation or other institutional pressures. Scheff (1966) appears to believe this is the case, although he acknowledges that negotiation may occur in the initial stages of labelling. He explains patients' acceptance of a deviant identity as arising both from patients' experience of institutional pressures within the hospital, and from their previous experience of stress as a result of their initial contacts with the medical (and possibly legal) system, which increases their vulnerability and reduces resistance to institutional pressures. In contrast to Scheff's belief in the inevitable acceptance of a deviant identity, Goffman (1961) suggests that patients in psychiatric hospitals do not necessarily accept the staff's views of them (see Chapter 5). Scott (1969) has similarly identified a pattern of responses among clients of rehabilitation services for the blind. These range from those who become 'true believers', who accept the agency's definition of their problem and organise their lives and identities around their blindness, to 'resistors' who attempt to monitor their dependence and may actually refuse help offered because it involves the redefinition of themselves as persons. However, even if people manage to resist professional definitions, they may be subject to redefinitions of themselves arising both from society's image of stigma bearers and from the reactions and responses of others with whom they interact.

Responses by Stigma Bearers

Goffman's (1963) classic study of stigma provides one of the most notable accounts of the management of stigma by individual stigma bearers. The fundamental distinction drawn by Goffman is between *discreditable* attributes, which are those that are not immediately visible or known about and are, therefore, only potentially stigmatising, and *discrediting* attributes, which are visible or otherwise known about and are, therefore, reacted to by others in terms of stigma. In some cases, a condition which is not immediately visible, such as history of mental illness, may form a discreditable attribute in relation to some groups of people with whom the individual interacts but a discrediting attribute to others who are aware of his/her past history.

Goffman, like Scheff, viewed stigma bearers as accepting the dominant social values and as a result, 'Shame becomes a central possibility, arising from the individual's perception of one of his own attributes as being a defiling thing to possess.' Goffman identified a number of responses by stigma bearers which may take place over a protracted period of time. These include the direct attempt to correct the basis of their failing, which may involve physically deformed people undergoing plastic surgery or mastering areas of activity, such as riding or swimming, ordinarily felt to be closed to a person with his/her condition. Another option is to break with what is called reality and to view one's differentness in unconventional ways, and particularly for secondary gain, as when a disability is used as an excuse for a lack of success in areas unconnected with one's condition. Goffman's primary concern was not however with such long-term adjustments, but rather with the way in which stigma bearers interact with normals (the non-stigmatised) when they are in one another's immediate physical presence, 'whether in a conversation-like encounter or in the mere co-presence of an unfocused gathering'. He identified the main problem in such situations for people with a discrediting condition as being the 'management of tensions' generated during social contacts. In contrast, when the condition is discreditable, the main task is to 'manage information' about the failing — 'to display or not to display; to tell or not to tell; to let on or not to let on; to lie or not to lie; and in each case, to whom, how, when and where'. Goffman identified three strategies — passing, covering and withdrawal — which are employed to cope with a stigmatising attribute in social encounters. These strategies are not unique to stigma bearers but whereas they may be employed occasionally by normals when their identity is threatened, they must be employed continually by stigma bearers.

Passing involves an attempt to conceal the disvalued attribute and gain acceptance as a normal. The possibilities of passing depend on whether the stigmatising condition is immediately visible or otherwise known about by those involved in the interaction, and secondly on its obtrusiveness, or the extent to which it interferes with the flow of interaction. For example, blindness may not affect a telephone conversation but may affect face-to-face interactions. Thirdly, the possibility of passing in particular situations depends on the 'perceived focus' of the stigma, or the particular sphere of activity from which an individual's stigma is regarded as disqualifying him.

Passing may sometimes be achieved through the use of artificial aids, such as a hearing aid, or by presenting stigmatised failings as signs of another attribute which is a less significant stigma. An example is when a person who is hard of hearing gives the impression that he is a daydreamer and unable to answer quiet questions. Passing may also require the construction of a biography or an acceptable explanation of aspects of life that may draw attention to the possession of a disvalued attribute, such as the need to explain away a period of unemployment due to imprisonment or admission to a psychiatric hospital. Edgerton's (1971) study of mentally handicapped patients discharged from hospital provides a good example of the attempt to pass by a discreditable group of people. These ex-patients were discreditable both from their pasts, having been patients in a psychiatric hospital, and through the bewildering demands of everyday life which were likely to reveal their defect. They were therefore faced with the task both of constructing an acceptable biography to conceal their past and of concealing their difficulties with everyday tasks, such as filling in official forms, finding a job and ensuring that they conformed to the requirements of punctuality and industriousness. Edgerton drew attention to the importance of a benefactor who knows of the discreditable condition, and forms what Goffman termed one of the 'wise', in assisting the mental retardate to pass, for mentally handicapped people are by definition unable to manage any of their own affairs. He claimed that, 'in general, the ex-patient succeeds in his efforts to sustain a life in the community only as well as he succeeds in locating and holding a benefactor'.

The process of passing often involves a high psychological cost. One aspect of this is that the person who passes may feel a sense of disloyalty and self-contempt in that he cannot take action against offensive remarks made by members of the category he is passing into against the category he is passing out of. Furthermore, inherent in passing is the constant danger of failure, disclosure and shame. In addition, the stigma bearer may believe that he is more fully accepted as a normal person than he is. As Edgerton (1971) wrote in relation to the mentally handicapped people he studied 'the cloaks that they think protect them are in reality such tattered and transparent garments that they reveal their wearers in their naked incompetence'.

Covering involves trying to reduce the significance of the stigmatising condition rather than denying its existence. Covering may be employed both by the involuntarily discredited and by those who feel that they should be above passing and voluntarily disclose their stigmatising attribute, thus transforming the situation from the management of information to the management of tension. One of the main methods of covering, as with passing, is reducing the visibility and obviousness of failings that are stigmatised. For example, a blind person may learn to look at the speaker so as to avoid violating codes of spoken interaction and thus draw attention to his/her condition.

On the basis of interviews with visibly handicapped informants, Davis (1961) identified three stages that may occur in a relationship based on covering over a period of time, which he refers to as the process of deviance disavowal or normalisation. The first stage consists of 'fictional acceptance', with interaction being kept to a minimum level of sociability. The second stage is 'breaking through' in which the discredited person encourages the normal to disregard his/her stigmatising condition. If this is successful it leads to a 'normalised relationship', with the normal either adjusting his/her perceptions so as to suppress his/her effective awareness of the areas in which the disabled person's behaviour deviates from the normal, or surrendering some of his/her normality by joining the handicapped person in a marginal existence. This latter situation often characterises those who are closely associated with disabled people. As with passing, the situation of normalisation is relatively precarious. If too successful, the strategy may itself cause problems, with disabled people being expected to perform activities they are unable to achieve because of their disabilities, which again gives rise to tension.

The strategy of *withdrawal*, or opting out of social activities with normals, may be resorted to if a benefactor is lacking, or if for any other reason passing or normalisation prove too difficult.

Higgins (1981), on the basis of a study of deaf people, has criticised Goffman's analysis of coping strategies for placing too much emphasis on the framework of stigmatisation. He argues that in many cases a primary concern of physically disabled people is to accomplish everyday activities, rather than to manage their spoiled identity. This overriding concern with and problem of accomplishing activities, such as dressing and getting out of bed, is graphically described by Locker's (1984) study of people with severe rheumatoid arthritis. Secondly, Higgins argues that in encounters between non-disabled and physically disabled people, the non-disabled's reactions are not merely to the disabled's putatively spoiled identities, but also to the disruption of the assumptions and routine practices of social interaction. The uncertainties associated with the disruption of normal roles and routines and the consequent tensions in the interaction have been depicted by Hilbourne (1973) in relation to a personnel manager interviewing a blind applicant. These uncertainties included whether or not he should guide the applicant to a seat, and, if offering a cigarette, whether he should light it for him. In situations of uncertainty, interaction has been shown to be characterised by a greater physical distance between participants, the avoidance of eye contact and a more abrupt termination of the encounter (Comer and Piliavin, 1969). In a study of the impact of the severity, type and visibility of the limitation of physically disabled people in encounters with the non-disabled, Zahn (1973) found that contrary to expectations, more severely impaired people were likely to have better interpersonal relationships than the less severely impaired. She suggested that this may be because severe physical limitation removes the ambiguity surrounding one's status and thus reduces the uncertainty in social relationships.

Goffman's concern with the consequences of social responses, rather than with the problems directly arising from a bodily disorder or dysfunction, can also be seen in relation to his notion of the effects of stigma on close associates of the stigma bearer. Goffman (1963) introduced the notion of a 'courtesy stigma' to refer to the extension of the spoiled identity to those closely involved with the stigma bearer, who often become 'tarred with the same brush'. Hilbourne (1973) suggests this notion is too limited. This is because close family members are often themselves disabled by the presence of a disabled person, in terms of the need to assume additional responsibilities and curtail some of their normal social activities.

A second major criticism of Goffman's interpretive analysis relates to his presentation of the recipient of social labelling. Although stigma bearers are not depicted simply as the powerless victims of social labelling but as exercising some control over these processes, the strategies he identifies are essentially defensive manoeuvres. As Gussow and Tracey (1968) explain:

Goffman's people are both other- and self-stigmatised and forever doomed. The basis for this dilemma or self contradiction lies in the fact that those stigmatised are apparently firmly wedded to the same identity norms as normals, the very norms that disqualify them.

Anspach (1979) has presented an analysis of responses to social labelling which incorporates both active and passive responses (see Table 2.2). When individuals accept the dominant social values and beliefs regarding their condition, their responses may be either normalisation or disassociation (broadly corresponding to withdrawal), depending on the individuals' self concept. When individuals reject the dominant social values, their response may be 'retreatism' (a term borrowed from Merton, 1968), which occurs when a person has a negative self image and neither accepts the dominant social values nor aspires to 'normal' attainments. Alternatively, they may engage in 'political activism', which represents a collective alternative to other individualistic responses, and seeks by repudiating social values to elevate the self concept of its participants. Whereas Anspach identified what can be viewed as the extremes of a continuum of responses, Rogers and Buffalo (1974) presented nine modes of adaptation to deviancy labels. They suggest the active rejection of a label may consist not only of the collective repudiation of the label but also of individual strategies to reduce the significance and personal effects of the label. They also draw attention to the way in which people may move between different strategies.

Table 2.2: Strategems for Stigma Management: Social Values

	Accepts	Rejects
Positive	Normalisation	Political Activism
Self-concept		
Negative	Disassociation	Retreatism

Source: Anspach (1979).

Three main conditions have been identified as necessary for individuals who share a similar situation to form an active political force and engage in collective action to repudiate deviancy labels (Schur, 1980). These are: (1) the existence of organisers, founders and leaders; (2) the existence of political conditions which permit organising activity to occur; and (3) the social conditions of organisation which have to be met. Among the most important of these social conditions of organisation is the development of a collective consciousness. This involves, firstly, the recognition on the part of the deviant group that their situation is caused by the prevailing institutions and interests, and, secondly, recognition of the necessity of collective action to achieve the desired change. An important determinant of the outcome of deviancy struggles is the social power of the conflicting groups, for any attempt to designate and treat behaviour as deviant, or action to remove stigma labels, must be backed up by social power if it is to have any real effect. The support of society's major power holders (politicians, media, etc.) will therefore be actively sought by the contending parties, especially in attempts to achieve various concrete goals, such as the passage or removal of a law, changes of policies on the part of the law enforcers, helping agencies or schools, or changes in mass media content. The success of deviancy defining (or re-defining) groups is also likely to depend on the extent to which the perceived deviance is congruent with the general social and cultural values and is thus likely to be viewed as a reasonable or justifiable goal.

Changes which are regarded as contributing to the development of collective consciousness and the growing political organisation since the 1960s among such groups as former mental patients and the physically disabled include the return in the USA of newly politicised disabled veterans of the Vietnam War who actively sought institutional reforms, and the increasing criticism of the medical model in psychiatry. Other conditions likely to favour political activism as a strategy are when the disvalued attribute is not severely restricting — thus permitting participation in collective efforts, close association with other handicapped persons, a lack of integration into the network of normals and the dominant response being one of exclusion rather than acceptance by normals.

Stigma, Disability and Handicap

Whereas Chapter 1 showed how definitions of disease can be viewed as socially constructed, this chapter has shown how the experience of illness is similarly surrounded by social expectations, which are particularly pervasive in the case of illnesses which attract a stigma. Recognition that the effects of impairment, such as the loss of a limb or visual problems, depend not only on the nature of the activity restrictions it imposes but also on its social consequences and interpretations, has led to the formulation of a model of disablement which encompasses the notions of impairment, disability, and handicap (see Figure 2.1). This serves to extend the traditional medical model and is regarded as facilitating policy development and clarifying the potential contributions of medical services, social services, and broader changes in housing, educational or employment policies in improving the functioning and reducing the disadvantage experienced by people with chronic conditions.

Figure 2.1: World Health Organisation Model of Disablement

Impairment: any loss or abnormality of psychological, physiological or anatomical structure or function.
Disability: any restriction or lack (resulting from an impairment) of ability to perform an activity in the manner or within the range considered normal for a human being.
Handicap: a disadvantage for a given individual, resulting from an impairment or a disability, that limits or prevents the fulfilment of a role that is normal (depending on age, sex, social and cultural factors) for that individual.

Source: WHO (1980), p. 30.

Impairment represents a deviation from some norm in the individual's biomedical status (e.g. a defect in or loss of a limb or a defect in mental functioning). Impairment does not, however, necessarily indicate that disease is present or that the individual is generally regarded as sick. Disability represents a departure from the norm in terms of the performance of the individual, as opposed to that of the organ or mechanism. It has been measured by assessing the individual's ability to perform specific tasks (or the movements required in their performance), or their ability to function in various spheres of activity and social life (see Chapter 1).

Handicap refers to the disadvantage for a given individual resulting from an impairment or a disability. Handicap is thus a social phenomenon, with the translation of impairment or disability into handicap depending on a variety of social, psychological and economic factors. Two people suffering from the same disability may, for example, differ in the handicap or disadvantage experienced because of differences in the extent to which the disability interferes with their normal activities. Thus, the amputation of a finger is likely to cause greater disadvantage to a typist or pianist than to a teacher whose work does not require such manual dexterity. A young person who has difficulty walking will also have greater problems fulfilling his/her normal role (going to work, etc.) and the social expectations surrounding people of his/her age (engaging in sports, etc.) than will an elderly person, and will thus experience a greater handicap. Disadvantage or handicap may also be influenced by economic and social resources. For example, the availability of a car may, by increasing mobility, reduce the disadvantage and handicap experienced as a result of conditions which limit a person's ability to walk.

Just as the activity restrictions imposed by a disabling condition may place the individual at a disadvantage in his/her everyday life, so the negative social responses or stigma associated with particular types of impairments and disabilities may constitute a handicap, through giving rise to discrimination, avoidance and exclusion. In some cases an impairment, although not giving rise to any activity restriction, may none the less constitute a social handicap as a result of the responses of others to the condition. This is often the situation experienced by patients discharged from psychiatric hospitals who carry the label of 'ex-mental-patient'. Similarly, the possession of a facial scar may result in a person being excluded from jobs involving contact with the public because of the reactions of potential customers or clients, although the condition does not in itself restrict a person's capacity to work. As we have seen, whereas Goffman emphasised the handicap experienced as a direct result of the social responses to a negatively valued condition, Higgins and others, focusing on people with physical disabilities, emphasised the handicap which arises from the physical inability to carry out 'normal' activities (p. 68). However, in cases of severe physical disability both types of disadvantages are likely to be experienced.

Figure 2.1 presents a model based on a one-directional flow between impairment, disability, and handicap. However, in some cases a feedback loop may occur. For example, research employing notions of individual susceptibility or resistance to disease suggests that people whose experience of impairments and disability is accompanied by social disadvantage, negative self conceptions and low self esteem are more likely to experience a worsening of their condition and decreased levels of functioning (see Chapter 8).

The primary aim of the medical services is to prevent the

occurrence of impairment through measures which either prevent or cure disease. In contrast, in cases of chronic illness the task becomes one of minimising the impairment and reducing its disadvantages for the individual. For example, hearing may be corrected by the provision of aids, muscle weakness improved through physiotherapy, and diabetes controlled by dietary advice and drug therapy.

A second approach is to reduce the disadvantage experienced by people whose impairment produces long-term disability, through a variety of social, economic and environmental measures. This may involve reducing the consequences of restricted mobility through the provision of transport, providing access into public buildings through ramps and adapting homes. Disadvantage in the economic sphere may similarly be reduced by providing financial benefits for disabled people and initiating policies to increase employment opportunities (Topliss, 1982).

A third approach is to undertake measures aimed directly at reducing the stigma associated with impairments. Such measures generally involve educational programmes and the use of the mass media to increase understanding and reduce negative stereotypes. In addition, attempts have been made to reduce negative images and responses through measures which promote the social integration of disabled people by reducing the physical barriers to social participation, or increasing employment opportunities in the general labour force. Another important factor influencing social attitudes is the responses of stigma bearers themselves and the ways in which they cope with their condition. This, as we have seen (pp. 65-70) is influenced by their social and psychological resources and by the nature of their health problem, in terms, for example, of the pain and activity restrictions experienced.

The considerable attention currently paid to the nature, effects, and experience of disabling illness can be viewed as forming a product both of the increasing numbers of chronically ill people, as the scope for medical intervention increases and as more people survive into old age, and of the increasing knowledge and awareness of the needs of disabled people as a result of community surveys and other research activity. This concern with the needs and problems of disabled people has in turn provided an opportunity for the application of knowledge which has been steadily accumulating concerning the nature and effects of stigma and handicap, and has stimulated further research, discussed in Chapter 8, examining the influence of social support in promoting coping behaviour. Questions of service and financial provision for disabled people and other dependency groups also form a major policy issue with implications for the health, housing, educational and employment services.

References

Anspach, R. (1979) 'From stigma to identity politics', *Social Science and Medicine*, *13A*, 765-73

Arluke, A., Kennedy, L. and Kessler, R.C. (1979), 'Re-examining the sick-role concept: an empirical assessment', *Journal of Health and Social Behaviour*, *20*, 30-6

Bittner, E. (1967) 'Police discretion in apprehending the mentally ill', *Social Problems*, *14*; 278-92

Blaxter, M. (1978) 'Disease as category and process', *Social Science and Medicine*, *12*, 9-17

Bloor, M. and Horobin, G. (1975) 'Conflict and conflict resolution in doctor/patient interactions', in C. Cox and A. Mead (eds.), *A Sociology of Medical Practice*, Collier Macmillan, London

Chalfont, H.P. and Kurtz, R.A. (1971) 'Alcoholics and the sick role', *Journal of Health and Social Behaviour*, *12*, 66-72

Comer, R.J. and Piliavin, J.S. (1974) 'The effects of physical deviance upon face-to-face interaction', in D. Boswell and M. Wingrove (eds.), *The Handicapped Person in the Community*, Tavistock, London

Davis, F. (1961) 'Deviance disavowal: the management of strained interaction by the visibly handicapped', *Journal of Health and Social Behaviour*, *7*, 265-71

Edgerton, R.B. (1971) *The Cloak of Competence*, University of California Press, Los Angeles

Eichorn, R. and Anderson, R. (1962) 'Changes in personal adjustment to perceived and medically defined heart disease', *Journal of Health and Human Behaviour*, *3*, 242-9

Freidson, E. (1970) *The Profession of Medicine*, Aldine Pub Co., New York

Goffman, E. (1961) *Asylums: Essays on the Social Situation of Mental Patients and Other Inmates*, Doubleday & Co., New York

Goffman, E. (1963) *Stigma: Notes on the Management of a Spoiled Identity*, Prentice Hall, Inc., Englewood Cliffs, N.J.

Gordon, G. (1966) *Role Theory and Illness*, College Press, New Hampshire

Gove, W. (ed.) (1975) *The Labelling of Deviance*, John Wiley & Sons, London

Gussow, A. and Tracey, G.S. (1968) 'Status, ideology and adaptation to stigmatised illness', *Human Organisation*, *27*, 873-84

Hern, W.H. (1975) 'The illness parameters of pregnancy', *Social Science and Medicine*, *9*, 365-72

Higgins, P.C. (1981) *Outsiders in a Hearing World*, Sage Publications, London

Hilbourne, J. (1973) 'On disabling the normal', *British Journal of Social Work*, *3*, 497-504

Kassebaum, G. and Baumann, B. (1965) 'Dimensions of the sick role in chronic illness', *Journal of Health and Social Behaviour*, *6*, 16-27

Lemert, E. (1951) *Social Pathology*, McGraw Hill, New York

Levine, S. and Kozloff, M. (1978) 'The sick role: an assessment and overview', *American Review of Sociology*, *14*, 317-43

Locker, D. (1984) *Disability and Disadvantage*, Tavistock, London

McKinlay, J.B. (1972) 'The sick role, illness and pregnancy', *Social Science and Medicine*, *6*, 561-72

Merton, R.K. (1968) *Social Theory and Social Structure*, Free Press, New York

Parsons, T. (1951) *The Social System*, Free Press, Glencoe, Ill.

Parsons, T. (1975) 'The sick role and the role of the physician reconsidered', *Millbank Memorial Fund Quarterly: Health and Society*, *53*, 257-78

Plummer, K. (1979) 'Misunderstanding labelling perspectives', in K. Plummer (ed.), *Deviant Interpretations*, Martin Robertson, London

Rogers, J.W. and Buffalo, M.D. (1974) 'Fighting back: nine modes of adaptation to a deviant label', *Social Problems*, *22*, 101-18

Scheff, T. (1966) *Being Mentally Ill*, Aldine Publishing Co., Chicago

Scheff, T. (1975) *Labelling Madness*, Prentice Hall Inc., Englewood Cliffs, N.J.

Scheff, R. (1970) 'Schizophrenia or ideology', *Schizophrenia Bulletin*, *2*: 15-19

Schur, E. (1980) *The Politics of Deviance*, Prentice Hall Inc., Englewood Cliffs, N.J.

Segall, A. (1976) 'Sociocultural variations in sick role behavioural expectations,' *Social Science and Medicine*, *10*, 47–51

Scott, R. (1969) *The Making of Blind Men*, Russell Sage, New York

Sontag, S. (1977) *Illness as Metaphor*, Allen Lane, New York

Topliss, E. (1982) *Social Responses to Handicap*, Longman, Harlow, Essex

Waitzkin, H. (1971) 'Latent functions of the sick role in various institutional settings', *Social Science and Medicine*, *5*, 45-75

Waxler, N.E. (1981) 'Learning to be a leper: a case study in the social construction of illness', in E.G. Mishler *et al.*, *Social Contexts of Health, Illness and Patient Care*, Cambridge University Press, Cambridge

World Health Organisation (1980) *International Classification of Impairments, Disabilities and Handicaps*, WHO, Geneva

Zahn, M. (1973) 'Incapacity, impotence and invisible impairment', *Journal of Health and Social Behaviour*, *14*, 115-23

3 LAY INTERPRETATIONS AND RESPONSES TO ILLNESS

The study of illness behaviour, and more recently of health behaviour, has been characterised by two main approaches. Traditionally, work in this area has tended to accept providers' definitions of how the health service 'ought' to be used and has generally sought to explain why these organisational solutions were not complied with. It has thus attempted to identify the social, cultural and psychological factors influencing patient delays, patient under-utilisation and patient over-utilisation of the health service.

A second approach, drawing on the theoretical perspectives of the sociology of knowledge and the interpretive paradigm, emphasises the cognitive and interactional processes involved in the management of signs and symptoms. Rather than accepting medical definitions of health and illness and a single value structure, this approach acknowledges both the differences between scientific medical knowledge and lay health knowledge and practices, and the pluralist nature of social life. Thus an attempt is made to examine how the actor(s) interpret(s) and make(s) sense of disturbances in body functioning, with the decision to seek medical care being viewed as one possible response among a number of alternative course of action.

Illness Behaviour as a Social Problem

The Emergence of the Concept of Illness Behaviour

Once the economic barrier to health care had been removed with the setting up of the National Health Service, it was assumed that all those in need of medical care would consult their doctor or other appropriate medical services. No one questioned whether an individual would be able to know whether he or she needed medical attention or not. The process of becoming ill was believed to be clear-cut. The majority of people were expected to perceive that they were obviously and normally healthy; a minority were assumed to be equally aware that they were ill because they could perceive their symptoms and appreciate their significance. The image of the lay person as portrayed in this type of perspective is clearly illustrated by Zola (1973). He states:

> We postulate a time when the patient is asymptomatic or unaware that he has symptoms, then suddenly some clear objective symptoms appear, then perhaps he goes through a period of self-treatment and when either this treatment is unsuccessful or the symptoms in some way become too difficult to take, he decides to go to some health practitioner (usually, we hope, a physician).

Studies of illness behaviour and help-seeking behaviour emerged out of concern expressed about the results from several health surveys. These surveys showed the prevalence of ill health was high throughout the community, with the existence of signs and symptoms of ill health throughout the general population being the norm. For example, Wadsworth, Butterfield, and Blaney (1971), in a study based on the population of two London boroughs, found that out of a total sample of 3,153 respondents only 5 per cent reported no health complaints. Thus, 95 per cent of the sample said that in the fourteen days prior to the interview they had suffered from one or more complaints. Of this group, 19 per cent suffered from ailments for which they had sought no advice or treatment, and of the remainder who took action of some kind about their complaints, 60 per cent resorted to self-medication. Such studies indicated that those people who seek medical care represent the tip of an iceberg of illness, with a large proportion of morbidity in any community never reaching the medical services.

One explanation of these findings was that the complaints which were not taken to the doctor were the less serious ones. However, results from several surveys show that many serious mental and physical complaints go untreated. For example, Williamson *et al.* (1964) carried out a clinical and psychiatric examination of 200 people aged 65 or over. They found a large minority of serious complaints which were not known to the doctor. For example, a quarter of the respondents with chronic bronchitis and a third of the respondents with heart disease were unknown to the doctor. Psychiatric complaints tended to be more likely to be unreported than physical complaints. For example, approximately 90 per cent of the people suffering from depression had not contacted their doctor.

These findings suggested that 'non-medical' factors may be influencing both the individuals' perception of ill health and the subsequent decision to seek medical care. The study of the influence of non-medical factors on individuals' perception of and reaction to clinical disorder has been described by medical sociologists as 'illness behaviour'. Illness behaviour has been defined in various ways but the more frequently cited definition is the one proposed by Mechanic (1968). He states:

> By illness behaviour we mean the way in which symptoms are perceived, evaluated, and acted upon by a person who recognises some pain, discomfort, or other signs of organic malfunction.

The study of illness behaviour has been influenced in recent years by concern at the delay between the appearance of symptoms and treatment for conditions such as breast cancer, in which early treatment may increase long-term survival. For example, in a study of women referred to hospital outpatients with breast symptoms, 40 per cent delayed more than four weeks between first noticing breast symptoms and first consulting the doctor (Nichols *et al.*, 1981). The current emphasis on prevention, self help and self care has also extended attention from the study of illness behaviour to include patterns of health behaviour. This refers to behaviour in relation to the adoption of officially recommended health actions, such as following a 'healthy' diet, giving up smoking, or using preventive health services.

Determinants of Illness Behaviour and Health Behaviour

Research into factors influencing the use of the health services may be broadly classified as adopting either an individualistic approach, in which variations in observed behaviour are explained by reference to the personal characteristics of the individual, or a collectivist approach in which individual behaviour is viewed as the outcome of social forces.

Individualistic Approaches. Various attempts have been made to develop socio-psychological models which predict people's responses to symptoms. For example, Mechanic (1962) on the basis of research with several student groups argued that people under stress have a repertoire of coping responses. One of these is to adopt the sick role and seek professional medical advice. He thus attributed differences in the use of medical services to differences in individual propensity to experience stress and to adapt to it by adopting the sick role. People who had a low inclination to adopt the sick role were therefore regarded as seeking treatment only if they experienced particularly unusual or severe symptoms.

In a later paper, Mechanic (1968) abandoned the attempt to develop a model of illness behaviour which specified the relationship between variables in favour of merely listing ten variables that studies have shown are associated with seeking medical advice. The variables are:

(1) Visibility, recognisability, or perceptual salience of symptoms. The more a symptom is visible or recognisable the more readily it can be defined and responded to.

(2) The perceived seriousness of the symptoms. The more the sufferer and others believe the symptoms to hold present or future probabilities of danger the more likely that the sufferer and others will respond to it.

(3) The extent to which symtoms disrupt family, work and other social activities. Symptoms which are disruptive and which cause inconvenience, social difficulties, pain and irritation are more likely to be responded to than those that do not. A typist may be more concerned about an injury to a finger than someone whose work does not depend on the use of their hands.

(4) The frequency of the appearance of symptoms, their persistance or frequency of recurrence. The more frequently a behaviour occurs or the longer a symptom persists the more likely the sufferer is to seek help.

(5) The tolerance thresholds of those who are exposed to and evaluate the deviant signs and symptoms. Mechanic argues that people's willingness to tolerate symptoms will depend on their values about independence and stoicism.

(6) Available information, knowledge and cultural assumptions, and understanding of the evaluator. Difference in levels of medical knowledge and understanding are associated with differential responses to symptoms.

(7) Perceptual needs which lead to autistic psychological processes. The relationship between anxiety and fear about symptoms and patterns of help-seeking behaviour is not straight-forward. For example, in studies of patients with possible signs and symptoms of cancer, delay in seeking medical care is associated with both a very high and a very low level of fear about the disease.

(8) Needs competing with illness responses. Concerns about health are not always major ones and may be overridden by economic concern or commitments to plans or projects. For example, soldiers may neglect their wounds in the heat of the battle, or perhaps, less dramatically, in one-parent households the parent may have to accommodate his/her illnesses because his/her priorities are with taking care of young children and no alternative caretaker is available.

(9) Competing possible interpretations that can be assigned to the symptoms once they are recognised. Mechanic argues that symptoms are evaluated according to the life situation of the sufferer. People who work long hours expect to be tired and thus tiredness is not seen to be a sign of anything abnormal. Thus, people will assess signs and symptoms according to their expectations which are in turn influenced by their life circumstances.

(10) Availability of treatment resources, physical proximity and psychological and monetary costs of taking action. The use of help facilities may depend upon the extent of the barriers to care, which may include financial costs, the time spent getting to the doctor and then waiting for treatment, the effort involved and the embarrassment, stigma or humiliation caused by the treatment.

Mechanic recognises the overlap among some of these variables but suggests that consideration of each individual category provides clues which might otherwise be neglected. He also points out that what may appear salient to the definer may not appear relevant to the physician. For example, the recognisability of symptoms is not necessarily correlated with medical views of their seriousness. In discussing each of these factors through which symptoms are recognised and help seeking is initiated, Mechanic distinguishes between 'other defined' and 'self defined' illnesses. With 'other defined' conditions, the definition of illness originates from others in the environment; the sick individual tends to resist the evaluation, and may have to be brought into treatment involuntarily. 'Other defined' illness is regarded as frequently occurring with psychiatric conditions, and also includes the illness of children and adult physical conditions accompanied by denial of symptoms and/or the need for care. Mechanic, however, maintains that 'the variables affecting definitions of a condition by the person himself or others in his social group are surprisingly similar, and that these variables equally pertain to the area of physical illness and to the mental disorders' (Mechanic, 1968 pp. 138-9).

One model which attempts to explain patterns of help-seeking in the use of preventive health services is the Health Belief Model (HBM), which is derived from psychological learning theory. The HBM was originally formulated by Rosenstock (1966) and has subsequently been developed by Becker *et al.* (1977) (see Figure 3.1). The model consists of a number of factors which comprise the concept of 'readiness to undertake recommended compliance behaviour'. These include motivation, value of illness threat reduction and the probability that complaint behaviour will reduce the threat. In addition, a number of modifying and enabling factors have been included, such as demographic (age of individual), structural (accessibility of regimen), attitudinal (satisfaction with doctor), interaction (type of doctor-patient relationship) and enabling (prior experience with action).

The theory underlying the HBM is that people who exhibit the appropriate combination of motives and beliefs will accept and undertake recommended behaviour designed to prevent illness in the absence of symptoms, or to restore good health after the actual diagnosis of illness. Furthermore, through the identification of specific factors associated with 'inappropriate' behaviour, health education programmes and service provision can be more closely tailored to the particular needs of the target group. The HBM has been employed to predict and explain behaviour in a variety of settings, including mothers' compliance with dietary advice prescribed for obese children, the take up of immunisation and the use of dental services (Becker *et al.*, 1977). However, although specific components of the model have often been shown to be associated with differences in behaviour, when taken together they often explain only a small amount of the variance in compliance behaviour.

Collectivist Approaches This approach emphasises the differences in the values and attitudes to health among social groups that have implications for illness behaviour, as well as the particular social and situational forces which prompt or delay professional help-seeking.

One example of a study which adopts a collectivist approach is Zborowski's analysis (1952) of the role of cultural factors in explaining differential responses to signs and symptoms. He examined cultural components in response to pain, based on a sample of male patients suffering from neurological ailments. The patients were either Italian, Jewish or of Old American origin. Zborowski found that, in hospital, Italian and Jewish patients responded to pain

Figure 3.1 Summary Model for Predicting Individual Health-related Behaviour

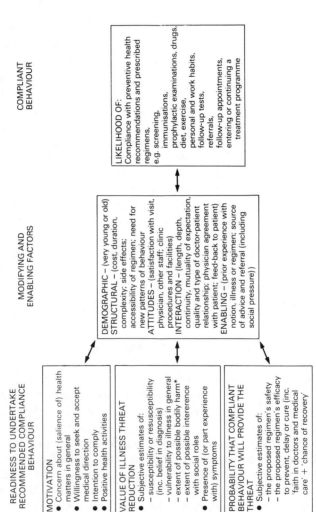

READINESS TO UNDERTAKE
RECOMMENDED COMPLIANCE
BEHAVIOUR

MOTIVATION
● Concern about (salience of) health
  matters in general
● Willingness to seek and accept
  medical direction
● Intention to comply
● Positive health activities

VALUE OF ILLNESS THREAT
REDUCTION
● Subjective estimates of:
  – susceptibility or resusceptibility
    (inc. belief in diagnosis)
  – vulnerability to illness in general
  – extent of possible bodily harm*
  – extent of possible interference
    with social roles
● Presence of (or part experience
  with) symptoms

PROBABILITY THAT COMPLIANT
BEHAVIOUR WILL PROVIDE THE
THREAT
● Subjective estimates of:
  – the proposed regimen's safety
  – the proposed regimen's efficacy
    to prevent, delay or cure (inc.
    'faith in doctors and medical
    care' + 'chance of recovery'

* at motivating but inhibiting levels

MODIFYING AND
ENABLING FACTORS

DEMOGRAPHIC – (very young or old)
STRUCTURAL – (cost, duration,
complexity; side effects;
accessibility of regimen; need for
new patterns of behaviour
ATTITUDES – (satisfaction with visit,
physician, other staff; clinic
procedures and facilities)
INTERACTION – (length, depth,
continuity, mutuality of expectation,
quality and type of doctor-patient
relationship; physician agreement
with patient; feed-back to patient)
ENABLING – (prior experience with
notion, illness or regimen; source
of advice and referral (including
social pressure))

COMPLIANT
BEHAVIOUR

LIKELIHOOD OF:
Compliance with preventive health
recommendations and prescribed
regimens,
e.g. screening,
     immunisations,
prophylactic examinations, drugs,
diet, exercise,
personal and work habits,
follow-up tests,
referrals,
follow-up appointments,
entering or continuing a
     treatment programme

Source: Becker *et al.* (1977).

'emotionally', although the Italians, apparently because of their authoritarian masculine role in the family, were stoic at home. In contrast, the Old Americans tried to conform to the medical notion of an ideal patient, seeking to co-operate with hospital personnel and to avoid being a nuisance. They therefore avoided expressing pain and tried to give clear and descriptive accounts of their ailments to meet the doctor's expectations.

In another study based on new patients to an outpatient clinic, Zola (1973) found that patients of Irish and Italian origin differed in the way they communicated about their complaints. Irish patients seemed to describe their problem in terms of a fairly specific dysfunction, whereas Italian patients conveyed a more general malfunctioning, emphasising the more diffuse nature of their complaints. However, both groups of patients appeared to have accommodated their ailments for long periods and something else needed to happen before they decided to seek medical care. Zola identified five different types of incident which 'triggered' the decision to seek medical care. Firstly, there was what he called an interpersonal crisis, for example, a death in the family. Secondly, there was a perceived interference with social or personal relations, where the sufferer decides to seek medical care because their complaint starts to disrupt their personal plans or their social relationships. Thirdly, there is sanctioning from others who put pressure on the sufferer to seek medical help. This can come from family members, neighbours, friends and workmates. Such sanctioning is illustrated by a respondent explaining why he decided to attend a hospital accident and emergency department after he had cut his hand. The respondent stated:

> If he [his father] hadn't pushed me into it I'd have just had a pint of milk and a couple of aspirins and gone to bed and I'd have been OK. My dad thought I looked rough and he said in between the thumb and forefinger is a dangerous place to cut as you get lockjaw and we couldn't remember when I'd had a tetanus injection (Calnan, 1983b).

The fourth trigger is perceived interference with vocational or physical activity. This is where an individual's complaint begins to interfere with his/her everyday activities, such as work roles. The final trigger involves the temporising of signs and symptoms where the sufferer has specific ideas about how long certain complaints should last, and if a complaint continues to persist after the experienced time then a decision to seek medical care is made.

Zola's identification of non-psychological triggers draws attention to the way in which social and situational factors may influence coping behaviour. He also identified specific triggers as being of particular importance to different ethnic groups. For example, the presence of an interpersonal crisis and the perceived interference with social or personal relations were more frequent triggers among the Italians, while sanctioning was of particular importance for the Irish, and perceived interference with work or physical functioning for patients of Anglo-Saxon origin.

Other studies adopting a collectivist approach have focused directly on the influence of significant others in illness behaviour. A recent example is the work of Pratt (1976), who studied the relationship between the family structure of the urban American family and the pattern of health behaviour. She was concerned with explaining why lower socio-economic groups had relatively poor health and tended not to conform to officially recommended health practice. The family characteristics most strongly associated with good health and compliance with officially recommended health actions were high levels of interaction, support and encouragement among family members and where there was a low level of family conflict. However, in general, the supportive role of the family was specifically associated with levels of health, whereas those aspects of family functioning which facilitated coping behaviour were relatively more important to the use of the health service.

In many cases the influence of significant others may extend beyond the individual's immediate family. Freidson (1970) argues that rates of use of health services are influenced by what he termed the lay referral system, and developed a four-fold typology relating characteristics of the lay referral system to rates of service use (see Figure 3.2). This typology was based on two characteristics: (a) the social distance between lay and professional medical cultures, and (b) the structure of the lay referral system, such as the degree of cohesiveness. Freidson described the four resulting categories as follows:

(1) A culture which is markedly different from that of the professionals in which there is a well-developed cohesive lay referral structure, e.g. where deviations are not regarded as symptoms of illness, and the problem resolved by referring the deviant to an indigenous practitioner. A high degree of resistance

to use of professional services is predicted.

(2) A culture which again differs from the professional culture but where there is only a limited lay referral system such that the individual is exposed to influences outside the local community. A greater degree of utilisation is predicted.

(3) A lay culture which is similar to the professional culture but where there is only a limited lay referral system. Although there are no or few lay consultants to support or discourage use of services, because of cultural similarity in definition of deviations as illness an individual will seek professional help after attempts at self-treatment. Utilisation of professional medical services is predicted to be even greater.

(4) A culture similar to that of the professional is reinforced by a large and cohesive referral system. Maximum utilisation is predicted for this group.

Figure 3.2: Predicted Rates of Utilisation of Professional Services by Variation in Lay Referral System

Lay referral structure	Lay culture	
	Congruent with professional	Incongruent with professional
Loose, truncated	Medium to high utilisation	Medium to low utilisation
Cohesive, extended	Highest utilisation	Lowest utilisation

Source: Freidson (1970).

There is some evidence to support Freidson's propositions that the structure and composition of the lay referral system will influence patterns of help-seeking behaviour. For example, McKinlay (1972) studied the use of maternity services by lower-working-class mothers in Aberdeen. He divided his sample of 87 women into two groups, utilisers and non-utilisers according to whether or not they had attended the antenatal clinic before the seventeenth week of pregnancy and had since been regular attenders. Mothers classified as under-utilisers were found to have more relatives living geographically closer and to visit friends more frequently. Utilisers lived closer to friends and were more likely to have friends of their own age. Answers to questions about whom, if anyone, they would consult about five hypothetical problems showed that utilisers appeared to make greater use of friends and husbands and less use of mothers and other relatives, and also tended to consult a narrower range of lay persons. McKinlay suggests that the association between lay consultation patterns and use of antenatal services can be explained by the fact that friends are likely to have more up-to-date health beliefs and greater knowledge about the availability of services, or in Freidson's terms, their culture could be viewed as more congruent with that of the medical profession. The lower rate of take-up preventive health services among lower class than middle-class people has similarly been explained in terms of a cultural hypothesis, with such behaviour reflecting the existence of culturally transmitted values and beliefs which are incongruent with those of the medical profession (see Chapter 7).

Although relatives, and particularly household members, form the main sources of lay consultation and advice, other lay people may exert an important influence on an individual's illness behaviour in special circumstances. For example, colleagues may form an important source of advice in the case of accidents at work, while illness behaviour may also be influenced by established procedures at the workplace and the administrative requirements for possible compensation claims (Calnan 1983a).

Collectivist approaches have primarily focused on the influence of cultural values and of significant others in determining illness behaviour among different ethnic, social class and age groups. However, situational factors in the form of the differential cost of utilising health services, arising from their differing circumstances, have also been advanced as a major determinant of differences in patterns of utilisation of health services by social groups. Such costs arise from problems of the inaccessibility of services, the unavailability of transport, and difficulties arising from the need to take time off work, or coping with children. These costs of service use are likely to be of particular significance in determining rates of use of preventive health services, where the benefits to be derived are often less immediately apparent. The relative importance of the characteristics of service provision and of differences in perceived benefits of service use in determining rates of service use among social class groups is however still unclear (see Chapter 7).

Problems of 'Over-utilisation'

In addition to concerns with patient delay and non-use of health services, there has been a concern that patients should not use services unnecessarily and should not waste the doctor's time consulting with 'trivia'. These two demands often put potential patients in a dilemma. On the one hand they may be uncertain whether their symptoms are serious or not and would like to go to the doctor to ease their minds, but on the other hand they do not want to be seen by general practitioners to be a 'bad' patient. For example, one respondent stated with reference to the early diagnosis of breast cancer: 'Oh, I would not think my doctor has time for that sort of thing. He would go mad if I bothered him with nothing' (Calnan and Johnson, 1983).

A second type of over-utilisation which has caused concern is the question of why the public do not comply with organisational solutions about when to use specific services. For example, there has been a plethora of studies trying to explain why people use the hospital accident and emergency department instead of going to their general practitioner. This problem is specifically concerned with 'over-utilisation' of the hospital accident and emergency department and why the departments have to deal with what are clinically defined as 'trivial' complaints. Studies carried out in both the United Kingdom (Calnan, 1982), and the USA (Torrens and Yedvab, 1970), have examined social factors that might influence patterns of use. They have shown that the role of the hospital emergency department situated in central urban areas is different from that of one situated in suburban and provincial areas. The latter departments perform the more conventional function of providing emergency care for the community and for those people who suffer ill health away from home, as well as acting as a substitute for a family doctor during off-peak hours when services are not available. However, an additional function of the hospital emergency department situated in the inner city area is to act as a family doctor for all those not registered with family doctors, which in the USA is usually the urban poor.

Weaknesses in the Traditional Approach to Illness Behaviour

The clearest and simplest point to emerge from traditional studies of illness behaviour is that the presence of signs or symptoms is not always sufficient either for people to define themselves as sick or to seek professional medical care. The studies have pointed to the influence of social, cultural and psychological factors on the way individuals and social groups respond to signs and symptoms, and suggest that the question of why some people seek medical help and others do not has to be understood within a framework which takes into account each of these three types of factors and their relationship to one another. However, these studies have been characterised by methodological problems and a lack of coherent theoretical models which serve to detract from their value.

Three main methodological weaknesses can be identified in traditional studies of help-seeking behaviour. Firstly, many studies have used data which are retrospective and based on respondents' recall after the decision to seek help or a decision to adopt a certain pattern of health behaviour. In the case of studies of illness behaviour, respondents' accounts of their behaviour may be coloured by their experience since the decision to seek medical care was made, and particularly through the knowledge gained from visiting the health service. In the case of studies of health behaviour, the problem is more serious as data collected through cross-sectional studies are used to explain the determinants of health behaviour. Since data on health beliefs are collected at the same time as statements of retrospective behaviour, it is difficult to identify whether beliefs determine behaviour or vice versa. This may account for the apparent effectiveness of the HBM in explaining the decision to use preventive health services and to adopt patterns of health care (Becker and Maiman, 1975). In order to overcome this problem, Calnan (1984) employed a prospective study design to examine the power of the HBM for explaining attendance at a clinic providing immunography and attendance at a class teaching breast self-examination. This showed that the predictive power of the HBM for explaining attendance at both the clinic and class was fairly low.

The second methodological weakness is that until recently many of the traditional studies have used samples of people who actually used professional medical care. They then compared the delayers with the non-delayers within these populations. Studies using a sample which included people who did not consult were rare. However, to explain the variation in demand for the health service adequately it is necessary to examine why some people do not consult and others do.

The third methodological weakness is that the majority of studies have attempted to characterise the attender and the non-attender (delayer, under-utiliser) in terms of a socio-demograophic profile, pyschological dispositions or general orientation towards health and medicine. Thus, although help-seeking is often referred to as a social process, the actual study of how and why certain decisions are made has tended to be neglected. This has meant that although large numbers of people resort to self medication as an initial response to symptoms, little attention has been given to the different course of action adopted prior to or instead of consulting the doctor, and the reasons for these alternative choices and assessments.

The major theoretical criticism of this traditional approach to illness behaviour has come from sociologists who favour the interpretive paradigm. Dingwall (1976), for example, emphasises the need for sociological enquiry to examine individuals' action and the meaning of that action and not to assume that actors are empty organisms responding passively to the demands of the social system. He also questions the assumption of many traditional studies of illness behaviour that medical explanations have a unique access to the truth. Following from this assumption, lay theories of illness are treated as in some way inferior to biological and medical explanations. Dingwall argues that since clinicians' accounts have no known relationship to the experiences of sick people they cannot advance the understanding of illness as social conduct. For Dingwall a biology of illness is therefore complementary to a sociology of illness and in no way a substitute for it. Each has an autonomous realm of problems, and once this is accepted a more pluralist approach to social life can be developed.

Theoretical criticisms of the traditional studies of illness behaviour have led to some important changes in the questions posed for study. One change has been from an emphasis on the need to explain or account for problems surrounding the use of services to an emphasis on questions such as 'What is health?', 'What is illness?', 'How do people come to feel ill?' and 'What do they do about it?' The use of professional medical care is thus viewed as only one response to the problematic experience of illness. Secondly, there has been greater emphasis on the cognitive and interactional components of illness behaviour. As West (1979) explains:

Very generally, this [shift] has involved a reformulation of the problem from one in which the task was viewed as the identification of social and psychological variables that impeded the [irrational] proto-patient from doing what he ought to do — consult the doctor, to another in which much greater attention is directed to the person as a conscious, reflective actor engaged in the process of making sense of various kinds of body changes within the framework of his own 'lay knowledge'.

This shift in perspective involves an acceptance that man's ability to evaluate, interpret, and define the meaning of his world and the world of others, will be influential in the course of action that is followed. Furthermore, disease and illness are viewed as conceptually distinct and derived from different social contexts. This is illustrated by Cassel (1976) who describes illness as 'what the patient feels when he goes to the doctor' and disease to mean 'what he has on the way home from the doctor's office'.

Not only are the entities of disease and illness conceptually distinct but the relationship between the two is not simple. There are many empirical examples where disease has been identified but illness has not been imputed. For example, in the case of screening for disease some pathology may be identified in medical terms but the sufferer may not have experienced any change in body functioning and not defined themselves as ill. Eisenberg (1977) identifies this difference and states:

> When disease is extreme, as in diabetic ketoacidosis or in the terminal stages of malignancy, its pervasiveness make illness inevitable. However, disease may occur in the absence of illness; the person with hypertension may by asymptomatic and therefore unconcerned when the physician who measures his blood pressure becomes alarmed; he may stop taking the prescribed medication because it makes him 'ill', even though he is told it will mitigate his disease. Only when the hypertension lead to congestive failure or hemiplegia will the person become a patient and agree with his doctor that he is sick, even when the agreement may be limited to a common perception that a problem exists which each is likely to formulate in quite different terms.

Lay Models of Health and Illness

The Structure of Health Beliefs

The application of the social construction approach to health and illness focuses on the way sufferers make sense of their body and bodily disturbances. Emphasis is therefore placed on examining lay interpretive processes within the context of lay knowledge and beliefs. Thus, rather than treating health beliefs as idiosyncratic, this type of approach emphasises their logic and integrity. The methodology, and in some respects this perspective, is more commonly associated with the ethnographic research found in anthropology where emphasis is placed on discovering the rules and meanings that populations or groups use to order their lives and make sense of their experiences.

A good illustration of this approach is provided by Lewis's (1976) description of the system of medicine of the Gnau villagers of New Guinea. He showed that illness was grouped with a wider class of undesirable conditions. Sickness was defined in terms of an impaired sense of well-being as a whole. The Gnau villagers did not classify the signs and symptoms of a complaint but were more concerned with eliciting information about the social circumstances of the sufferer and identifying the causes of the illnesses. Thus, sufferers could present various types of signs or symptoms but if the cause was the same then the illness might be classified in the same way. The explanation of causes usually identified external factors such as conflict between families or being attacked by an evil spirit. The nature of the cause influences the type of treatment offered. The ill person follows a ritualised procedure which to the Gnau symbolises wretchedness. This involves the sufferer withdrawing from the social life of the village and covering the body with ash and dust. The Gnau's system of knowledge about body processes is a general one and contrasts markedly with the Western scientific approach which focuses on knowledge of specific body processes.

Studies within Western cultures where scientific medicine has a monopoly have also shown variation in the way health and illness are defined among different social groups. For example, Blaxter and Paterson (1982) in their study of socially disadvantaged families found that for the majority of respondents (both mothers and daughters) health was defined in a functional way in terms of the ability to carry on normal roles such as continuing to work. Health was seen as the absence of illness and particularly of illnesses which seriously disrupt practical and necessary activities. Blaxter and Paterson state:

> The norms of the majority continued to be low. One, whose daughter had suffered recurrent ear infections, scarlet fever and coughs, said that she had 'never had a day's illness', and another, with one child who was crippled and other with chronic conditions, described them as 'very healthy children'. Healthy children were those who were never kept off school, or for brief periods only, or at least managed to be active.

There was, as Blaxter and Paterson (1982) point out, no evidence of a positive conception of health. Illness was also seen in functional terms and a distinction made between normal illnesses and more serious illnesses. The former were familiar and common ailments, which were an expected and accepted part of daily life. Some conditions were not defined as bad health at all, especially those associated with 'normal' stages of life — child-bearing, the menopause, or wear and tear over the years. Illnesses consisted of the serious illnesses such as cancer, heart disease and tuberculosis. Blaxter and Paterson also found that health and illness were moral categories. Health was a good quality and few respondents wanted to say that they were anything but healthy. Illness was conceived of in terms of a state of spiritual or moral malaise. They state:

> People were not ill if they did not 'lie down to it', 'dwell on it', or 'let it get them down'. Illness was not so much the experience of symptoms as the reaction to symptoms. The adoption of the rule of a sick person by staying off work, taking to bed, or allowing one's functioning to be disturbed.

The lack of a positive conception of health and the accommodation of minor illnesses might explain why lower-working-class groups have a lower rate of participation in preventive health programmes than other classes. These conceptions are clearly influenced by the experience of a high prevalence of ill health among this group.

Studies examining the way middle-class groups or wealthy groups conceive of health and illness are rare. Herzlich (1973) carried out one of the few such studies based on interviews with 80 subjects — 68 lived in Paris and 12 lived in Normandy. She analysed the content of these repondents' accounts about health and illness and found that illness was conceived of as something external to the individual. The way of life of modern urban society was regarded as the principal and active determinant of disease, through its effect in exposing people to risks of pathological agents, accidents and injury. In contrast, health was seen to be something internal to the individual determined by their constitution, temperament and heredity. These two elements are in opposition, determining states of health and illness. Although illness is determined by factors external to the individual, people were seen as having a certain margin of freedom to respond to illness with the resistance of health. Since illness was caused by external agents respondents did not regard catching illness as blameworthy, although people were regarded as responsible for having lost their health.

Herzlich not only examined lay people's distinction between health and illness but also looked at the meaning of each of these terms. She identified three distinct dimensions of health in the respondents' accounts. The first dimension she referred to as 'health-in-a-vacuum', which implies an absence of illness. The second dimension was called 'the reserve of health', and refers to an individual's capacity to maintain good health. This capacity is made up of two aspects — physical strength and a potential for resistance to illness — and is regarded as determined by individual attributes, such as a person's constitution and temperament. The third dimension is what Herzlich described as 'equilibrium'. This forms a more positive conception of health and is regarded as constituting the full realisation of the individual's reserve of health. People described a state of equilibrium in terms of happiness, relaxation, feeling strong, and having good relations with people. At the biological level, it is a state of perfect well-being, where there is an absence of awareness of the body.

Herzlich also identified a three-fold classification of illness based on respondents' responses to illness. First, there were those who explained illness in terms of what Herzlich described as an 'occupation', which occurred when the respondents emphasised the need to fight and control the impact of it. This suggested that the respondent would do anything possible to manage the illness, including seeking medical care, and that he or she formed a conception of illness most common among people who were currently ill or had been severely ill in the past. The second group were those who saw illness as a 'destroyer'. This group emphasised the destructive influence of inactivity and the need to avoid it or ignore it at all costs. It might include people with diseases such as breast cancer who have been described as deniers, refusing to accept or acknowledge the problem. The third group were those who saw illness as a 'liberator'. In this case illnesses or inactivity freed them from their everyday commitments. As Herzlich notes, 'destructive illness' and 'illness as an occupation' seem to correspond to different stages of illness, with destructive illness primarily operating at the beginning of the illness and illness as an occupation at later stages. The conception of 'illness as a liberator' may be tied to the patient's struggle with benign, short, and painless conditions. However, the precise determinants and implications of these different lay conceptions of health and disease remain to be examined.

An investigation carried out more recently in Aberdeen by Williams (1983) into the way elderly people identify states of health produced a similar classification to the one identified by Herzlich (1973) in France. The evidence about lay concepts of health came from intensive open-ended interviews with 70 informants, aged 60 and over, who lived in the city of Aberdeen. Three major dimensions of health were identified. These were: (a) health as the absence of illness and disease; (b) health as a dimension of strength, weakness and exhaustion; and (c) health as functional fitness. The relationship between these three dimensions was a complex one. For example, health as strength was seen as being logically distinct from health as an 'absence' of disease, because the former notion of 'good' health was seen as involving the 'strength' to overcome a disease that is already present. Functional fitness was described in terms of what a person was fit for which, in relation to the age group involved, was usually work in the home and garden. Thus, fitness had a simple relationship to sickness and disease, in that to be disabled is to be unfit for normal roles. However, its relation to health was more complex, in that having weakness or vulnerability in their constitution did not, on its own, imply being unfit.

In contrast to studies which have looked at the lay person's general conceptions of health and illness are studies which have examined the system of knowledge used by lay people to make sense of common signs and symptoms. Helman (1978), based on research carried out in a London suburb, examined lay theories about colds and 'flu'. Colds were found to refer to a state when you feel colder and 'flu' or fever when you feel hotter. Helman describes how colds are perceived:

> chills and colds are due to a by-product of one's personal battle with the natural environment — particularly with areas of lowered temperature. In this view, damp or rain ('cold/wet' conditions) or cold winds or draughts ('cold/dry') can penetrate the boundary of the skin and cause similar conditions within the body.

The conditions believed to cause colds are cold, rainy days, or sitting in a draught or night air, or changes in the season. Colds and fevers are also one's own responsibility, from carelessness or lack of foresight. By contrast, fevers are due to germs or bugs which travel through the air between people, entering the body of their victim and causing fever:

> Because germs, unlike colds, originate in other people rather than in the natural environment, germ infection implies some sort of

relationship of whatever duration. Infection is an inherent risk in all relationships though neither party is to blame if one picks up a germ.

Victims of germ infection are viewed as less blameworthy than in the case of colds and more able to gain sympathy. This again reflects notions of the degree of individual responsibility for and control of health and illness, which appear to be present in most lay beliefs.

Lay Theories about the Causation of Illness

Studies examining lay beliefs about health and illness have discovered a complex system of theories about the causation of illness, which comes into use when sufferers try to make sense of a change in body functioning.

Chrisman (1977), in a review of several studies, identified the following theories of causality found among populations from different cultures. They were:

(1) Invasion — such as germ, cancer, something I have eaten, or object intrusion.
(2) Degeneration — such as being run down or accumulating toxins.
(3) Mechanical — such as blockage of gastro-intestinal tract or blood vessels.
(4) Balance — such as maintaining 'a proper diet', enough vitamins, enough sleep, as well as maintenance of harmony in the patient's life and relationships.

More recent research in Britain by Blaxter (1983), based on interviews with 46 lower working-class women, attempted to identify the structure of women's thinking about causes of disease. In her analysis of the 46 transcripts she found 587 examples of named disease, although in only 432 of these examples was the cause imputed explicitly or implicitly. In some of these cases the disease was too common or too trivial to be worthy of discussion. However, two diseases, cancer and tuberculosis, stood out as being the most frequently mentioned without discussion of cause. While many of the women were still concerned about tuberculosis, cancer had replaced TB as the incurable disease. Blaxter argues that many feared it because it was mysterious and they had no idea what caused it. There was a suggestion that its causes were random and it was all the more frightening because it could happen to anybody.

Of the diseases where a cause was imputed, Blaxter (1983) identified twelve categories of cause. Infection was the most common cause followed by heredity or family tendencies, and environmental agents, such as climate, working conditions and drugs. It was noticeable that stress and strain were one of the more popular categories of cause, and as Blaxter (1983) argues, her respondents were very conscious of the mind/body link. In conclusion, she suggests that although the women's models of causal processes were often inaccurate from a scientific point of view, they were not in principle unscientific. She argues that not only are women's models of disease causation sophisticated but they in many ways parallel modern scientific explanations, particularly those that link the environment and ill health.

Lay people's theories of illness causation not only contain ideas about the causes of illness but also often contain stereotypes of the type of people likely to get an illness. For example, West (1979) shows how parents with epileptic children sometimes doubted the clinical diagnosis, as their child's identity did not match up with what they considered to be the identity of the typical epileptic. Similarly, Calnan and Johnson's (1983) study showed that some women had images of a type of person who is likely to get breast cancer. For example, one woman said:

> Well, these two women I know, they are both of a similar . . . they are both highly nervous people. When I say nervous I do not mean that they are frightened of their own shadows but they were both very thin. Well, they were both wiry people, probably people that tend to live on their nerves.

Lay theories about the causes of ill health have implications for what people feel they can do to manage or even prevent ill health. This is clearly illustrated by recent research which has investigated the feasibility of government policies on prevention (Pill and Stott, 1982) These authors have suggested that for government propaganda about prevention, with its emphasis on individual responsibility, to have any meaning then people's ideas about the causation of illness must be examined. A sample of working-class mothers were asked what they thought the main reasons for illness were. The majority of women subscribed to the belief that germs are the main causes of illness. This constitutes an 'amoral' theory of causality where nobody has to feel responsible for illness onset. This amoral concept appears to conflict with official conceptions about health, with their emphasis on individual responsibility. The notion of blame and individual responsibility tended to be attributed to cases when either sufferers did not go to the doctor or delayed going, or where the sufferers had taken unnecessary risks with their health.

Lay theories about causation of illness also have other implications for explaining individuals' health behaviour. For example, one of the key dimensions in understanding health behaviour is how people conceptualise threats to their health. Data collected in a study of health beliefs (Calnan and Johnson, 1985) suggest that people often make a distinction between diseases they fear getting at a general level and those that they feel personally vulnerable to. For example, many respondents identified cancer as the disease that they feared and dreaded getting but did not always feel personally vulnerable to it. As one respondent stated: 'Well, I fear getting it but I don't believe I will get it.' This distinction between a general fear of cancer and feelings about personal vulnerability stems from the respondents' ideas about the causes of cancer. Far from believing that everyone was at risk, the most common theory of causality invoked was a hereditary theory, as the following respondent explained:

> I do worry about getting cancer simply because there is so much of it in my family. And I do think, every time I get something — I wonder if it is cancer. I must admit that I do worry about it.

This adoption of a heredity theory of cancer may be the product of the way people construct and develop their own theories of causality, for the respondents tended to base their theories on personal experience rather than official information. Thus, heredity explanations may be invoked simply because they tend to involve personal experience. This use of personal experience as a basis for making sense of health and illness is important because the underlying philosophy in many health education campaigns stems from a different model of disease causation. Such campaigns tend to use an epidemiological model of disease causation, with the emphasis on reducing the chances of getting the disease. This probability model was not used by any of the respondents (Calnan and Johnson, 1985).

The origins of lay beliefs about illness in Western industrialised society are difficult to pinpoint. The dominant scientific medical beliefs seem to have been accepted by many groups, with the germ theory of disease being one of the more commonly used. However, the scientific medical belief system does not appear to totally dominate the way lay people think about health and illness. Alternative theories sometimes reflect humoral notions of balance, or are products of a particular subculture, or may be created as a result of experience.

Theoretical Models of Illness Action

Fabrega (1974) and Dingwall (1976) have developed theoretical models of illness and illness behaviour from an interpretive perspective which provide a useful framework for approaching the study of illness. Because of their theoretical stance, which emphasises the importance of taking a pluralist and a phenomenological approach, they cannot provide any substantive material on the rules used by people when they interpret and respond to signs and symptoms. However, their models do outline a form in which the decision-making process might occur.

Fabrega's approach concentrates on the information a person might be expected to process during an occurrence of illness. He states:

> Concentrating in a theoretical way on informational correlates of illness can be seen as articulating a set of rules that organise the data of illness (i.e. sensations, perceptions, beliefs, circumstances, etc.), and explain the culturally specific acts of behaviour associated with illness occurrences in various contexts.

For Fabrega, the person monitors happenings and processes through four analytically distinct but connected systems. These are:

(1)   biological system which includes chemical and physiological processes;
(2)   social system which includes relations between the person and other groups or institutions;
(3)   phenomenological system which involves states of awareness and self-definition;
(4)   memory system which is a unique history of the person that includes experiences gained from deviations in the other three systems.

Using these interlinked systems a person is continually capable of monitoring happenings and processes in the functioning of the various systems. A new deviation can be evaluated because of the availability of information experienced and internalised from other deviations in functioning, or through the availability of 'illness categories'. The information available to the individual during an illness occurrence is processed in nine stages:

(1) Illness recognition and labelling — conviction that an undesirable state of affairs exists.
(2) Illness disvalues — evaluation of illness's meaning or significance.
(3) Treatment plans — each person is believed to have available a set of treatment actions that can be implemented for the purpose of managing an illness.
(4) Assessment of treatment plans — each person is capable of estimating the probability that a treatment plan will alleviate a negative component of illness.
(5) Assessment of treatment benefits.
(6) Assessment of treatment costs.
(7) Assessment of net benefits.
(8) Selection of treatment plans.
(9) Set up for recycling.

Fabrega's approach is taken from traditional economics and elementary decision theory. People are viewed as basically rational, evaluating instances of illness using the principle of cost-benefit analysis and reaching a decision regarding the best course of action that might eliminate the illness.

Dingwall's model of illness action is similar to Fabrega's in that it distinguishes between the occurrence of biological events in the human body and the meaning of these events. However, unlike Fabrega, Dingwall focuses almost entirely on the cognitive aspects or lay responses to disturbances in body functioning. He thus gives a more detailed account of how a disturbance in body process might become a problematic experience for the actor. Dingwall's model (see Figure 3.3) shows that when a biological disturbance affects the body this may disrupt the stable and predictable relationship between a person and his/her body. The extent of this disruption depends on the priorities given to the disturbance, with every actor having his/her own range of priorities. Dingwall argues that individuals need to present a 'normal' identity to others, but a significant biological disturbance may disrupt this 'normal' identity. Thus, remedial action is required to repair this disruption.

Dingwall views the sufferer as undergoing a series of interpretive and assessment processes (see Figure 3.3) similar to those set out by Fabrega. However, Dingwall places greater emphasis on the influence of the interpretive work of lay others and the introduction of official health knowledge (see Figure 3.4). The process of interpretation can be interpersonal, involving significant others such as family, friends and neighbours, which also involves an input of lay health knowledge. This interpersonal decision-making process can also involve other, more formal, contacts when the illness or injury episodes occur outside the network of informal contacts in a more public setting such as when an accident occurs in the street. Dingwall suggests that such episodes may involve a short-circuiting of the lay interpretive process due to the input of official health knowledge. The options for action which result from this decision-making are three. The disturbance can be ignored, the person can wait and see what happens, or a decision to seek help can be made.

Figure 3.3: Basic Structure of Illness Action Model

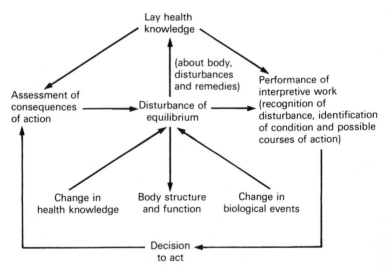

Source: Dingwall (1976).

Secondly, Dingwall, unlike Fabrega, makes no *a priori* judgement about the structure of decision-making in illness episodes and implies that the cost-benefit model of decision-making may only be one among several forms. Evidence to support this view has been

Figure 3.4: Some Pathways through Illness Action Model.

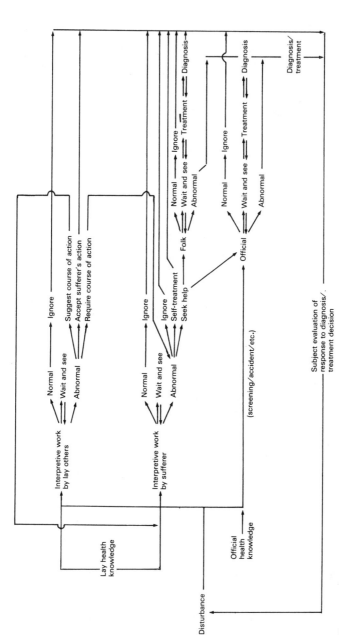

Source: Dingwall (1976).

provided by a study comparing the pre-patient careers of sufferers with lacerations to those with illnesses (Calnan, 1983a). This showed that in the former cases decision-making tended to be routinised rather than taking the form of a long-drawn-out series of assessments. In the cases involving lacerations, the decision-making was brief and usually straightforward, with the three stages of identification that something is wrong, assessment of significance and decision to act all being compressed. Although the decision-making about other illness was more elaborate and tentative than with lacerations, the cost-benefit type of process was not found with these types of complaints either.

A major contribution of the interpretive approach has been to show that lay people have their own complex systems of theories which are in some respects different from medical scientific theories, and that these exist even in societies where scientific medicine has a monopoly over the delivery of health care. In searching for the causes of disorders which they or others experience, lay people may employ specific theories of causation which form part of the lay culture, as well as relying on typifications about the sorts of circumstances and sorts of people who are most likely to suffer these disturbances. Furthermore, this approach has shown how the meaning attached to signs and symptoms often depends on the context in which they occur, while certain actions can also only be understood by reference to specific contexts. For example, in the case of a bleeding traumatic wound caused by an accident, lay people usually have clear ideas of what is wrong and why it happened, and have a recipe for action. In other cases, where symptoms are unfamiliar, self diagnosis becomes more problematic. This is illustrated by Cowie's (1976) study of 23 cardiac patients. In his examination of the interpretation of symptoms during the critical incident involving a sudden increase in pain he found that seven patients immediately diagnosed that they might be having a heart attack because they recognised that the symptoms were unfamiliar and could not be explained in terms of less serious complaints. However, sixteen patients initially applied a common-sense lay diagnostic category. Some explained the disturbance as a bout of indigestion and others related it to a recurrence of other illnesses that they had recently had which were not serious. For example, Mr O. explained what he thought was wrong: 'I just felt rotten and I had a pain in my chest and I thought it was indigestion. I'd been mowing my lawn in the lunch hour and lifted a heavy box and all this sort of thing, and it was three-quarters of an hour after the actual mow that I felt the pain.'

In cases where patients initially normalised their symptoms, this process of normalising was eventually upset by their failure to understand the physical experience in terms of the interpretive framework available to them. There was thus a break in accommodation between interpretation and experience. In many cases sufferers' spouses also played an influential part in the normalisation and evaluation of symptoms and tended to know something serious was wrong when their conception of their partner in his/her everyday activities was upset. These sixteen patients thus eventually decided to seek medical care when they could no longer explain their symptoms in terms of their own common-sense knowledge and when their recipes for action were unsuccessful.

Illness Behaviour and the Medical Model

This chapter has shown how the study of illness behaviour has evolved. The earlier approach, characterised by an acceptance of medical definitions and a positivist perspective, was valuable in identifying the importance of 'non-medical' factors in explaining illness behaviour, although it failed satisfactorily to account for and predict responses to illness. This approach posed no real practical problems for medicine, as it accepted the 'problems' as defined by those providing the service and took for granted professional medical definitions of health and disease.

Later changes in the study of illness behaviour have been marked by a shift away from an emphasis on explaining behaviour in terms of medical rationality, towards attempting to understand the lay person's actions in terms of their own logic, knowledge, and beliefs. The image of the lay person in this approach is of one who is active and critical, who has his/her own complex system of theories about health and illness, who manages his/her own health requirements and who is discriminating in his/her use of medical knowledge, advice and expertise. This change in the image of the lay person appears to pose considerable practical problems for the medical profession. For example, it has been argued (Armstrong, 1984) that the discovery that lay theories about disease are both rational and theoretically sophisticated necessitates a change in clinical practice in at least two ways. The first involves a change in technique in that good clinical practice should involve considering and responding to the patients' theories about illness, and not just being concerned with diagnosis and treatment. This is particularly important if the medical profession is concerned with increasing patients' satisfaction and compliance. The second requires a more fundamental change, in that it involves a reassessment of the value of the conceptual framework used in present-day clinical practice. This reassessment is required as patients' experience of symptoms and illness does not completely correlate with organic disturbances, often being influenced by their social relationships and adjustments to life changes. Biomedical theory of the relationship between symptoms and the organic lesion thus needs to be re-examined, as does the idea of the doctor as a technical expert and his patient as 'a passive repository for organic pathology and uncomplicated soak for medical explanation and reassurance' (Armstrong, 1985).

References

Armstrong, D. (1985) 'Illness behaviour revisited', *Journal of Psychosomatic Research* (forthcoming)

Becker, M.H. and Maiman, L.A. (1975) 'Sociobehavioural determinants of compliance with health and medical care recommendations', *Medical Care, 13*, 10

Becker, M.H., Haefner, D.P., Kasl, S.V., Kirscht, J., Maiman, L. and Rosenstock, I.M. (1977) 'Selected psychological models and correlates of individual health-related behaviours', *Medical Care, 15*, no. 5, Suppl. 27-46

Blaxter, M. (1983) 'The cause of disease: women talking', *Social Science and Medicine, 17*, 59-69

Blaxter, M. and Paterson, E. (1982) *Mothers and Daughters: A Three-generational Study of Health, Attitudes and Behaviour*, Heinemann Educational Books, London, Ch. 4, pp. 26-39

Calnan, M. (1982) 'The hospital accident and emergency department. What is its role?', *Journal Social Policy, 11*, 483-503

Calnan, M. (1983a) 'Social networks and help-seeking behaviour', *Social Science and Medicine, 17*, 25-8

Calnan, M. (1983b) 'Managing "minor" disorders: pathways to a hospital accident and emergency department', *Sociology of Health and Illness, 5*, 149-67

Calnan, M. (1984) 'The Health Belief Model and participation in programmes for the early detection of breast cancer: a comparative analysis', *Social Science and Medicine, 19*, 823-30

Calnan, M. and Johnson, B. (1983) 'Understanding non-compliance with cancer education campaign', UICC, TRS, *Public Education about Cancer*, Geneva, 76, 49-68

Calnan, M. and Johnson, B. (1985) 'Health, health risks and inequalities: an exploratory study of women's perceptions', *Sociology of Health and Illness, 7*, 1 (in press).

Cassell, E.J. (1976) *The Healer's Art: A New Approach to the Doctor-Patient Relationship*, Lippincott, New York

Chrisman, N.J. (1977) 'The health-seeking process: an approach to the natural history of illness', *Culture, Medicine and Psychiatry, 1*, 351-77

Cowie, B. (1976) 'The cardiac patient's perception of his heart attack', *Social Science and Medicine*, *10*, 87-96

Dingwall, R. (1976) *Aspects of Illness*, Martin Robertson, London

Eisenberg, L. (1977) 'Disease and illness: distinction between professional and popular ideas of sickness', *Culture, Medicine and Psychiatry*, *1*, 9-23

Fabrega, H. (1974) *Disease and Social Behaviour*, MIT Press, Boston, Mass.

Freidson, E. (1970) *The Profession of Medicine*, Dodd Mead and Co., New York

Helman, C.G. (1978) 'Feed a cold, starve a fever — folk models of infection in an English suburban community and their relation to medical treatment', *Culture, Medicine and Psychiatry*, *2*, 107-37

Herzlich, C. (1973) *Health and Illness*, Academic Press, London

Lewis, G. (1976) 'A view of sickness in New Guinea', in J.B. Loudon (ed.), *Social Anthropology and Medicine*, Academic Press, London

McKinlay, J. (1972) 'Social networks, lay consultation and help-seeking behaviour', *Social Forces*, *51*, 275-81

Mechanic, D. (1962) *Students Under Stress*, Free Press, New York

Mechanic, D. (1968) *Medical Sociology*, Free Press, New York

Mechanic, D. (1982) 'The concept of illness behaviour', *Journal of Chronic Disorders*, *15*, 189-94

Nichols, S., Waters, W., Fraser, J., Wheeler, M. and Ingham, S. (1981) 'Delay in the presentation of breast symptoms for consultant investigations', *Community Medicine*, *3*, 217-25

Pill, R. and Stott, N.C.H. (1982) 'Concepts of illness causation and responsibility: some preliminary data from a sample of working-class mothers', *Social Science and Medicine*, *16*, 13-51

Pratt, L. (1976) *Family Structure and Effective Health Behaviour. The Energized Family*, Houghton Mifflin Co., Boston

Rosenstock, I. (1966) 'Why people use health services', *Millbank Memorial Fund Quarterly*, *44*, 54-127

Suchmann, E. (1965) 'Stages of illness behaviour and medical care', *Journal of Human Health Behaviour*, *6*, 114-22

Torrens, P.R. and Yedvab, D.G. (1970) 'Variations among emergency room populations: a comparison of four hospitals in New York city', *Medical Care*, *8*, 1-12

Wadsworth, M.E.J., Butterfield, W. and Blaney, H. (1973) *Health and Illness: The Choice of Treatment*, Tavistock, London

West, P.B. (1979) 'Making sense of epilepsy', in D.J. Osborne, M.M. Grunberg and J.R. Eiser (eds.), *Social Aspects, Attitudes, Communication, Care and Training*, Academic Press, London

Williams, R. (1983) 'Concepts of health: an analysis of lay logic', *Sociology*, *17*, 185-204

Williamson, J. *et al.* (1964) 'Old people at home: their unreported needs', *The Lancet*: 1117-20

Zborowski, M. (1952) 'Cultural components in response to pain', *Journal of Social Issues*, *8*, 16-30

Zola, I.K. (1973) 'Pathways to the doctor: from person the patient', *Social Science and Medicine*, *7*, 677-89

4 DOCTORS AND MEDICAL PRACTICE

Doctors differ from other groups of health service staff in terms of their professional status and, together with lawyers, have been regarded as the foremost professions. This chapter thus begins by examining the nature and attributes of professional groups and considers a number of different, and sometimes conflicting, socio-logical theories about professions, which have tried to explain the power, status and authority of the medical profession. The chapter then focuses on the relationship between doctors and patients. This relationship has been viewed as one form of a particular type of provider-consumer relationship and attention has been paid to understanding the sociological problem of how this form of relation-ship is socially organised. Other work has stemmed from the medical professionals' realisation that the nature of their relationship with their patients may influence whether the consultation has a successful outcome or not, and has focused particularly on the factors affecting the communication of information in the consultation.

Doctors as a Professional Group

Characteristics of Doctors as a Professional Group

The Attribute Approach. This is primarily an empirical approach which involves an attempt to list the essential features of those occupations which are conventionally defined as professions, so as to achieve a universal definition of professions. An early example of the attribute approach was Carr-Saunders and Wilson's (1933) identifi-cation of five characteristics that they regarded as distinctive of professional occupations. These were the presence of: (1) specialised skill and training; (2) minimum fees and salaries; (3) professional associations; (4) a code of ethics; and (5) work consisting of the provision of a skilled service or advice. Subsequent attempts to identify traits which distinguish professions, such as Greenwood's (1957) five attributes and Gross's (1958) list of six attributes, included many of those identified by Carr-Saunders and Wilson. One of the most notable attempts to develop the attribute approach was provided by Goode (1960) who argued that professions should be defined in terms of two core characteristics and ten derived characteristics. The two core characteristics consisted of the presence of a prolonged, specialised training in a body of abstract knowledge, and a collectivity or service orientation. The ten derived characteristics identified by Goode were:

(1) The profession determines its own standards of education and training.
(2) The student professional goes through a more extensive socialisation experience than students in other occupations.
(3) Professional practice is often legally recognised by some form of licensure.
(4) Licensing and admission boards are run by members of the profession.
(5) Most legislation concerned with the profession is shaped by that profession.
(6) The occupation gains in income, power and status and can demand higher calibre students.
(7) The practitioner is relatively free of lay evaluation and control.
(8) The norms of practice enforced by the profession are more stringent than legal controls.
(9) Members are more strongly identified and affiliated with the profession than are members of other occupation with theirs.
(10) The profession is more likely to be a life-time occupation. Members do not care to leave it, and a higher proportion asserts that if they had to do it over again they would again choose that type of work.

A brief examination of the characteristics of the occupation of medicine might suggest that it possesses many, if not all, of these characteristics, and using these criteria alone it is a good example of what a profession is. However, this congruence between medicine and a classification of the essential features of a profession is hardly surprising, given that occupations such as medicine were used as the examples from which the classification was created. An additional weakness is that many of the characteristics also describe other occupations which do not have medicine's status, authority, and power. This classification is thus of doubtful value if used as a means of distinguishing professions from other occupations. Other classifications adopting an attribute approach share similar problems, and consist of *ad hoc* constructions of lists of attributes.

Functionalist Approach. The major problems with the attribute approach are the lack of an explicit theoretical framework, and the neglect of the historical conditions which gave rise to these special occupations called professions. One approach which, although it has much in common with the attribute approach, has both a theoretical and historical perspective, is the functionalist approach, among whose influential exponents are Barber (1963) and Parsons (1951). This approach locates the position of the professions in the wider social system and accounts for the special position of professional groups in terms of the vital functions that professions perform for the society as a whole. For example, functionalists argue that expert knowledge is imperative to the development and organisation of industrial society. However, specialist knowledge can be powerful, particularly in sensitive areas such as health and illness, where the community is vulnerable to exploitation. The professions perform the function of using their expert knowledge in the community's interest and the altruistic and service orientation of the profession protect the community from exploitation. Thus, the medical profession is given exclusive control of matters of health and illness in industrial societies because it works in the interest of potential patients and is committed to the maintenance of the health of the community. In repayment for performing this special and valuable role, the medical profession and other professions are accorded higher status and given greater financial rewards than other occupational groups. The functionalist explanation of the establishment of the professions thus suggests that the professions automatically developed out of the functional differentiation generated by the division of labour. The change in the division of labour came about because of changes in values or owing to technological factors. The profession of medicine developed as a response to the system's requirements for the control of 'illness'. The requirement was for a group with access to technical knowledge which could be used in the interests of the community and thus be functional for the system. Technical knowledge brings with it power and status, and while all illnesses were not controllable, the doctor was legitimised in practice on the grounds of technical competence and the institutionalised expectation of 'doing everything possible'.

Professionalism as a Form of Occupational Control. Recent sociological writing on professions and professionalism has rejected the idea that the medical profession emerged naturally and automatically out of the division of labour. Instead it is suggested that the actual rise of the medical profession occurred as a result of a historically specific process which involved a power conflict among a number of different interest groups. Thus, far from seeing medicine emerging naturally because of its superior skills and knowledge and thus its ability to perform vital functions in industrial society, these writers have characterised the process in terms of a political struggle between groups intent on achieving higher status. Rather than assuming that medicine's attainment of professional status was an inevitable one, it therefore attempts to explain why medicine was so successful in attaining professional status compared with other competing groups. Freidson (1970), who is one of a number of authors to have adopted this latter approach, conceives of a profession as a structural position which has to be attained and maintained through a process of political struggle and persuasion. He suggests that the most strategic distinction between professions and other occupations lies in legitimate organised autonomy. A profession can be distinguished from other occupations in that it has been given the right to control its own work. Freidson states:

> Unlike other occupations, professions are deliberately granted autonomy including the exclusive right to determine who can legitimately do its work and how the work should be done. Virtually all occupations struggle to obtain both rights, and some manage to seize them, but only the profession is granted the right to exercise them legitimately.

The right of autonomy is usually granted by a dominant elite or by the state. It is this patronage or protection by the dominant elite, according to Freidson, that aids occupations in the pursuit of professional status, rather than an intrinsic quality of an occupation which makes it superior to competing occupational groups.

Freidson argues that expert knowledge and other attributes which have been identified as distinctive features of a profession are used by these groups as ideological ammunition for attaining the powerful position of professional status, as well as for maintaining it. Freidson illustrates this proposition in an examination of Goode's list of core and derived characteristics which are put forward as essential features of a profession. He suggests that Goode's two core characteristics, a prolonged specialised training in a body of abstract knowledge and a collectivity or service orientation, 'are critical criteria for professions in so far as they are said to be causal in producing autonomy'. However, he argues that Goode's criteria are not in themselves sufficiently specific to determine whether particular occupations should be regarded as professions. Taking the three traditional professions of medicine, law and the ministry, the degree of specialisation and the amount and type of theory and abstract knowledge is in each case sufficiently wide that many other occupations not recognised as professions would fall within it. Nursing, for example, is specifically excluded from the professions by Goode on the basis of training, but falls within the range manifested by the three established professions. However, as Freidson notes, Goode excludes nursing because he feels its training is nor more than a 'lower level medical education', which implies more the lack of autonomy it is supposed to produce than the specific attributes of nurse training. Thus, it is not what nurses learn or how long it takes, but the fact that the bulk of what they learn is ultimately specified by physicians that is important. As Freidson concludes:

> It does not seem to be the actual context of training that explains or produces the differences ... the possibilities for functional autonomy and the relation of the work of an occupation to that of dominant professions seem critical. And the process determining the outcome is essentially political and social rather than technical in character — a process in which power and persuasive rhetoric are of greater importance than the objective character of knowledge, training and work.

Johnson (1972) also argues that professionalism is not an expression of the qualities inherent in specific occupations but a type of occupational control which emerged out of a specific set of historical conditions. However, while Freidson emphasised that professional autonomy is derived from an occupation being given the right to control its own work and sometimes the work of others, Johnson suggests that professional control and autonomy are specifically derived from the ability of the producer to define and cater for the needs of the consumer. Johnson (1972) argues that the type of occupational control found in provider-consumer relationships depends upon two factors. These are the social distance between the two parties, which is the distance created by the difference in specialised knowledge and specialised skills between the producer and consumer. The greater the distance between producer and consumer, the greater will be the level of uncertainty in the relationship, and thus the greater the dominance of the provider and the dependence of the consumer. The structure of the provider-consumer relationship is also dependent upon the social and economic resources available to the two parties. Using these two elements Johnson developed a threefold typology of occupational control:

(1) Collegiate control. This is where the producer defines the needs of the consumer and the manner in which these needs are catered for — e.g. medicine.

(2) Patronage. This is where the consumer defines his own needs and the manner in which they are met — e.g. accountancy.

(3) Mediation. This is where a third party, such as the state, mediates in the relationship between producer and consumer, defining both the needs and the manner in which the needs are met — e.g. probation officer.

Medicine is described as a form of collegiate control because of its ability to impose on the consumer its own definitions of need and how it should be catered for. Johnson (1972) argues that this ability of the provider to define needs is due in part to the acute problems of uncertainty that consumers face in matters of health and illness, which help create consumer dependence and also heightens the social distance between the consumer and provider. The powerlessness of the consumer is further compounded by the demand for medical services being fragmented and disorganised, whereas the providers are organised and powerful due to their ability to draw on social and economic resources which are associated with their class position.

The view that one of the major sources of a profession's power is its ability to create social distance between itself and the consumer has been developed by other writers, specifically in relation to medicine. For example, Waitzkin and Stoeckle (1972) argued that the 'competence gap' (i.e. discrepancy in knowledge between doctors and patients) leads to the potential for exploitation. The doctors's ability to control and manipulate information creates a basis asymmetry in the doctor-patient relationship. Professional dominance is thus grounded in a stratified distribution of technical 'knowledge'. Waitzkin and Stoeckle argue that the perpetuation of uncertainty by physicians serves to maintain a professional's power. The provision of information, according to these writers, not only reduces the patient's uncertainty, but in generating a greater degree of control in decision-making about the illness the physician's power in the doctor-patient relationship is correspondingly reduced. They state:

> Although both physician and patient experience uncertainty, the competence gap — which derives from a discrepancy in technical knowledge — means that uncertainty generally is greater for the patient than for the physician.

Professional Power and the Needs of the Economy. A different explanation of professional dominance suggests that professional power is tied up with the requirements of the economic system. For example, Johnson (1977), in his more recent writings, argues that professionalism can only arise when the political processes which create and maintain uncertainty in the producer-client relationships coincide with the needs of the capitalist system. In other words, for professionalism to develop the occupation must not only sustain a dependent clientele but also must meet some of the requirements of the economic system. Johnson illustrates this approach by using the case of medicine as an example. He states:

> The professionalisation of medicine — those institutions sustaining its autonomy — is directly related to its monopolisation of 'official' definitions of illness and health. The doctor's certificate defines and legitimates the withdrawal of labour. Credentialism, involving monopolistic practices and occupational closure, fulfils ideological functions in relation to capital and reflects the extent to which medicine in its role of surveillance and the reproduction of labour power is able to draw upon powerful ideological symbols in the creation of indetermination.

Navarro (1978), in his analysis of the role of medicine in capitalist society, places little emphasis on the division of knowledge between doctor and patient as a means of maintaining dominance. Instead, the power of the medical profession is regarded as based on its ability to perform effective social control functions. For Navarro, the medical profession's major social control function is to translate the collective and political problem of health and illness into an individual one. Medicine, according to Navarro, 'ameliorates or makes palatable those diswelfares generated by the economic system' and legitimates them in the eyes of the general population. He argues that the idea that the power of the profession derives from exclusive control of trades and skills is misguided, as he believes that it simply serves to reinforce the power already implicit in the class position of doctors.

Several writers, particularly Freidson and Johnson, have identified different but interrelated aspects of the type of occupational control that is conventionally described as professionalism. The following section describes how and under what conditions medicine gained control over its own work and gained a monopoly over the definition of the population's medical needs and how to provide for them.

The Rise of the Medical Profession

The passing of the Medical Registration Act in 1858 is generally regarded as providing the conditions necessary for the development of professional autonomy. This Act marked the legitimisation of the medical profession by the state as the official body to deal with matters of health and illness, and it legitimised the medical profession's right to be self-regulatory. It also provided for the unification of the profession, if only formally, which in itself was crucial in the development of a single and powerful medical body. The Act may also have eliminated other competing medical groups although, as will be shown, it did not reduce competition within the profession itself. The unification in 1858 involved the formal amalgamation of the three occupational groups which had been predominant in medical practice up until then. They were the physicians, surgeons and apothecaries. Each occupational group had its own corporate body which controlled training and education, as well as entry to the occupation. The physicians, although few in number, were the recognised leaders of the medical profession and their clientele consisted of the wealthy middle class. In contrast, the apothecary surgeons were low status with little training, whose clientele consisted of the mass of the population. The differences between the approaches of the physicians and the apothecaries is clearly illustrated by Honigsbaum (1979). He writes:

The main division within the profession was thus between physicians and apothecaries but it cannot be said that the higher social status accorded to physicians derived from the treatment they gave. Since medical science then had little to offer, all doctors tended to employ the same procedures and drugs. The main difference came in the way drugs were supplied. Physicians who received a classical education, traditional to their class, wrote their prescriptions in Latin and left dispensing to others — whereas apothecaries, who underwent only a limited apprenticeship-type of training, supplied the drugs themselves. In this way, the extent to which a doctor freed himself from dispensing became the hallmark of professional status, paralleling the class division that existed in medical ranks.

The status of the physicians in the medical hierarchy was founded on a system that had its roots in the eighteenth century. Unlike the present doctor-patient relationship, where the patient is dependent on the doctor, in the eighteenth century the physicians' legitimisation was based on the support or patronage of their patients. Jewson (1974) argues that a two-way network of dependence existed. The gentry and artistocracy held ultimate control over the consultative relationship and the course of medical innovation, due to their political and economic power. On the other hand, Jewson argues that the patient was also dependent. He states:

> Physicians enjoyed a measure of counter power over their patients, for the promise of physical and mental health held out by the profession was highly sought after by the sick. The systems of nosology and pathology were founded upon concepts of disease which upper-class patients could readily identify, while legitimising the provision of therapy and the collection of fees by practitioners.

It is difficult to judge why the high status physicians and the surgeons agreed to formal unification with the low status apothecaries. Gill (1980) points out that the physicians and surgeons were relatively unaffected by competition from other medical groups during the first half of the nineteenth century. On the other hand, it was the apothecaries who suffered most from the competition from the unqualified doctors such as druggists and chemists. Thus, according to Gill (1980), it was the apothecaries who were most concerned about achieving legislation to protect their interests whereas the physicians and the surgeons were concerned that legislation would mean a loss of their privileges. The reason why physicians and the surgeons agreed to the formal unification in 1858 was probably because they began to realise that reform was inevitable, prompted by the changes achieved by the political activities of the Poor Law Medical Officers in their struggle against unqualified medical practitioners. The physicians and surgeons thus agreed to legislation once they realised that their special position might be compromised. Furthermore, the 1858 Act itself did not greatly reduce the authority of the two Royal Colleges. However, the Act did not resolve any of the conflicts within the profession, as there was still competition between medical groups for patients, and unorthodox medicine, such as homoeopathy, was not outlawed.

The emergence of the medical profession as a unified group is seen as a good example of the use of professionalism as an ideological strategy for gaining upward social mobility. Thus, Parry and Parry (1976) suggest that the rise of the low-status apothecary-surgeon provides a particular example of how a group of doctors achieved upward social mobility and attained higher status and greater financial remuneration. The processes of collective social mobility and social closure may describe how the medical profession achieved unification and legitimisation by the state. However, it is still not clear why the medical profession was more successful than others in achieving a monopoly.

The Use of Science in the Development of a Medical Monopoly. The means of achieving a monopoly of the marketplace are, according to Larson (1978), tied to two interrelated factors. These are: (a) the potential market for a professional service; and (b) a cognitive basis to which the service is or can be tied. The potential market for medicine in the early part of the nineteenth century was expanding rapidly due to an increase in effective demand from the middle class. Other characteristics of the medical marketplace that help maintain monopolistic control once it has been achieved include the private and individual form of relationship between doctor and patient which limits direct external control, the universal need for medicine and the special problems of uncertainty for the patient in matters of health and illness (Larson, 1978). However, the problem for medical groups was to convince not only the state but also the public as a whole that their medical commodity was superior to others'. Larson argues that not only must the product be superior but also it must be standardised, so as to differentiate clearly the distinct identity of the service. Standardisation requires a uniformity and reliability in what the producers produce, as the commodity in the professional market is a service provided by a producer, and in effect the producer makes up a significant part of the commodity. It was also necessary to have a body of knowledge which was uniform and specialised if standardisation was to be achieved. The specialised nature of the knowledge aids the occupational group's autonomy from both clients and other competing groups.

The need to persuade the consumer that the medical commodity is superior is, according to Larson, particularly important in the medical marketplace. This is because medicine is a consulting profession, and its credibility needs to be deep and widespread, so as to motivate the vast majority of individuals to consult when in need. However, the superiority of the profession's skills does not necessarily need to be entirely based on objective knowledge because of the nature of the exchange between doctor and patient. Larson explains:

> Modern medicine more than any other profession illustrates how functionally rational elements of legitimisation such as scientific expertise and proved technical superiority in healing blend with traditional, irrational or substantively rational supports. What is to be stressed here is that medicine is relatively exceptional in this sense because of the persistently private and purely individual basis on which professional services are provided.

The medical profession went some way towards convincing the public and possibly the state that it had a superior medical commodity by tying itself to science which formed its cognitive basis. Until the early nineteenth century there was little evidence that one medical theory was superior to others, while fashionable medical theories tended to be tied to metaphysical speculation rather than to the scientific method. However, the nineteenth century saw a spate of scientific discoveries which proved invaluable to the development of medicine. For example, anaesthesia and antisepsis began to be used, which expanded the range of surgical procedures that could be carried out and increased survival rates. A further aid to surgeons came with the discovery of the X-ray in 1895. These scientific discoveries occurred at a time when the remedies used by public health authorities were beginning to have some success. For example, the improvement in sanitary conditions and the development of a pure water supply led to the control of cholera. The spread of typhoid, scarlet fever, and diphtheria was controlled by the pasteurisation of milk.

The scientific discoveries coupled with the successes of the public health movement may have increased the credibility of the medical profession, in that they suggested that it had access to a superior body of knowledge and expertise. However, the use of science, and in particular the germ theory of disease, proved invaluable in other ways for the development of the medical profession's control over the medical marketplace. For example, the adoption of the germ theory of disease by medical practitioners led to a shift away from patient-centred medicine towards a system which reduced patient involvement and created greater patient dependence, which in turn increased professional autonomy. Thus, the medical profession's power not only rested on its claims to having access to a superior body of knowledge and expertise but the nature of the knowledge itself helped maintain dominance by encouraging patient dependence. The use of science as a whole provides a number of other functions which maximise the favourable characteristics of a professional market, and, for Larson (1978), it provides the perfect cognitive base for a profession. This is because it is 'esoteric, yet formalised and standardised enough to be, in principle, accessible to all who would undergo prolonged training'.

Larson's identification of the role of scientific discoveries and knowledge based on science in promoting doctors' professional status is shared by other analyses which differ in their view of the mechanisms by which science promoted professionalisation. For example, as Chapter 1 showed, the social constructionist perspective identified the new medical gaze based on the scientific paradigm as serving to extend and consolidate the power of the medical profession. Similarly, whereas Larson identifies the particular characteristics of scientific knowledge which make it a perfect cognitive base for a profession, and hence serve the interests of doctors, Navarro emphasises the way in which the ideology of science, and the success of doctors in convincing the state of their superior medical knowledge, is shaped by and reflects the needs of the economic system and its ruling class (p. 35). Thus for Navarro, the key characteristic in explaining the link between the development of science as a cognitive base and the professionalisation of medicine is the social control functions of this form of knowledge.

The Medical Profession and Its Relationship with the State. The early part of the twentieth century saw the expansion of the medical profession and further consolidation of its monopoly. The medical profession during this period became increasingly involved with the state, a relationship which might have threatened the power of the profession through controls on professional autonomy. However, the profession managed to use its involvement with the state to achieve its own ends. This is illustrated by the Health Insurance Act of 1911 which set up the panel system. This enabled workers with low incomes to contribute, along with their employers and the state, to an insurance fund and receive sickness benefit and free medical care provided by a panel doctor. The panel doctors were general practitioners, with specialist and hospital services not being included in the scheme. The Act, although imposing some regulation on the doctor and eliminating free bargaining between doctor and patient over treatment and payment for it, strengthened the profession and in particular the general practitioners' position. Bowling (1981) argues that the profession's overall monopoly was strengthened by further state recognition of the medical profession as the providers of care for the working sector of the population. She also described the Act as reinforcing the general practitioners' position:

> It substantially increase the income of these doctors, led to an increase in their number and brought the mass of the working population into contact with them. By doing so, it established the concept of the family doctor and reinforced the referral system. General practice was thus given support at a time when it was being seriously threatened by hospital practice.

In contrast to the 1911 Act, the National Health Service Act of 1946 strengthened the position of the hospital doctors at least in comparison with general practitioners and the public health doctors. The Act also enhanced the overall power of the medical profession, particularly in that there was considerable medical representation at all levels of the service. However, while the general practitioner did receive a better income and a more secure position, the Act gave greater support to the hospital doctor who received both a guaranteed salary and financial incentives. The 1946 Act thus perpetuated the division between the hospital doctor and also made the hospital doctor less financially dependent on the general practitioner for the referral of private patients (Bowling, 1981).

The Medical Profession in Contemporary Britain

The medical profession's position after the creation of the National Health Service was a strong one, in the sense that the state had by then completely legitimised its claim to autonomy and to dominance of the health field. However, the division within the profession between hospital doctor and general practitioner was still very much in evidence. The hospital doctor was in a particularly powerful position, which was enhanced by the increasing specialisation that had occurred in many branches of hospital medicine during the post-Second World War period. In contrast, the general practitioner's position, although secure, was of lower status than that of the hospital doctor. In their early attempts to professionalise, and to achieve parity with the hospital doctors, the general practitioners attempted to adopt a model of health care similar to that used in hospital medicine. This concern with developing a model of health care in general practice which paralleled that developed in the hospital reflected the dominance of hospital ideology. For example, Armstrong (1979) shows how hospital ideology influenced the way the problems or crises in the general practitioners' service were conceptualised. He identifies three themes which emerged in the debate over general practice. These were: (1) the desire for hospital work; (2) a concern with trivia; and (3) a search for an appropriate role. Each of these themes illustrates how the hospital controlled the way in which 'problems' were defined in general practice. However, while involvement with the state had removed the general practitioners' entrepreneurial status and made them subordinate to hospital medicine, this involvement also freed the general practitioner from being dependent on the patient for income, and enabled the general practitioner to take the dominant role in the relationship. As a result, the general practitioner, through the forum provided by the Royal College of General Practitioners, developed an alternative model which Armstrong (1979) describes as biographical medicine. The emphasis was on the need to consider the patient as a whole and to concentrate on the signs and symptoms in the context of the patient's own biography and environment. This ideology is one which has been adopted by the Royal College of General Practitioners, although only in their most recent reports has this ideology has been proposed as a real alternative to the approach of the hospital.

A further change which influenced the position of general practitioners was the Charter of 1965 which gave them higher incomes and better working conditions. Changes in the organisation of the general practitioner service, such as the increasing use of deputising services, appointment systems and receptionists, as well as the proliferation of health centres and the increasing number of group practices also radically influenced the general practitioners' working conditions and particularly the way in which they could control their work and workload. Thus, the early part of the post-war period has, in some respects, witnessed an increasing consolidation of the power of the hospital doctor and the professionalisation of the general practitioner service.

Threats to Professional Autonomy

During the course of the nineteenth century and the first half of the twentieth century, the profession of medicine made steady progress towards the present position of power. Potential barriers to this progress, such as the increasing involvement of the state in the provision of medical care, proved to be of little consequence and were even used to enhance the medical monopoly. Since the 1960s various challenges have been made to the medical profession's autonomy by developments in the health care field. Three different but closely related challenges to medical autonomy have been identified (Elston, 1977). The first challenge stems from recent critiques (see Chapter 1) of the effectiveness of modern medicine. These criticisms may undermine both the public's and the health workers' belief in the legitimacy of medical dominance, but more important the challenge has led to a call for a change in the allocation of resources. The apparent ineffectiveness of curative medicine, coupled with changes in patterns of morbidity, have led to a greater emphasis being placed on preventive medicine and care which has involved a loss of resources for those involved in curative medicine. This shift in emphasis also entails greater responsibility and involvement in decision making both for patients and other health workers, and a consequent reduction in the power of the doctor.

A second, and possibly the most serious challenge to medical autonomy, is identified as arising from the increasing professionalisation of the paramedical occupations, which have managed to achieve some autonomy and independence from the medical profession. One of the reasons why a degree of autonomy has been achieved is the change in the structure of training of paramedicals and the change in the composition of recruits. For example, the inclusion of non-medical subjects in the syllabuses and the development of degree courses have meant that medical control over the knowledge of paramedicals has been challenged. A further development which served to increase the autonomy of paramedical workers was the view expressed in a series of government reports published during the 1970s that many of the paramedical occupations, such as remedial therapists, should have a type of 'contractual' relationship with the medical profession. This type of relationship involves the paramedical serving a range of specialities rather than being tied to specific medical specialities. The contractual relationship means that no one clinical speciality has a monopoly over access to the service, and thus the doctor is no longer in the position of manager controlling what services should be provided. Other administrative changes which aided the paramedicals' attempts to professionalise included the passing of the 1974 NHS Reorganisation Act. This changed the medical division of labour from one organised according to function to one reorganised on the basis of expertise. Armstrong (1976) explains the importance of the change in principle and states:

> With a service based on function the doctor's claim to dominance over other skills groups could be legitimated by the claim to be necessary for the efficient management of health problems. By organising instead on the basis of skill, any group gaining official recognition of its particular expertise could claim a measure of organisational independence. Although the claim to a particular skill is an essential part of this process it is the official recognition of that skill which indicates a decline in the strength of medical hegemony.

The third challenge to medical autonomy came in the early 1970s from within the medical profession itself. Junior hospital doctors, dissatisfied with their working conditions and the uncertainty of their career prospects owing to the lack of expansion in consultant posts, claimed the profession's leadership was not adequately representing their interests. In an attempt to gain some independence from their leaders, they negotiated the terms of their own contract which specified the number of hours worked and payment for overtime. This reduced the financial advantages of promotion from senior registrar to consultant and also limited the junior hospital doctors' dependence on consultants.

Despite these threats to autonomy there is little evidence of a decline in the power of the medical profession, with one of the strengths of the profession lying in its ability to resist attempts to limit its own autonomy. For example, the medical profession has successfully restricted controls on its clinical freedom under the NHS to prescribe or request X-rays, tests, special diets or beds, while at the local level they have successfully influenced the allocation of resources and restricted attempts to change the balance of expenditure, from hospital services to facilities in the community (see Chapter 6). The most recent challenge to the health professions comes with the proposals of the Griffiths Report (1983) to restructure management in the Health Service. The most important recommendation, at least from the point of view of health professionals, is the proposed introduction of a general manager at the level of unit, district, and regional health authority. One implication for the health professions is that this proposal may limit their potential influence on decision-making. However, the strong negotiating power of the medical profession, coupled with the vociferous resistance of its political representative, the BMA, suggests the impact of this policy may be to undermine the power of other occupations with less political strength, such as the nursing profession. The Griffiths proposals may thus further bolster professional dominance by increasing the inequalities between medicine and the other health professions.

The Doctor-Patient Relationship

The consultation between doctor and patient forms the meeting between professional and layman, and thus between groups who differ in their knowledge and power. Sociological analyses of the relationship between doctor and patient can be divided into those which attempt to locate the position of medical practice in the wider social structure, and those operating at the micro-level which have concentrated on the dynamics of social encounters between doctors and patients.

Models of Doctor-Patient Relations

Consensus Models. Parsons (1971) portrays the doctor-patient relationship as one of reciprocity where the doctor and the patient have certain obligations and privileges which are attached to their respective roles. The relationship is based on the two parties being socialised into their roles. The patient, as part of the obligations attached to the sick role (see Chapter 2 for a more detailed discussion), is expected to seek technically competent help, usually from a doctor, and to trust the doctor and accept that the doctor is a competent help-giver. Conversely, the doctor is expected: (1) to act in accordance with the health needs of his or her patient; (2) to follow the rules of professional conduct; (3) to use a high degree of expertise and knowledge when dealing with health problems; and (4) to remain objective and emotionally detached. The privileges attached to the professional's role are that they are granted access to intimate physical and personal problems, and that they have both professional autonomy and dominance. The doctor also controls access to the sick role, and thus legitimises the privileges associated with acceptance into the sick role, such as exemption from the performance of normal social activities. The doctor-patient relationship is depicted by Parsons is one characterised by harmony, even though it is an unequal relationship. The doctor's authority is accepted by the patient because of the doctor's superior knowledge and skills and the patient cooperates fully with the doctor, as the doctor works according to the needs and interests of his or her patients. It is thus a consensus model reflecting the wider assumption of a shared value system which is found in much of Parsons' functionalist approach.

A more elaborate conceptualisation of the doctor-patient relationship was subsequently developed by Szasz and Hollender (1956). However, their approach also adopts a functionalist perspective and once again portrays the relationship in terms of harmony and consensus. Szasz and Hollender identify three different models of the doctor-patient relationship, namely: activity-passivity, guidance-cooperation and mutual participation (see Figure 1). The type of relationship which occurs is regarded as determined by the patients' illnesses. For example, the activity-passivity type is found in circumstances where patients are in comas, collapses or states in which they cannot participate in the encounter. In these cases a patient is a recipient of medical expertise as the doctor does something directly to the patient. The guidance-cooperation types involves illnesses, such as infections, where the doctor instructs the patient and the patient cooperates. The final type — mutual participation — usually involves chronic illnesses where the doctor helps the patient to help himself or herself. Such a relationship can also be found in other areas, such as alcohol problems, where the emphasis is placed on the need for the sufferer to want to stop drinking heavily and be willing to do something about it himself or herself, as well as in the general area of 'health behaviour', where the doctor may advise the patient about the need to give up smoking but the responsibility is placed on the smoker for actually doing so. Thus, according to the model proposed by Szasz and Hollender, the structure of the doctor-patient relationship varies with the type of health problem involved. However, in each instance there is an assumption that the relationship is a reciprocal one, with the patient accepting the doctor's authority.

One of the major criticisms of Parsons' approach to doctor-patient relations is that it is based on the medical profession's image of what the relationship should be like. For example, Bloor and Horobin (1975) argue that the Parsonian portrayal of the doctor-patient relationship is formulated from Parsons' 'common-sense' typfications of how patients should behave given the undisputed rationality of medicine. It therefore reflects the doctors' image of the 'good' patient — a person who defers to medical competence and cooperates in the process of minimising illness. They go on to show the double bind for the patient in his or her role prescriptions which brings with it a potential conflict between doctor and patient. This double bind is a result of contradictory expectations of patient behaviour. Empirical studies have shown that a major source of frustration of British GPs is the large number of patients who present with trivial conditions. Thus, the expectation is that the ideal patient should be able to distinguish between serious and trivial illnesses prior to consultation. However, a corresponding sense of dissatisfaction is the decline in respect accorded to doctors, which conflicts with the expectation that patients should display deference. The 'double-bind' is found in the contradiction between the expectation that people should be sufficiently well informed to assess the seriousness of their condition and then, if and when consulting, should as patients defer to and comply with the doctor. Thus, the assumption of reciprocity between doctor and patient is problematic, precisely because of the potential for conflict implicit in these contradictory role prescriptions.

Figure 4.1: Szasz and Hollender's Typology of the Doctor-Patient Relationship

Model	Role of doctor and patient	Type of problem
1. Active-passive	Doctor does something to patient. Patient passively receives treatment.	Surgery Trauma Coma
2. Guidance-cooperation	Doctor tells patient what to do and patient complies	Acute illnesses (respiratory complaints)
3. Mutual participation	Doctor helps patient to help him or herself and patient uses expert help.	Chronic illnesses (diabetes) and psychotherapy

Source: Szasz and Hollender (1956).

Freidson (1970) has also suggested that Parsons' model of the doctor-patient relationship is derived from doctors' own idealised notions of what the doctor-patient relationship should be like. He believes a similar criticism applies to the models put forward by Szasz and Hollender. He points out that these models fail to take into account the logical possibility of there being a relationship where the doctor is passive and the patient active, or where the patient guides and the doctor cooperates. The failure to recognise such a logical possibility is, according to Freidson, a reflection of the normative stance of the authors in that they represent the views of how medical professionals think the relationship ought to be organised.

A 'Clash' of Perspectives. Freidson (1970) is one of the principal exponents of a perspective which portrays the doctor-patient relationship in terms of a 'clash' of perspectives between lay and professional conceptions about the organisation of illness. He explains (1970):

> Conflicts in perspective and interest are built into the interaction and are likely to be present to some degree in every situation. They are at the core of the interaction, and they reflect the general structural characteristics of illness and its professional treatment as a function of the relations between two distinct worlds, ordered by professional norms.

The conflict Freidson refers to is between the diverse perspectives of the doctor and the lay person. On the one hand, the doctor views the patient as another case in a general framework of clinical knowledge. On the other hand, the patient assesses his or her illness within the context of his or her own cultural background and in the context of his or her own daily activities. One example of this difference in clinical and lay perspectives can be found in the way the significance or seriousness of signs and symptoms is assessed.(see Chapter 3 for more detail). Doctors working in general practice and in hospital accident and emergency departments are continually claiming that they are having to treat too many 'trivial' conditions. However, from the patients' point of view their complaint is not trivial, as their assessments are derived from a different body of knowledge and a different set of assumptions and priorities. For example, a study of new patients attending at a hospital accident and emergency department showed that of the 628 different complaints presented by patients only 6 per cent were defined as 'emergencies' using strict clinical criteria, whereas 59 per cent of the complaints were defined as 'emergencies' by patients (Calnan, 1984).

In Freidson's earlier empirical work he presents patients as active and critical. For example, in his study of patients' views about a health care scheme in New York (Freidson, 1961), he argued that patients rejected professional services when they did not fit into their own scheme of things, such as contradicting their own conceptions of illness and treatment or having to sacrifice personal convenience. In some cases patients perceived lay alternatives to be superior to professional medical treatments. This view of doctor-patient is different to that of Parsons and Szasz and Hollender, not just because it identifies conflict in the relationship but because the patient is active and critical and uses lay alternatives rather than being passive and dependent on professional medical expertise.

In Freidson's later writing (1970) less emphasis is placed on empirical findings, and his portrayal of the doctor-patient relationship is derived directly from his theoretical approach to professional dominance and professional autonomy. This leads him to extend Szasz and Hollender's typology, arguing that the structure of the doctor-patient relationship varies according to the degree of divergence in the cultural background of doctors and patients. Thus, the active-passive relationship would be found where there is a marked difference in cultural background between the two parties, whereas a mutual participation type of relationship would be more likely to be found when the cultural backgrounds of the two parties are similar. Freidson also suggests that the social organisation of the doctor-patient relationship may depend upon structural characteristics, one of which is the setting in which the two parties meet. For example, in settings such as general practice or hospital accident and emergency departments where the patient has, at least in theory, direct access to the doctor and medical facilities, the practitioner is more likely to be client-dependent. In these settings the professional is dependent on lay referrals and the consultation process is likely to involve the patient as an active participant. Freidson says the consultation will be characterised by bargaining and negotiation as the patient has, at least in theory, the option of going to another doctor or another consultant. On the other hand, in settings where the practitioner is dependent on professional referrals, such as in outpatient clinics (colleague-dependent practices), the patient has few options open to him or her and the consultation may be characterised by an active doctor and passive patient.

Micro-level Analyses of the Doctor-Patient Relationship

Sociological studies of the doctor-patient relationship at the micro-level have also been concerned with conflict and consensus in the encounter and have examined the way professional and patient interests have been organised. Symbolic interactionism and ethno-methodology have formed the dominant perspectives. Research based on an interactionist approach is considered here, while examples of the study of doctor-patient relations from an ethno-methodological perspective can be found in Atkinson and Heath (1981).

Doctor-Patient Interaction as a Form of Negotiation. Some writers have portrayed the doctor-patient relationship as a form of negotiation. The doctor and the patient are depicted as actors who are conscious and intentional, and who are striving to maximise their own interests by means of strategic action. There is therefore as much potential for conflict in the encounter as there is for consensus.

Negotiation has been identified in various medical contexts, one of which was in a study of tuberculosis patients who were inmates of a sanitorium (Roth, 1963). These patients conceptualised their illnesses in terms of time, and attempted to influence doctors' decisions about cure by achieving career states which were regarded as evidence of medical progress. The ultimate aim of the patients was to influence their discharge date. Roth shows how doctors and patients bargained over the timetable and how the outcome was negotiated. Other areas of medical practice where 'negotiation' is evident is where the treatment regime necessarily involves the patient as an active participant. For example, in some treatments of alcoholism emphasis is placed on the responsibility of the patients for the occurrence of their condition and patients' strength and will-power are implicitly invoked in the treatment. Davis (1979) describes the encounters between a psychiatrist and an alcoholic and shows how the psychiatrist continually tells the patient that it is up to him or her to give up drinking. However, the emphasis on the patient's involvement means that the patient continuously negotiates with the psychiatrist. Davis (1979) shows how the psychiatrist and his or her patient are sometimes in dispute about the best possible treatment, with the patient laying emphasis on the need for medical help and the psychiatrist emphasising that he or she cannot do anything until the patient himself or herself decides to give up drinking.

The portrayal of the doctor-patient relationship as a form of negotiation suggests the encounter is open, with each party having the scope to influence the outcome significantly. However, this approach neglects the powerful position of the doctors and the patients' more limited ability to negotiate. Thus, Stimson and Webb (1975) concluded on the basis of an observational study in general practice, involving 50 consultations and five doctors, that although patients had some opportunity to negotiate:

> In general, the patient tends to be the more passive of the two . . . .
> Patients rarely give open expression to feelings of disagreement or
> dissatisfaction to the doctor's face but may mask them behind
> muttered or mumbled comments which are barely audible.

Stimson and Webb (1975) suggest that negotiation does not go in an 'open arena', with there being a number of constraints on the negotiability of the encounter as perceived from the patient's point of view. They show how doctors control not only information but also access to themselves through organisational procedures. As they state: 'The doctor maintains control by acting in such a way that the patient is continually aware of "who is the doctor".' Stimson and Webb also note there was rarely open conflict in the negotiation in the consultation. Even when patients were unhappy with their treatment they rarely confronted the doctor directly. For example, they describe a patient who felt that her doctor tended to overprescribe and phrased her question in this way to the doctor when he gave her a prescription: 'Are those tablets really necessary, doctor? Because, if they're not, I'd rather not take them, if it will clear up anyway.' Stimson and Webb interpret this statement in this way: 'Rather than being openly critical of the doctor's behaviour this patient tactfully pivots her doubts back upon herself.'

Other authors have used a concept developed by Scheff to explain how professional maintain authority. Scheff (1968) emphasised the negotiable nature of interactions and that definitions of reality are produced through interaction rather than skilful interrogation. However, Scheff argues that the transaction between interactants take place against the background of a 'hidden agenda', known to the more powerful participant, which comprises information, rules and procedures pertinent to achieving a successful outcome acceptable to the subordinate. The 'hidden agenda' may remain undisclosed, it may be revealed for purposes of imposing a workable definition on a client or it may be discovered, in some cases to the disadvantage of the more powerful party. In the case of the doctor-patient relationship the hidden agenda consists of information about diagnosis, prognosis and treatment and, by controlling access to it, the doctor can maintain control over the encounter and its outcome. In the majority of consultations the hidden agenda may remain undisclosed, although in some circumstances, and particularly in chronic conditions when patients become knowledgeable about the condition, it can be opened up. West (1976), in an observational study of doctor-patient encounters where the child had epilepsy, showed how after a succession of visits to the doctor the parents became increasingly active participants in the encounter. The doctor in his initial contact with the parents was able to rely on routine solutions for maintaining control of the encounter. However, by the third consultation parents began to initiate questions themselves and force information out of the doctor. The doctor was increasingly having to work hard to maintain his claim to competence. The hidden agenda was slowly opened up as there was a gradual release of information about diagnosis, prognosis and treatment. As a result, the negotiating power of parents increased and the structure of the encounter changed from one characterised by an active doctor and passive patient to one of negotiation where both parties had equally strong bargaining positions.

Some of the routines employed by doctors to maintain 'functional autonomy' were identified by Bloor (1976) based on observations of 500 consultations. He identified three main routines employed by ENT (ear, nose and throat) specialists to reduce the likelihood of parents initiating a discussion around the question of their child's need for tonsillectomy which might lead to parental influence on the outcome of the consultation. The routines which work against this eventuality are, first, 'inhibitory routines' or strategies which restrict parental influence, such as a clinic organisation that denies face-to-face contact, the transfer of responsibility for communicating the decision to the GP pending the results of investigations, a question format requiring affirmative or negative rather than elaborate replies. Second, specialists who operate with a more open agenda employ 'reactive routines' which serve to nullify the impact of parental influence; for example, simply ignoring a parent's definition of the situation. Third, in instances where parents manage to question a disposal decision, doctors make use of 'reconciliatory routines', such as spelling out their expertise in a manner which persuades parents of the correctness of the decision. Whilst these routines are not invariate features of ENT consultations they occur often enough to suggest they constitute features of the production of 'functional autonomy'.

The use of routines has been found in other areas of medical practice, such as in the communication of information about fatal disease. The communication of a diagnosis of cancer by a doctor to a patient is said to be a particularly difficult problem because of the public's conception that the disease is painful and incurable and usually leads to death. McIntosh (1976) in an observational study of staff-patient encounters on a cancer ward identified the routines employed by the staff in their attempts to manage these communication problems. The staff only informed patients in those cases when the condition was known to be benign and eminently curable, and only in those cases did the clinical details of the case influence what the patient was told. In all other examples of the disease doctors had no intention of disclosing information even when certain of the diagnosis and prognosis. Doctors explained the withholding of information in terms of the patients' desire for information and the patients' probable reactions to disclosure. McIntosh states (1976):

> Quite simply, where the doctors accepted that some patients would genuinely want to know and would not react adversely they did not know which patients really wanted to know or which of them would react well to being told.

McIntosh describes the ways doctors coped with this problem of uncertainty. Firstly, doctors adopted a rule of not disclosing to any of the patients unless absolutely necessary. This rule was based on the principle that not telling a patient was better than telling a patient who didn't want to know and could not cope with bad news. Secondly, all communication was routinised and geared to limiting the amount of disclosure to patients. This perpetuation of 'uncertainty', as West has pointed out in his study of epilepsy, may put the doctors' professional credibility at risk in that the patients may begin to lose faith in the doctors' ability to diagnose their complaint. However, McIntosh describes how this problem is dealt with:

> The use of this sort of terminology (terms such as 'suspicious cells' or 'it might have become dangerous' or 'activity') also solved a potential dilemma for the doctor: namely, how could he use a pretence of uncertainty to restrict information while at the same time conveying to the patient that he knew what he was doing. The

method accepted was, as we have seen, to use terms which, while implying uncertainty in sufficient degree to allay patient fears, also avoided a more explicit professon of it. The doctors could not openly profess to be uncertain about the diagnosis after having completed their investigations without the risk of losing the patients' confidence in their ability to treat them.

Doctors control access to information not only where diagnosis and prognosis is certain but also to conceal medical uncertainty. Scheff (1963) has described the informal norm for handling uncertainty as forming part of the subculture of the medical profession. He states the role of medicine as 'when in doubt continue to suspect illness'. Scheff adds: 'Most physicians learn early in their training that it is far more culpable to dismiss a sick patient than to retain a well one.' This rule is so pervasive and fundamental it goes unstated in medical textbooks. A second way in which doctors handle uncertainty is through the development of a belief system to guide actions. As Posner (1977) notes, there are considerable uncertainties surrounding the reliable diagnosis of diabetes and the effectiveness of treatment, while some of the common treatments are claimed to be ineffective or even potentially dangerous. In spite of these uncertainties the hypothesis guiding the treatment of diabetes has not been seriously questioned. Posner (1977) suggests this is because when doctors are faced with a situation of great uncertainty and the possibility of serious and life threatening complications, it is understandable that they need to feel they can control it. Thus, Posner concludes that: 'the medical theory of the treatment of diabetes is a belief system which is sustained by certain medical assumptions and like any other, by social, structural and cultural factors.'

Doctors may not only share a general belief system but also establish individual routines to cope with diagnostic uncertainties. Bloor (1976) in a study of doctors' interpretation of signs and symptoms as indicating a need for adenotonsillectomy among children drew attention to the substantial variations in doctors' decision-making due to the problematic activity of applying general disease entities to specific cases. This 'diagnostic uncertainty' applies to all cases, not just the idiosyncratic ones, and is a form of uncertainty which is common to all cognitive activity. Bloor found that even when doctors agreed on what signs or symptoms were indicators of the need for surgical treatment there was still variation in the interpretation of these signs and symptoms.

Doctor-Patient Communication and the Problem of Patient Compliance

The medical profession, like social scientists, has begun to take an increasing interest in the doctor-patient relationship or, more specifically, in communication between doctors and patients. The medical profession's interest stems from its recognition that the patients' major source of dissatisfaction with medical practice is the lack of information that they receive, and that 'bad' medical communication can influence therapeutic outcomes. Of particular concern to the medical profession has been the apparent link between poor communication and the degree to which the patient complies with medical advice and medical solutions. The problem of non-compliance can thus be defined as any deviation from medically prescribed rules, procedures, programmes or regimens. It includes behaviour as varied as non-attendance, non-participation, failure to take medicines as indicated, failure to cooperate with the doctors' instructions and so on. More recently, as the medical profession has become involved in health education, non-compliance refers to those who do not follow instructions to give up smoking, cut down on alcohol consumption or follow a healthy diet. However, the term usually refers to patients who do not follow doctors' orders.

Research on patient compliance has tended to focus on attempting to identify the extent of the problem, or the deviance, and on trying to characterise the defaulter. Studies suggest there is a significant level of defaulting. For example, Ley (see Tones and Davison, 1979) in a review of 68 studies found the median percentage of patients not following advice varied from 35 to 57.5. A similar conclusion was drawn by Stimson (1974) who focused on 19 investigations specifically concerned with drug defaulting and attempted to identify the characteristics of non-cooperators. However, he found an inconclusive and contradictory pattern and concluded that it was not possible to identify an uncooperative type; almost anyone can default at one time or another. Stimson argues that the reason for the failure of much of the defaulting research is the dominance of the medical perspective, which suggests that the cause of the default must reside in the patient. The ideas of the doctor as the legitimate expert and the patient as passive and obedient are simply taken for granted, ensuring that attention is not directed either to the patient's view of the situation or the nature of doctor-patient interaction. If the patient's perspective is taken seriously, non-compliance can be seen either as resulting from an aspect or aspects of the medical encounter, or from a rational decision made by the patient that the treatment might not be useful. Stimson argues, therefore, that patients may have good reasons why they choose not to follow doctors' orders. These reasons have, however, received little attention.

The focus of compliance has shifted in the last few years away from the patient towards the communication strategies used by the doctor. The reason for this shift was the increasing evidence that patient compliance was related to patient satisfaction and that patient satisfaction was associated with the level and quality of information given to the patient by the doctor. For example, Korsch and Negrete (1972) carried out a study examining 800 patient visits to an emergency paediatric clinic involving the first attendance of children with various acute disorders. The majority of the consultations were tape-recorded. In addition, mothers were interviewed immediately after the consultation to ascertain their perceptions of the encounter and later to find out about their levels of compliance. On the basis of an overall assessment, 76 per cent of the sample were classified as 'highly' or 'moderately' satisfied with the doctor's performance. Satisfaction was unrelated to the nature of the complaint, to demographic factors, such as social class or educational level, and to the duration of the consultation. It was, however, related to the degree to which doctors met the mothers' expectations. Dissatisfaction was high when doctors were perceived as unfriendly, when they failed to understand the mothers' concern, when they employed technical or short-hand terms and particularly when the doctor did not provide information about the child's disorder, which was, according to the authors, of immense importance to mothers. Analysis of the actual exchanges indicated that paediatricians displayed limited concern with relieving parental worries and, in maintaining tight control over the structure of the interaction, restricted the opportunities mothers had in raising such issues. Furthermore, levels of satisfaction were related to subsequent compliance; 53 per cent of mothers who were 'highly satisfied' cooperated fully with medical instructions, compared with 17 per cent of those who were 'highly dissatisfied'.

Doctor-Patient Relations and the 'Problem' of Communication

Some of the reasons for 'bad' medical communication that were initially put forward were the short time the doctor could give to the patient, or that the patient did not ask for information or was not interested in gaining further information, or that the doctor believed the patient did not want to be told. More recently, explanations of 'bad' medical communication have focused on the doctors' awareness of the patients' perspective and the doctors' communication skills, or lack of them. Research sponsored by the British government has focused on doctors' communication styles in an attempt to increase doctors' communication skills. In addition, exhortations have come from within the medical profession itself to include communication training, particularly in the education of general practitioners. The weakness of this approach to communication and compliance, at least from a sociological point of view, is its failure to explain the 'problems' of communication and compliance in terms of the wider issues of professional autonomy and medical control. Such neglect is not surprising given the managerial bias in much of this research, where the model of doctor-patient relations reflects the medical profession's ideas about what the relationship should be like.

Sociological explanations of the communication 'problem' between doctors and patients tend to describe the issue in terms of informational control and of the perpetuation of uncertainty. Various explanations have been offered for the perpetuation of uncertainty (Calnan, 1984b). One explanation is that in some areas of medicine there are considerable problems of uncertainty about diagnosis, prognosis and the value of medical treatment. In these circumstances the doctor has the option of informing the patient of these uncertainties, and thus running the risk of the patient questioning the doctor's professional credibility and professional authority. On the other hand, the doctor may wish to perpetuate patient uncertainty for as long as possible so as to protect their professional authority. This latter strategy is however also risky in terms of its implications for professional status. This is because it places the doctor's credibility at risk, which can lead to patients becoming increasingly dissatisfied with the professional's performance and consequently withdrawing legitimacy. Alternatively, doctors may perpetuate uncertainty 'way beyond the stage at which clinical uncertainty about prognosis is resolved'. Such a strategy is often adopted with diseases such as cancer, because, among other things, it is functional for the doctor in that it minimises the time, effort and emotional difficulties involved in explaining the diagnosis to the patient or a parent, and maintains patient and parental hopes for a full recovery. The final explanation suggests that information control, or the perpetuation of uncertainty, is a device used by professionals, and doctors in particular, as a means of maintaining professional autonomy by creating social distance between doctor and patient and creating patient dependence.

Other sociological approaches to doctor-patient communication have tied the nature of communication strategies used by the doctor to his or her perception of the role of the professional and the type of relationship which they try to maintain with their patients. For example, Comaroff (1976) examined the different strategies used by a sample of general practitioners to communicate information about non-fatal illness. She found two extreme types of strategy. First, the unelaborated strategy where the doctor had simple stereotypes of his patients and a limited number of alternative forms of communication. This type of strategy is illustrated by the response of a doctor to a question asking him to describe his approach. He stated: 'My patients are told only what is good for them; and I'm the best judge of that.' The second type of strategy, the elaborated strategy, emphasises the uniqueness of each patient's needs and the problems involved in describing a specific set of rules to embrace the wide range of modes of communication. Comaroff's study identified links between these strategies and how the doctor conceived of the control of knowledge and the nature of the doctor-patient relationship. For example, those doctors who tended towards an unelaborated strategy emphasised the marked difference in knowledge between the doctor and patient and the need to maintain autonomy by keeping tight control in the encounter. On the other hand, those doctors who followed a more elaborated strategy held more doubts about the value of their knowledge and skills and recognised the importance of the patient's contribution. The relationship was therefore seen as more symmetrical, with each party having something to offer. Comaroff argues that these different strategies, although a product of the doctors' views about their role and their relationship with their patients, are also used as a means of coping in a context of uncertainties about medical diagnosis and treatment.

The explanation that information control in the doctor-patient relationship suits the professional interests of the doctor through the maintenace of autonomy and power has implications for the study of patient compliance. For example, Pratt (1976) argues that conventional approaches to patient compliance assume that doctors communicate the recommended course of action to the patient. However, there is evidence that doctors withhold information. This suggests that the notion of patient compliance and non-compliance is of little value, for patients have often not been adequately informed about what instructions he or she should comply with. Pratt therefore believes that the study of non-compliance should be reformulated into a problem in communication between two participants. However, she depicts the doctor as only one source of expertise within the consumer's network of consultants, and suggests that while the medical practitioner has some specialised expert knowledge the consumer should comply selectively (not automatically), as the medical professional has only limited knowledge of and limited interest in the patient's health requirements.

The Doctor-Patient Relationship: A Need for Change?

One of the most important findings to emerge from this review of theoretical and empirical approaches to the doctor-patient relationship is that the nature of the relationship has a considerable influence on patient satisfaction. Levels of satisfaction are believed to have declined over the past decade, mainly because patients have become more knowledgeable and therefore critical (Cartwright and Anderson, 1981; Jefferys and Sachs, 1983). While patients have expressed concern, particularly in relation to general practice, about organisational arrangements, such as waiting time being too long, a major concern has been about the personal characteristics of the doctor and his or her style in consultation. The ability to listen, to be sympathetic and reasoning and to give the information the patient requires are all attributes that patients judge to be good qualities in a family doctor. For example, Jefferys and Sachs (1983) found that among the patients they interviewed at home in 1975, 33 per cent viewed the opportunity to discuss non-medical problems with their doctor as very important (compared with 28 per cent in 1972), and that of patients attending the surgeries in 1975, 48 per cent wanted reassurance from their doctor (compared with 42 per cent in 1972).

The requirement to be able to understand and meet the needs of patients is becoming increasingly important as doctors are asked to become more involved in preventive medicine. General practitioners in particular have been encouraged to carry out more health education with their patients, such as giving advice about the way to keep healthy or prevent illness. The image of the general practitioner in his or her role as health educator that has been portrayed in policy proposals is one where the doctor is to help his or her patients to help themselves. The form of doctor-patient relationship which would be most conducive to this aim would be one which is similar to that described by Szasz and Hollender (1956) as the mutual participation type. This type is characterised by the doctor helping the patient to help himself or herself through advice-giving, and the patient becoming responsible for controlling his or her own health through the use of the knowledge gained through the consultation with the doctor. The emphasis is on the doctor and the patient in an equal partnership, with the perspective of the patient being of equal partnership, with the perspective of the patient being of equal importance to the perspective of the doctor, as it is the patient who will be ultimately responsible for following a healthy life style (Calnan and Johnson, 1983).

Evidence presented in the previous section shows that the most prevalent form of relationship is one characterised by a dominant and active doctor and a passive and dependent patient. The image of the doctor as health educator freely giving out information is not one which appears to have a realistic basis. This type of relationship may change as a result of the practice of health education in the consultation. However, the structure of the present-day doctor-patient relationship seems to have been produced not just by the substance and content involved in the consultation but also by the structure of professional-client relations in Western industrial society. Thus, it may not be enough to argue that this problem of patients receiving inadequate information is due to the poor communication skills of the doctor and that this can be remedied by teaching these skills during medical training. More radical solutions may be required. For example, those who feel that the problem lies with professionalisation might argue the need for deprofessionalisation.

References

Armstrong, D. (1976) 'The decline of medical hegemony: a review of government reports during the NHS', *Social Science and Medicine*, *10*, 157-63

Armstrong, D. (1979) 'The emancipation of biographical medicine', *Social Science and Medicine*, *13A*, no. 1, 9-12

Atkinson, P. and Heath, C. (1981) *Medical Work, Realities and Routines*, Gower, London

Barber, B. (1963) 'Some problems in the sociology of professions', *Daedalus*, *92*, 669-88

Bloor, M.J. (1976) 'Professional autonomy and client exclusion: a study in ENT clinics', in M. Wadsworth and D. Robinson, *Studies in Everyday Medical Life*, Martin Robertson, London

Bloor, M.J. (1976) 'Bishop Berkeley and the adenotonsillectomy enigma: the social construction of medical disposals', *Sociology*, *10*, 43-61.

Bloor, M.J. and Horobin, G. (1975) 'Conflict and conflict resolution in doctor-patient interactions', in C. Cox and A. Mead (eds.), *A Sociology of Medical Practice*, Collier-MacMillan, London

Bowling, A. (1981) *Delegation in General Practice; A Study of Doctors and Nurses*, Tavistock, London

Calnan, M. (1984a) 'The functions of the Hospital Emergency Department: a study of patient demand', *Journal of Emergency Medicine*, *2*, 57-63

Calnan, M. (1984b) 'Clinical uncertainty: is it a problem in the doctor-patient relationship?', *Sociology of Health and Illness*, 6, 1, 74-85

Calnan, M. and Johnson, B. (1983) 'Influencing health behaviour: how significant is the general practitioner?', *Health Education Journal*, 42, 39-45

Carr-Saunders, A.M. and Wilson, P. (1933) *The Professions*, Clarendon Press, Oxford

Cartwright, A. and Anderson, R. (1981) *General Practice Revisited*, Tavistock, London

Comaroff, J. (1976) 'Communicating information about non-fatal illness; the strategies of a group of general practitioners', *Sociological Review*, 24, 269-90

Davis, P. (1979) 'Motivation, responsibility and sickness in the psychiatric treatment of alcoholism', *British Journal of Psychiatry*, 134, 449-58

Elston, M. (1977) 'Medical autonomy: challenge and response', in K. Barnard and K. Lee, *Conflicts in the NHS*, Croom Helm, London

Freidson, E. (1961) *Patients' Views of Medical Practice*, Russell Sage Foundation, New York

Freidson, E. (1970) *The Profession of Medicine*, Dodd Mead and Co., New York

Gill, D. (1980) *The British National Health Service — A Sociologist's Perspective*, National Institute of Health, New York

Goode, W.J. (1960) 'Encroachment, charlatanism, and the emerging profession: psychiatry, sociology and medicine', *American Social Review*, 25, 902-14

Greenwood, E. (1957) 'Attributes of a profession', *Social Work*, 2, 44-55

Griffiths, R. (1983) *NHS Management Inquiry: Recommendations for Action*, DHSS, London

Gross, E. (1958) *Work and Society*, Thomas Crowell Co. Inc., New York

Honigsbaum, F. (1979) *The Division in British Medicine*, Kogan Page, London

Jefferys, M. and Sachs, H. (1983) *Rethinking General Practice*, Tavistock, London

Jewson, N. (1974) 'Medical knowledge and the patronage system in eighteenth century England', *Sociology*, 8, 369-85

Johnson, T. (1972) *Professions and Power*, Macmillan, London

Johnson, T. (1977) 'The professions in the class structure', in D. Scase, (ed.), *Industrial Society: Class, Cleavage and Control*, Allen and Unwin, London

Korsch, B.M. and Negrete, V.F. (1972) 'Doctor-patient communication', *Scientific American*, 227, 66-74

Larson, M.S. (1978) *The Rise of Professionalism: A Sociological Analysis*, California University Press, Los Angeles

McIntosh, J. (1976) *Communication and Awareness in a Cancer Ward*, Croom Helm, London

Navarro, V. (1978) *Class Struggle, the State and Medicine*, Martin Robertson, London

Parry, N. and Parry, J. (1976) *The Rise of the Medical Profession*, Croom Helm, London

Parsons, T. (1951) *The Social System*, Routledge and Kegan Paul, London

Posner, T. (1977) 'Magical elements in orthodox medicine', in R. Dingwall, C. Heath, M. Reid and M. Stacey (eds.), *Health Care and Health Knowledge*, Croom Helm, London

Pratt, L.V. (1976) 'Reshaping the consumers' posture in health care', in E. Gallagher (ed.), *The Doctor-Patient Relationship in the Changing Health Scene*, US Department of Health, Education and Welfare, NIH, pp. 197-214

Roth, J. (1963) *Timetables: Structuring the Passage of Time in Hospital Treatment and Other Careers*, Bobbs-Merrill, New York

Scheff, T.J. (1968) 'Negotiating reality: notes on power in the assessment of responsibility', *Social Problems*, 16, 3-17

Stimson, G. and Webb, B. (1975) *Going to See the Doctor: The Consultation Process in General Practice*, Routledge and Kegan Paul, London

Stimson, G.V. (1974) 'Obeying doctors' orders – a view from the other side', *Social Science and Medicine*, *8*, 97-105

Szasz, T. and Hollender, M.H. (1956) 'A contribution to the philosophy of medicine', *AMA Archives of Internal Medicine*, *XCVII*, 585-92

Tones, K. and Davison, L. (1979) 'Health education in the National Health Service', in D. Anderson (ed.), *Health Education in Practice*, Croom Helm, London

West, P. (1976) 'The physician and the management of childhood epilepsy', in M. Wadsworth and D. Robinson (eds.), *Studies in Everyday Medical Life*, Martin Robertson, London

Waitzkin, H. and Stoeckle, J. (1972) 'The communication of information about illness', *Advances in Psychosomatic Medicine*, *8*, 180-215

5 THE HOSPITAL AS A SOCIAL ORGANISATION

Modern medical practice is heavily concentrated in hospitals. As already noted in Chapter 1, the use of the general hospital as the centre for medical practice both encouraged and contributed to the development of biomedicine as the dominant approach to health, and can thus be viewed in social constructionist terms as a secondary manifestation of a certain way of viewing illness. Also, as shown in Chapter 4, hospital doctors maintain a dominant position in comparison with the general practitioner colleagues.

There are currently just under 2,000 hospitals in England, of which 80 per cent are non-psychiatric. They range in size from under 50 beds (36 per cent of all hospitals) to over 1,000 beds (11 per cent). Although comprising only one-fifth of all hospitals, psychiatric hospitals contain more than one-third of total beds — an indication of their large average size. Altogether, hospitals employ more than half of NHS doctors, 400,000 nursing and midwifery staff and 60,000 other professional and technical staff.

Hospitals are typically large institutions with a diversity of activities and personnel within them. They have been analysed from a variety of perspectives, such as management structure, staff attitudes and communications, and resource planning. However, sociological work has focused on the hospital as a social organisation, drawing on general sociological work on organisations, and on the experiences of patients and staff in psychiatric hospitals, often with a zealous commitment to reform. Early analyses of the hospital conceptualise it as a 'formal organisation', assuming that it is set up with the intention and design of accomplishing certain goals, and that people who work in an organisation believe, at least part of the time, that they are striving towards these same goals through intentionally rational behaviour (Simon 1955). While the hospital is chiefly a setting for medical practice, it has therefore, by virtue of being an organisation, many characteristics of its own. Organisation theory applied to hospitals is the subject of much debate, and has been characterised by a general shift from positivist to interactionist and radical approaches. The former takes the administrative and medical views of the hospital for granted, examining its more or less successful operation. The latter two views question such assumptions, exploring alternative

140

experiences of different people in the hospital, and questioning wisdom about their appropriate activities.

This chapter examines these different approaches to understanding the hospital as an organisation, and relates them to the situation and experiences of patients and staff in hospitals. Finally the major critiques of the psychiatric hospital and suggestions for substantial changes in its organisation are discussed.

The Hospital as a Bureaucratic Organisation

Organisation theory has generally employed a positivist approach, and views the hospital as consisting of a structured set of relationships which exist independently of the viewpoint of the observer. The primary aim is thus to understand the nature of the organisation as it operates in a more or less independent fashion. The classic work for the start of such an analysis is Max Weber's (1949) analysis of bureaucracy as a hierarchical system of authority, based on a rational and explicit set of rules. Weber argued that in modern industrial society systems of authority based on tradition or charisma give way to bureaucratic dominance, which forms the most efficient way of organising the nation state, the armed forces or the factory. He identified specific features of bureaucratic organisation as:

(1) The staff members are personally free, observing only the impersonal duties of their offices.

(2) There is a clear hierarchy of offices.

(3) The functions of the offices are clearly specified.

(4) Officials are appointed on the basis of a contract.

(5) They are selected on the basis of a professional qualification, ideally substantiated by a diploma gained through examination.

(6) They have a monthly salary, and usually pension rights. The salary is graded according to position in the hierarchy. The official can always leave the post, and under certain circumstances it may also be terminated.

(7) The official's post is his sole or major occupation.

(8) There is a career structure, and promotion is possible either by seniority or merit, and according to the judgement of superiors.

(9) The official may appropriate neither the post nor the resources that go with it.

(10)   He is subject to a unified control and disciplinary system.
(Albrow, 1970)

In so far as the hospital is a large-scale organisation in modern society, it can be seen to exhibit many aspects of Weber's ideal type of bureaucratic institution. However the hospital also exhibits both general and specific exceptions to Weber's model. These are centred around two areas. First is the modification of these principles, in so far as many hospital personnel are members of a profession which is organised in a different way to a bureaucracy, and in particular is characterised by professional autonomy and non-bureaucratic relationships (Chapter 4). Second is a related point, that hospital rules do not specify all the possibilities for action for every person
in the hospital. Thus staff have to exercise professionally guided discretion from time to time and negotiate these actions with colleagues.

The inappropriateness of Weber's bureaucratic model for hospitals has given rise to various reformulations. Of particular importance has been Etzioni's (1975) analysis. Etzioni accepts that organisations have rules, but is concerned with the question of how members of the organisation are persuaded to accept the rules and conditions (including technology) of their work. Etzioni explains the nature of this compliance by separating Weber's single concept of authority into two variables of power and involvement (Table 5.1). Etzioni suggests members can accept or reject the power position to which they are subjected. Those who reject their position are subject to coercive power; those who accept their position at a price are subject to remunerative power; and those who positively accept their position are subject to normative power. Members of an organisation consequently develop a positive or negative emotional commitment giving rise to three related kinds of personal involvement: alienative if their commitment is negative; calculative if their commitment is neutral; and moral if their commitment is positive. Etzioni suggests that these variables are fairly closely related. Thus, for example, those who reject the power exercised over them, such as prisoners, are also likely to have an alienated involvement with their organisation, whereas those who accept their power position, such as hospital patients or doctors, are likely to have a positive involvement or moral commitment to their organisation. Etzioni suggests that hospitals are most effective when their members (staff and patients) both accept power exercised over themselves and in addition have a positive moral involvement. However Etzioni provides no criteria by which effectiveness is to be judged and merely assumes that willing compliance by hospital staff and patients to the system of authority is best — an assumption that has been questioned particularly with regard to psychiatric hospitals.

Table 5.1: Typical Compliance Relations

		Kinds of involvement		
		Alienative	Calculative	Moral
Kinds of power	Coercive	Prisons		
	Remunerative		Factories	
	Normative			Hospitals

Source: Etzioni, 1975, p. 12.

Recognition that hospitals are characterised by two lines of authority, a bureaucratic one represented by the hospital adminisstrators, and a charismatic/traditional one upheld by doctors, with nurses being subject to both systems of authority, has led Bucher and Stelling (1969) to suggest that organisations such as hospitals in which professionals predominate cannot be usefully understood as bureaucracies at all. They argue that such organisations, which they describe as professional organisations, should be understood as unique in their own right. However, rather than attempting to elaborate further the structure of such an organisation, they dissolve the problem of alternative lines of authority by considering the general processes through which actions and meanings are agreed upon in the hospital. This conception suggests a much greater fluidity within an organisation, with power residing as much in the person as in his or her office. The role of doctor, for example, is not seen as a structural box into which an individual is fitted, but rather consists of a set of actions which an individual negotiates for him or herself within the hospital, and which may vary considerably from one person to another. Competition and conflict for resources are thus resolved more in the style of a parliamentary political process than a bureaucratic hierarchy.

In a more recent paper, Stelling and Bucher (1972) reject the notions of authority and hierarchy entirely. Instead they suggest that professional action within hospitals can be better understood in terms of 'elastic autonomy' which is negotiated by each person, and the monitoring of professions by each other to mutually justify the amount of negotiated autonomy exercised. This involves the processing of information rather than the following of rules. In other words, if an action can be justified by virtue of a negotiated shared meaning (e.g. 'this is an emergency'), then the actor or professional involved may expand the amount of autonomy he or she can exercise in that area. It can be seen that this line of argument has moved sharply away from the notion of an independent existing structure, but still focuses very much on those members of an organisation assumed to be the key factors, namely the professionals. The implications of this argument are developed later in considering the hospital as a 'negotiated order'.

The Hospital as a Goal-oriented Organisation

A second approach to analysing the nature of the hospital has been to focus on the output or effects of a hospital rather than its internal workings. For example, Parsons (1957) uses functionalist theory to judge the outputs or effects of any social institution by the functions it performs with regard to the achievement of widely shared social values. Parsons suggests that with regard to the hospital there is a widespread expectation that it can provide effective therapy. However, he notes that mental hospitals are also expected to perform additional functions which correspond to other social values. The public expects mental hospitals to provide custody for dangerous or frightening patients, and to protect patients who are vulnerable as a result of their disorder from social demands which they cannot meet and from actions which may be a danger to themselves or to other patients. Finally, Parsons suggests that mental hospitals have the job of re-socialising patients so that they can be returned to normal social roles in the wider society.

The failure of a hospital to perform these functions should lead to changes, since in functionalist theory social change is brought about as a result of the relative effectiveness with which functions are fulfilled. Stotland and Kobler (1965) provide a detailed study of such a case. This involved a mental hospital founded in a small town in the United States amid high expectations from professionals and public about its performance. However, these expectations changed rapidly after its opening in the 1950s in favour of treatment and prevention in a variety of community based facilities, reflecting general changes in policies towards mental illness. Since the hospital proved unable to adapt to these changed expectations about its functions it suffered a steady loss of confidence and internal conflict, and finally closed.

A failure to fulfil functions does not however always lead to closure, particularly where, as Parson suggests, there are multiple functions. While a hospital may fail to provide effective therapy or re-socialisation, it may continue to be custodial and hence satisfy public expectations.

Parsons' approach has been criticised for focusing too exclusively on factors external to the hospital (Whyte, 1961). Any variation between and within hospitals, particularly in a uniform structure such as the National Health Service, is consequently difficult to explain. In particular his approach has been criticised for ignoring the effects of technology on the organisational structure of the hospital. While functionalists would argue that such technology is controlled by the hospital in the pursuit of overall goals, some critics have suggested that the 'high techology' of modern medicine may have exerted an independent influence on hospitals. Indeed Perrow (1965) has argued that changing technology is the overall factor which most completely explains the changing social structure of the mental hospital. Whatever the traditions or history of the hospital, it would ultimately have to adapt to the impact of new technology.

Coser in her classic study of *Life in the Ward* (1962), showed in the same way that in a general hospital a different social structure corresponded to the different technology used on medical and surgical wards. Surgical wards involved the use of potentially dangerous treatments. Decisions had to be taken unequivocally and obeyed rapidly. Emergencies were not uncommon. This was associated with a social structure resembling Weber's description of an ideal-type of bureaucracy. Social relations amongst the staff, and between staff and patients, were governed by an explicit hierarchy of authority in which the predominant rationale for decisions was based on medical interpretation of the physical needs of the patients. These decisions were arrived at by senior staff and communicated as instructions which junior staff and patients were expected to obey. But in the medical wards treatments were less dramatic, required more thoughtful consideration, and could benefit from the opinions and observations of all grades of staff. The structure of authority was thus more participative on medical wards and characterised by a social structure of the kind described by Stelling and Bucher (1972). Decisions were not made only by senior staff, but negotiated amongst those individuals concerned with any particular patient. Authority, then, depended as much on the relevance of the information an individual (including a patient) possessed, as on his or her expertise in relation to decisive action.

This focus on the effects of technology on the social structure of the hospital has been criticised on the grounds that it assumes that technology is developed and applied without regard to its social effects. However technology is not neutral and often includes political, social and economic inputs which are part of that technology. For example, the use of drugs, anaesthetics and forceps in maternity wards is related to the social routines of ward staff, who wish to minimise the number of babies born at inconvenient times, such as at night or at weekends when staff do not want to work, although this may have adverse effects on babies and mothers (Oakley, 1979). Medical techniques, although generally justified in terms of their contribution to patients' care, can thus be heavily influenced by other factors.

An important contribution of approaches to hospitals which focus on goals is to draw attention to the existence of basic goal conflicts. Probably the major conflict is between goals focusing on patient care, and those focusing on the control of the patient or the education of the staff. The former are related to the interests of the patient, while the latter are related to the interests of the staff or other people outside the hospital. Of course, these two sets of interests may well overlap. For example, patients may wish to be cured, and staff and others also wish them to be cured, and similarly for some mental patients there may well be shared interests (including those of the patient) in control. Studies of hospital life have revealed, however, that conflict between goals is more common. A classic example of the conflict between patient care and control is in terms of the broad goals of institutions, as with the use of Soviet psychiatric hospitals for the punishment of dissidents. The conflict between cure and care is however also evident in relation to therapeutic regimes. In a recent study of psychiatric wards in general hospitals this manifested itself in different advice being given simultaneously. Consultants offered drugs for symptom control, while more junior doctors offered psychotherapy for cure, and each saw their therapeutic advice as a rival to, rather than a complement of, the other's (Baruch and Treacher, 1978).

A second way of viewing the conflict between care and control is in terms of what Goffman (1961) describes as the tension between 'humane standards' and 'institutional efficiency'. This tension is evident in all people-processing institutions, such as hospitals and prisons, since the objects processed are human beings to whom are attached rights and moral obligations and who possess an ability to react. However, concern with institutional efficiency is most likely to become a paramount and prolonged determinant of the social organisation of hospitals where the level of technology is low, and the opportunities for cure and the discharge of patients are limited. McKinlay (1975) has neatly encapulated this relationship between goals and technology in terms of the dimensions of social time and social space (Table 5.2). A team's interest in its patients can range from a very short space of time — for example the casualty clinic in a general hospital which is generally concerned only with immediate first aid work — to an indefinite span of time as in the care of chronically ill patients. The dimension of social space refers to the extent of involvement in the patient's biography, and ranges from very limited involvement, as with a patient with a broken leg who would not expect other parts of their anatomy, aspects of their personal history or considerations of their personal life style to be considered relevant, to more extensive involvement as with long-term mental hospital patients.

Table 5.2: Extent of a Patient's Time and Personal Space (Biography) Involved in Different Hospital Settings

	Social space	Social time
Acute general hospital	−	−
TB hospital, rehabilitation hospital, etc.	−	+
Short-term therapeutic psychiatric hospital	+	−
Long-term therapeutic hospital	+	+

Source: McKinlay, 1975, p. 343.

Conflicts between goals also have significant effects on the social organisation of staff. Perrow (1965) suggests that changes in technology, particularly as they relate to the general goals of the hospital, are important in understanding the role and status of staff. Despite some spectacular successes, such as modern surgery and antibiotics, or rather because of them, the expectations held of modern scientific medicine have continually outstripped its effectiveness. Coser (1963) argues that this has given rise to certain structural responses, using a model developed by Merton (1957). Merton suggested that in modern society in which there is an overarching goal of material success, combined with extremely varied means for its achievement, there would be a variety of different kinds of responses according to the disjunction between this goal and the means of obtaining it. For example, those who could achieve the goal by conventional means were most likely to be conformists, whereas those who had access to illegitimate means might turn towards criminal activity. Coser argues that within medicine there is a similar generalised goal towards curing patients, but again there are various means towards this goal, depending on the nature of the illness and the technology available. Where there is a goal/means disjunction, Coser suggests that a process of alienation develops whereby staff retreat from the goal and merely commit themselves to a ritualistic practice of institutional routines.

Coser's analysis has been extended to include other effects of the disjunction between goals and means in hospital (Table 5.3). Gralnick (1969) has shown that staff generate new means to existing goals. This is common in the field of hospital psychiatry, for example, which has witnessed a variety of therapies of dubious effectiveness in recent years, such as insulin shock therapy, lobotomy, a variety of mood-altering drugs, electro-convulsive therapy and psychotherapy. Brown (1973) has extended this model to suggest that staff can have a third kind of reaction. Not only may they become alienated and adopt a 'realistic' attitude towards what can be done for the patient, or generate new technology to meet therapeutic goals, but they can accept their disenchantment and give up medical work. Brown suggests that the particular reactions of staff members depend crucially on the nature of the reward system in the hospital. In effect, he is suggesting that only if these rewards are high enough, whether financial, intrinsic (such as scientific research) or incidental (easy hours, good accommodation and so on), will staff stay in the job.

There are two further solutions to Brown's dilemma. First, there can develop what Goffman (1961) describes as a moral division of labour. He derived this from Hughes' study of the nature of work (Hughes, 1958). Hughes observed that in work organisations there was very often a division of labour between those who did the 'dirty work', and those who epitomised the higher aspirations of the organisation. Goffman suggests that in mental hospitals there is a similar division of labour in that senior staff members, such as doctors, work towards more laudable goals such as therapy, while more junior staff, such as attendants or nurses, are assigned the more unpleasant tasks of managing and controlling patients. In other words, senior staff displace the goals/means disjunction on to junior staff.

Secondly, Brown's dilemma may be resolved ideologically. For example, Goldie (1977) suggests that while paramedical staff, such as social workers or physiotherapists, may have more to offer patients than doctors, they frequently acquiesce in doctors' definitions and prescriptions which they have declared in research interviews they disagree with. This acquiescence is not overtly demanded by doctors, but results from paramedicals accepting an ideology of medical dominance. In short, therapeutic optimism is maintained by the device of believing that medical activities are more effective than they really are.

Table 3: The Effects of the Disjunction between Goals and Means on Hospital Staff.

Means	Goals	Effects	Sources
Accept	Reject ➡	alienation	Coser, 1963
Reject	Accept ➡	innovation	Gralnick, 1969
Reject	Reject ➡	resignation	Brown, 1973
Displace	Accept ➡	moral division of labour	Goffman, 1961
Accept	Displace ➡	ideology	Goldie, 1977

The Hospital as a Negotiated Order

In contrast to positivist analyses which have emphasised formal structures, the interactionist perspective views organisations as no more than the intentions, actions and meanings of those people within it. Organisations thus become much more flexible and uncertain phenomena, owing any continuity in their existence to continuities in shared meanings. However, these do not arise spontaneously, but are determined largely by those individuals and groups that are successful in getting their own meanings accepted by the rest of the organisation. This approach, rather than taking an organisation such as a hospital as given, is therefore concerned with the question of how the activities and relationships of the hospital are continually recreated. Thus rather than focusing exclusively on the key professional workers, attention is paid to the interactions and relationships of all its members, regardless of their particular place or position within the organisation.

We saw earlier that Bucher and Stelling (1969) began to explore this approach in their criticism of models of the hospital as a bureaucratic organisation. They suggested, along with other critics of Weber's ideal-type of bureaucracy, that there is considerable room for autonomous action to develop between the lines of conduct specified by the official rules. Similarly, as Coser's (1962) study showed, in medical wards the organisation of social relations was far more negotiable than in surgical wards. In order to understand this aspect of hospitals, Strauss (1963) introduced the concept of the hospital as a 'negotiated order', which now forms the dominant sociological approach to understanding hospitals and hospital life. The analysis of the hospital as a negotiated order is based on the assumption that within hospitals the official rules are rarely specific enough to guide the detailed daily or hourly interactions of people, which are therefore subject to negotiation. Thus Strauss suggests that daily life is organised around a series of bargains, struck and forgotten or renegotiated from time to time, as desired by the individual. One of the most important notions this approach develops is of the ways in which lower level participants within the organisation, such as patients, attendants, visitors and paramedical staff, can influence the formal organisation through bargaining and negotiation. The ways in which patients, and especially long-stay patients who are knowledgeable about their condition and treatment, may bargain and negotiate with medical staff is discussed in Chapter 4. Low level staff may also exert considerable power, although having no formal authority. For example, Hall (1977) shows how attempts to introduce play leaders for children in hospitals were modified by nurses. The very notion of play, and the arrangements required for its occurrence, threatened the conventional routines of ward life. As a result nursing staff successfully renegotiated the opportunities that children had for play, and confined play leaders to a more marginal position within the ward than official policy decreed. An important implication of this is that lower level members of staff have more power than would appear to be the case, given the formal structure of the hospital and their position in the hierarchy of authority. While this might appear to be a democratising influence in the hospital, this power is frequently exercised by staff in a negative or obstructive fashion.

Negotiated order theory, although widely regarded as contributing important insights into the working of the hospital, has been criticised for over-emphasising the fluid nature of negotiations. Bittner (1979) suggests that ordinary staff and patients do in fact adhere to some kind of formal structural description of the organisation they are in. They do not necessarily believe the organisation is actually like this model, but rather they draw upon such a 'scheme of interpretation' to make sense of that part of the organisation out of their reach, so that they may identify with unseen actions elsewhere and gain a sense of uniform purpose. For example, nursing staff were formally organised into a bureaucratic hierarchy by the 1966 Salmon Committee recommendations (Ministry of Health, 1966). At the bottom of this hierarchy, nurses work with patients and doctors to a timetable, little of which they can negotiate over, since these basic aspects of their working environment are controlled by senior staff elsewhere. However, this process makes sense to junior staff through their acceptance of the Salmon hierarchy as a legitimate representation of the hospital organisation outside their immediate experience. Nevertheless, Bittner argues that this hierarchy is only a representation, and cannot be taken as a real structure in the sense that a positivist analysis would.

Day and Day (1977) also point out that while negotiated order theory gets away from the idealisation implicit in formal organisation theory, it focuses upon only one aspect of the reality of hospital life, namely a rather low level, immediate daily experience of that hospital. Negotiations over this daily experience are then extrapolated as an explanation for the hospital order in general, under-emphasising those considerable portions of hospital life which are non-negotiable, non-fluid and may well not be immediately symbolically meaningful. In other words, structural constraints, both political and economic, which may exist beyond the ken of the individual participants being studied, or indeed beyond the control of or boundaries of the hospital, are under-emphasised. A second weakness identified by Day and Day is the idea of negotiation as the basis for social order within a hospital, which suggests that adaptation and adjustment are the key elements. It is thus difficult to conceptualise from this point of view any notion of conflict or resistance to the agreements being negotiated. This conservative bias, shared with symbolic interactionism generally, arises from focusing at a level from which it is difficult to conceptualise and measure unequal distributions of power or the sources of that power.

Psychiatric Hospitals: Critiques and Alternatives

Sociological interest in hospitals has been particularly strong in the psychiatric field. This has been a result partly of a commitment to analyse and expose oppression in all areas of social life. In addition, psychiatric hospitals have provided a rich source of data about the limits of medical activities in practice, and the social dynamics of organisational life. This section first briefly reviews the history of institutional care for the mentally ill, and then examines sociological analyses of psychiatric hospitals and the nature of alternative 'therapeutic communities'.

Historical Development

The state has provided for lunatics since 1744, when it recommended in the Vagrancy Act of that year that each county should be allowed to set up an asylum to which both criminal and pauper lunatics could be sent, the term 'lunatic' to be determined by the local Justices of the Peace, rather then physicians. During the early part of the nineteenth century the gradual development of county asylums not only occurred without medical influence, but they indeed developed a quite sophisticated non-medical approach to mental illness, termed 'moral treatment'. From this point of view, the experience of madness was to be corrected by providing a calm and ordered life, in which the mad person was treated in so far as was possible in a humane and respectful manner. Symbolised by the dramatic removal of the chains of the mad in 1794 by Pinel in the asylums of Bicêtre and Saltpetrière, this approach was developed by Tuke in the Retreat at York into an educational process, using kindness and respect to help mad people re-establish self-control of their 'animal natures' through moral force. In *Description of the Retreat* (1813), Tuke argued that a patient's 'desire for esteem' rather than 'the principle of fear' guided the organisation of treatment.

Partly in response to this example, and partly in reaction to the excesses of the private mad-houses revealed in Parliamentary Select Committee reports in 1807 and 1815, a strong reform movement developed to press for the construction and regulation of public asylums. The construction of these was made compulsory in the 1845 Lunatics Act; within three years nearly three-quarters of English counties had complied, and the rest followed suit within ten years. While it might be expected that the non-medical system of 'moral treatment' would naturally be adopted in these new asylums, in fact the medical profession soon came to dominate them.

The Asylum Movement drew its inspiration not only from medicine and moral treatment, but also from the Utopian hopes which inspired socialist and religious communards of the early nineteenth century, such as Robert Owen. Yet by 1877 a Lancet Commission set up to investigate asylums recorded that 'everywhere attendants, we are convinced, maltreat, abuse and terrify patients when the backs of the medical officers are turned. Humanity is only to be secured by the watching officials' (Jones, 1972). The asylums had rapidly become overcrowded during the middle of the century, as a result both of pressure on them to take increasing numbers of admissions, and the failure of the asylum doctors to cure many of their inmates. While at the end of the first quarter of the nineteenth century there were six public asylums, of an average size of 116 inmates, this became 24 asylums averaging 300 inmates by 1850, and 60 asylums averaging 650 inmates by 1880 (Scull, 1979, p. 198).

Although the asylum movement had developed in the early nineteenth century with a positive idea — literally an asylum or retreat from an increasingly stressful world — in reality the incarceration of lunatics became a sub-branch of the general nineteenth-century use of institutional control. Clearly such a place was not attractive, and in the later decades of the nineteenth century considerable concern developed about the possibility of individuals being erroneously locked away. This gave rise in 1890 to the Lunacy Act which was addressed to the proper process of admission so that mistaken confinement could not occur. Its focus on safeguarding those outside could not be more of a contrast with the 1845 Act's intent of bringing the benefits of the asylum experience to mad people.

From the 1930s mental hospitals began to move away from their social welfare function to become more concerned with active therapeutic measures. Over the following 25 years there were further developments in somatic treatments for mental illness: insulin coma, electro-convulsive therapy, drugs and brain surgery. Drugs in particular have enabled doctors to control the disabling symptoms of mental illness sufficiently to reduce the need for hospitalisation. In addition, the establishment of income security and free health care in the 1940s substantially weakened the logic of supporting the mentally ill in hospital. Therefore the 1957 Royal Commission and 1959 Mental Health Act suggested that, with help from the welfare state and new medical treatments, the mentally ill could now be returned to, or retained in, the community, and the asylums were to become more flexible in taking voluntary patients. Logically, given the ageing physical structure and forbidding reputation of the old asylums, Enoch Powell announced in 1961 that he was going to substantially empty them by 1975.

Although this target was not met, a 40 per cent reduction in the asylum population has been achieved to date, despite higher admission rates, as a result of reduced lengths of stay.

Current state policy is to maintain the mentally ill in the community through the support of the welfare state, while making medical care available through brief in-patient treatment and out-patient support. However, policy for community care has only been slowly implemented in comparison with estimates of need. Wider concerns, such as shortage of money for public expenditure, have been crucial constraints on state policy; although official views have rationalised that this is in any case appropriate: 'Psychiatry is to join the rest of medicine . . . People go into hospital with mental disorders and they are cured' (Sir Keith Joseph, 1971, quoted in Jones, 1972, p. 340).

The history of psychiatric hospitals as a struggle between humanitarian concern and enlightenment on the one hand, and neglect on the other, has been challenged in more recent work on the way in which medical interests and definitions of mental illness developed in the nineteenth century. The medical profession had officially become involved with madness as early as the late eighteenth century when official (though ineffective) inspection of private mad-houses was set up. In addition, many of these used medical claims in their competition for trade and were often built near infirmaries. However, the development of moral treatment at the turn of the century posed a considerable threat to such medical expansion, and it is remarkable therefore to find that by 1830 existing public asylums (built under the 1744 Vagrancy Act) mostly had medical directors, and that the 1845 Act required the keeping of medical records and encouraged medical dominance within the Lunacy Commission. By the 1850s, two new journals devoted entirely to a medical approach to insanity had been founded, taking the line that 'insanity is purely a disease of the brain. The physician is now the responsible guardian of the lunatic and must ever remain so' (*Journal of Mental Science*, 2 October 1858). However, as Scull (1979) documents, at no point during the nineteenth century did the medical profession ever come up with any convincing treatment for mental illness.

The involvement of doctors in the early asylum movement survived the pessimism of the late nineteenth century by an appeal to the achievements of medical science for physical disorders. It seemed indeed that this would soon spill over into the psychiatric field. The identification of syphilis as the cause of general paralysis of the insane in 1894 and its confirmation as an infection in the nerve-cells of the cortex in 1913, and the identification of the neuroses in the early 1920s, enabled the medical profession to dominate the 1924-7 Royal Commission on Lunacy and Mental Disorder. The subsequent Mental Treatment Act of 1930, as its title implies, began to prise the control of asylum admissions away from lawyers in favour of doctors (Treacher and Baruch, 1981).

Nevertheless modern medical care in the psychiatric field is still of limited effectiveness, even in its own terms, and hence another interpretation of this history has been suggested by Scull (1977). He argues that improved medical treatment has not been the major cause of this change in the pattern of treatment of mental illness. Scull cites evidence to show that modern treatments are not very effective, and that the reduction in the number of patients in hospitals began before such treatments appeared in the late 1950s. Furthermore he argues that criticism of the negative effects of hospitalisation (discussed in the next section) had been available since the 1870s, but only stimulated policy changes in the 1960s. Therefore, he concludes, the real reason for community care is an economic one. The establishment of the welfare state provides an infrastructure of social control in the community which is far cheaper than hospital care, particularly as many of the old asylums are badly in need of physical refurbishment. Scull thus suggests that the incarceration and decarceration of the mentally ill has been shaped by the relative costs of different methods of social control, of which medical care is but one possibility, rather than any medical logic. Indeed he argues that medicine has merely provided a rationalisation for other changes.

Humanist Critique of the Psychiatric Hospitals

Concern about the overcrowded and poor condition of hospitals was being voiced in England as early as 1877. Despite such early observations, the conditions in psychiatric hospitals were not subject to systematic analysis until the 1940s. Important early works included those of Bateman and Dunham (1948), and Belknap (1956), which focused on the American state mental hospital. They disregarded the medical view of hospital life in favour of viewing mental hospitals in terms of a human community. Many mental hospitals were situated in rural settings and provided the majority of local workers with employment. Jobs were 'spoken for' from generation to generation within families, who frequently lived on or near the hospital site. Traditional and routine approaches to nursing work became very stable, and difficult to change. Their findings thus pointed to the existence of rigidly stratified community. Patients being at the bottom of a hierarchy of power were thus unable, either individually or collectively, to press their needs and claims within the community. Cumming and Cumming (1956) argued that this typical experience was a result of a 'granulated' social structure: the hospital was split up horizontally into separate 'caste'-like strata of staff and patients with different statuses. In addition, there were rigid vertical divisions between different functional groups such as therapists, nurses, administrators, and male and female patients. As a result, the hospital social structure was made up of separate granules, between which there was little communication.

Detailed anthropological work developed these observations more carefully to suggest that there was a relationship between the level of disturbance of individual patients and certain conflicts within this rigid social structure. For example, Stanton and Schwartz (1954) suggested that disagreement between staff about appropriate treatment methods caused apparently inexplicable disturbance in some patients from time to time. The reason for this was that staff members were often unaware that they were giving conflicting advice to patients, since there was little coordination of their work if they were on different shifts, or in different departments. At other times they were aware of these disagreements but were unable to resolve them, so that patients became the focus of their conflicts.

Miller (1957) and Caudill (1958) elaborated this idea to suggest a more collective link between the general level of disturbance in whole groups of patients, and conflicts within and between whole sections of the medical staff concerned with them. This relationship seemed to move in a cycle over a period of months during which tension and conflict fluctuated between apparently low levels and peaks of collective disorder.

These studies had cumulatively established that the American state mental hospital was a particularly static routinised place, in which patients had little autonomy, punctuated from time to time by explosive eruptions of tension, and the corresponding deterioration of some patients. The theoretical orientation of most of the work was anthropological functionalism, in which the hospital was viewed as an autonomous, integrated community, or as Caudill (1958) termed it 'a small society'. However, two subsequent studies were to take a rather different emphasis. First was the well-known work of Goffman (1958) based on a year's participant observation of a hospital in Washington as a remedial gymnast, and subsequently elaborated as a major theoretical statement about the nature of 'total institutions' (1961). The second study, by Strauss (1963), was also based on mental hospital observation and gave rise to the first outline of 'negotiated order theory', discussed earlier in this chapter. Both these studies are significant in two respects. They were both concerned with theoretical elaboration, as much as empirical observation, in contrast to the earlier studies mentioned. In addition, they were to give rise subsequently to two very influential streams of work.

Goffman's work combined both an acute eye for detail in noticing the similar structures and processes in mental hospitals, prisons, monastic orders and so on, and an explicit moral condemnation of the impact of those total institutions on the lives of people in them. His argument was based on the use of ideal-types, suggested by Max Weber (1949), in that he built up a model of the total institution from a variety of empirical and literary sources. He suggested that the key process — the totality — was established by collapsing the normally separate spheres of work, home and leisure, into one monolithic social experience: a kind of 'batch living' of the kind found in factory farmed animals. The crucial phase in this process is the entry of the patient into hospital. This process shares many similarities with the entry procedures experienced by all clients going into total institutions, from army camps to prisons and hospitals (Jones, 1972b). In essence, this amounts to the common severance of social relations on the outside and the entry into new social relations on the inside. More particularly with respect to hospitals, Goffman (1961) referred to this transition as a 'moral career'. He means by this that the changed social relationships resulting from movement into hospital include an important alteration in the patient's own identity, which becomes completely submerged by the requirements of the institution. Goffman identified three distinct aspects of this career in total institutions such as mental hospitals:

Mortification of the Self. This was achieved through the literal degrading of the person's previous status and identity, brought about by the removal of their normal social props such as clothing and personal effects, the restriction of activities and movements and the requirement to engage in various demeaning practices, such as asking permission to smoke or post a letter.

Reorganisation of the Self. The hospital replaces those aspects of the patient's identity it has removed: hospital clothes, hospital friends, a new status as patient, etc.

Patient Response. Goffman was well aware that his ideal-type of total institution did not always operate fully. In particular, in his discussion of the 'underlife' of asylums, he acknowledges that there are numerous means of working the system or 'making out' within the officially designated routines. Thus whereas some patients respond to the institution by *colonisation*, or the acceptance of their new position without enthusiasm, others become positively identified with their allotted identity in a process of *conversion*, while a third response is to reject the hospital's requirements, and either become *withdrawn* or *intransigent*.

Psychiatric hospital patients are expected in Etzioni's terms (Table 5.1) to be powerless and to exhibit a positive moral commitment to their position in the hospital. There is a strong moral image of the good patient who is seen as co-operative and totally acquiescent to this system of rules. Any attempt to reject this authority system, either by opposing the distribution of power or by moral rejection, elicits powerful negative sanctions, including personal unpopularity (Fairhurst, 1977).

The reorganised conception of the self which long-stay patients in psychiatric hospitals may come to accept has been termed 'institutionalisation' or 'institutional neurosis', which broadly corresponds with Goffman's notion of 'conversion'. Barton (1959) gave the following definition:

> Institutional neurosis is a disease characterised by apathy, lack of initiative, loss of interest most marked in things and events not immediately personal or present, submissiveness, and sometimes no expression of feelings of resentment at harsh or unfair orders. There is also a lack of interest in the future and an apparent inability to make practical plans for it, a deterioration in personal habits, toilet and standards generally, a loss of individuality and a resigned acceptance that things will go on as they are — unchangingly, inevitably and indefinitely. (Barton, 1959, p. 2)

Barton, like Goffman, believed that the behaviour and attitudes referred to as institutionalisation, or institutional neurosis, are a product of the environment and pattern of care characteristic of custodial institutions. An alternative view is that behaviours and attitudes of patients described as institutionalised are a product of the disease process which brought them into institutional care in the first place. In order to unravel the causes of this condition, Wing and Brown (1970) examined the relationship between the hospital environment and institutionalism among women schizophrenic patients. These patients had spent between two and six years in one of three mental hospitals which differed markedly in their social environments. They found environmental poverty (measured in terms of ward restrictiveness, lack of occupation, lack of personal possessions, lack of contact with the outside world and unfavourable nurse attitudes) highly related to the poor clinical condition of patients (measured in terms of flatness of affect, poverty of speech, and social withdrawal); and the hospital with the richest social environment contained patients with the fewest negative symptoms, even though patients did not appear to have differed in the severity of their illness at the time of admission. They also found that attitudes to discharge became progressively more unfavourable with increasing length of stay, regardless of the patient's clinical condition.

To ascertain whether a poor environment caused a poor clinical condition (or vice versa) they undertook a follow-up survey four years later to see if efforts to improve the social environment of these three hospitals over this period had been associated with an improvement of the patients' clinical condition. The follow-up was based on 233 patients who had been in the original study and were still in one of the three hospitals. They found that the improvement in the environment of hospitals was associated with improvement in the patients' clinical condition, and this improvement could not be explained by changes in drug treatment. Therefore they concluded that the patients' environment does have a significant effect on their clinical condition, although a patient's clinical condition and the strength of ties to the outside community were also important.

Further support for Goffman's criticism of institutions is provided in a study by King, Raynes and Tizard (1971) of residential care for mentally handicapped children. They compared hospital wards for such children with local authority homes. They found that hospital wards were organised on institutional lines, with batch management, little communication or mixing between staff and children and rigid rules and routines. Local authority homes, however, were child-oriented and characterised by a household type of organisation in which staff mixed with children and shared in the activities of the home and the person in charge was responsible for budgeting and purchasing toys and clothes for individual children. These two patterns of care were found to be associated with differences in the abilities of children, such that the children in homes had better speech and were more able to feed and dress themselves than children in hospital wards. These differences could not be attributed to differences in the severity of the handicap, but resulted from the institutional environment and pattern of care. There was also no difference in staff-patient ratios in the children's homes and hospital wards. However, a re-analysis of the data has shown that the effective staff ratios (ESR — the staff available at peak times) were higher in children's homes (Kushlick, 1973). The ESR is important because below a certain staffing level an individual-oriented pattern of care becomes impossible.

The variety of responses to institutional pressures in psychiatric hospitals identified by Goffman has been viewed by some writers as throwing doubt on the validity of his general model. For example, Perry (1974) has suggested that Goffman attempts to develop both a detailed study of the mental hospital as a unique institution, and a general model of the common elements in different kinds of institutions. However, this dual project led to considerable confusion between unique and common elements, such that neither is satisfactorily portrayed. The compelling style of his analysis is achieved rather through a more literary use of metaphor and symbol: 'In Goffman's work there is an unresolved tension between socio-logical etiquette and metaphysical concerns [which] constitutes an important basis of [its] appeal' (Perry, 1974).

It is precisely the question of these unofficial institutional interactions on which Strauss's (1963) study focused. This started out from the position that what was most important, rather than incidental, was the 'underlife' of the asylum. This was *de facto* the social reality for its members, staff and patients alike. Thus, Goffman's horrifying vision of the dominating totality of life in the asylum, and its associated moral condemnation, might turn out to be a sociological 'strawman' in the light of the real, rather than ideal-typical, 'negotiated order'. The theoretical adequacy of Strauss's work has been discussed earlier in this chapter (pp. 150–1). However, it is important to note here that its practical implication is that the underlife of the asylum could soften the totalising experience for its members sufficiently to make life at worst tolerable, and at best comfortable. For example, something akin to a 'black economy' has been noted by many observers of institutional life, such as the tobacco currency in prisons. A similar circulation of material goods amongst both staff and patients is common in mental hospitals, providing at the very least greater flexibility than the official routines allow.

The celebrated problem of 'institutionalisation' introduced earlier thus needs some careful qualification, in so far as patients can renegotiate the negotiated order they have joined. For example, the entry of patients into hospital and their subsequent 'moral careers' include the acquisition of hospital time. Since negotiations between patients and staff focus heavily upon progress towards leaving, institutionalisation can be defined as a moral career that has become stuck, so that the patient no longer tries to negotiate his or her way through and beyond institutional time. This is the experience of institutionalisation from the interactionist view, however it may be located in the hospital structure.

In some hospitals, patients do not however uniformly accept institutional time without question. As Strauss has suggested, there is room for negotiation — not merely over daily or weekly routines, such as the length and frequency of visiting hours, but, more importantly for some patients, the total amount of time they will be spending in hospital before being deemed recovered. In particular, Roth (1962) pointed out that for long-term illnesses both staff and patients often measure the depth of illness and extent of recovery in terms of time done, or to be done, and hence negotiations between staff and patients about dates of departure or home visits become highly significant and occupy a central place in the patient's identity. To the extent that staff successfully maintain uncertainty about these events they can prevent patients from making informed judgements about particular medical policies to which they are subjected. However, patients can successfully undermine such staff ploys by comparing treatments, playing off staff against each other, and so on. Indeed, as we have seen, Goffman recognised this in his description of patient responses other than conversion (institutionalisation): colonisation, withdrawal and intransigence.

A further exception to Goffman's model has been identified by Tobin and Lieberman (1976). They conducted a careful study of the way old people come to be rejected by their families and placed in hospital when home nursing becomes too difficult. They show that the self-identity of such patients begins to be undermined months before their physical removal, in their interactions within the family, particularly those leading to a decision to seek hospital care. Subsequently their social interactions begin to atrophy as the date for moving comes closer. Tobin and Lieberman argue that the hospital cannot therefore be seen as the only relevant agent, but that the process of mortification is caused by an interaction between at least three parties: the hospital, the patient and his or her family.

Therapeutic Communities

The most complete attempt to restructure the internal life of the mental hospital was developed soon after the Second World War. In America, this approach was termed 'milieu therapy', and in Britain the 'therapeutic community'. These developments attempted to change many of the processes identified in this chapter: to reduce goal conflict, develop a new technology of group therapy, democratise the authority structure and expose previously hidden negotiations to public discussion and democratic control.

The therapeutic community was committed to a critique both of psychiatric practice, and the hospital setting in which much of it took place. The assumption was that mental illness was fundamentally located within disordered social relations, rather than deep intra-psychological or chemical processes. It followed from this that not only was conventional psychiatric practice empirically invalid, but it allowed the incarceration of patients in a hospital setting which aggravated their problems, located as these were in the very social relations which the hospital created. The solution therefore was a double one. Both a new technology of treatment and the liberation of incarcerated patients could be achieved through radically restructuring the social relations of the hospital.

The new principles to be used were recorded in a study of the pioneering British hospital in this field by Rapoport (1960) as: 'everything is treatment'; 'all treatment is rehabilitation'; 'all patients should get equal treatment'. These statements mean that, firstly, since mental illness was caused by and manifested through social relations, all the patient's relationships of any kind should be used as opportunities for treatment. Consequently, the normal distinction between special treatment relationships (e.g. psychotherapy) and social rehabilitation disappeared. Finally, it was felt that the common cause of various mental illnesses (in social relations) required equal treatment, whatever the specific symptomatology of the patient.

Rapoport subsequently identified four objectives which he suggested were used to implement these new principles. First was the democratisation of the hospital, through which the patients would get a greater and ideally decisive share of power. As a group, the professional staff were to become the employed helpers, rather than controllers, of patients. Second, the hospital should be very permissive of deviant actions, so that, third, a real community could flourish, unimpeded by the requirements of 'proper' behaviour. Finally, the rich social and cultural life which would (and does) flourish under such conditions would be subject to communal reflection (aided by staff expertise), such that patients would be helped to confront the reality of their disordered social relationships, and come to try out new and more satisfactory ways of living.

These objectives were operationalised via an elaborate system of small and large group meetings through which patients circulated with a wide variety of other members of the hospital (Figure 5.1). The activities of these groups ranged from a kind of parliamentary administration of hospital business (conducted by an elected patient leader), to psychotherapy, to working groups concerned to repair the fabric of the building, or to decide on the admission of new patients (also under the control of a patient). At any time day or night emergency meetings could be called by any member of the hospital to discuss a personal or collective crisis.

Clearly, such a hospital was very different from the traditional style. However, in reality it operated within definite limits controlled by senior staff members. Rapoport showed that some of the principles were self-contradictory and incompatible. For example, for the sake of democracy, some behaviours such as intimidation, could not be permitted. Again, treatment and rehabilitation could not be entirely the same, since the social relations within the community, however desirable, were not likely to be found back in the patient's family, friends or workplace.

Other writers have raised more extensive critiques. From the traditional technology-input position, Perrow (1965) has argued that the therapeutic community has little effective technology and that there is little evidence to suggest that using social relationships is any better a therapy than conventional psychiatric practice. Consequently, he suggests that the patient is surrounded by an optimism and enthusiasm which are at best utopian and misleading, and at worst render the patient de-skilled with respect to the harsh realities of the world outside.

Figure 5.1: Therapeutic Community Activities

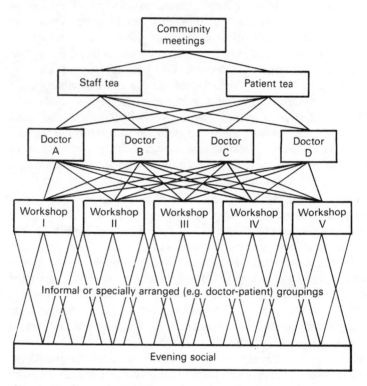

Source: Rapoport, 1960 (p. 83)

The role of staff in therapeutic communities can also be viewed as giving rise to considerable stress. Staff provide and sustain the culture which sets up the therapeutic relationships, but in doing so they become very committed to the success of treatment, dependent as it is on their personal involvement. This is not only very demanding, indeed draining enthusiasm and commitment, but can lead to spectacular personal collapse from time to time. Lewis Coser (1974) has identified this process in a variety of institutions which demand a high level of personal devotion. He analyses the way strongly motivated staff can be exploited through institutions he describes as 'greedy', in much the same way Goffman analysed the effects of 'asylums' in patients. This is a particular danger in therapeutic communities where zealous commitment can give rise to what Hobson (1979) terms a 'messianic' delusion that the staff or their leader will become the 'saviour' of the community and its patients.

Not only is technology failure a problem, but the very conditions for the existence of such radical communities pose some insoluble dilemmas for them. Therapeutic communities necessarily require financial and moral support from their own immediate environment, such as the National Health Service. They must therefore maintain legitimacy by fulfilling the function of social control of patients, providing career opportunities for professional staff, undertaking scientific research and so on. These requirements conflict with the ideal principles of democracy, communalism and permissiveness, and thus place great strain on the community's leadership which has to manage such contradictions (Manning, 1980). At times, this can lead to a breakdown of the commitment of community members to the collective enterprise in exactly the way that nineteenth-century religious communes frequently foundered (Kanter, 1972).

Other difficulties are those generated entirely within the community that may undermine its activities. For example, Punch (1974) has suggested that a sociology of the 'anti-institution' can be constructed which focuses on the central dilemma of setting up a set of social rules specifically devised to create a community in which the mortifying rule-bound routines of the traditional institution are eliminated. But there is obviously the possibility that the new rules can become as 'totalising' as the old ones and lead to what Perrow (1965) describes as 'utopian institutionalisation'. For example, the mortification and reconstruction of the self which Goffman described as a negative effect of the traditional institution can occur even more forcefully in the therapeutic community. Both patients and staff may become so bound up with the new experience of their community life that they exhibit Goffman's 'conversion' in the opposite sense to that in which he used it, that is they become unrealistically committed to the exclusion of their previous or outside social ties.

A further problem for therapeutic communities is of sustaining a sufficiently anti-institution culture and preventing its contamination by old patterns of interaction. For example patients may resurrect their deference to medical staff or institutional rules, while the staff themselves may reinstate conventional patterns of authority through exercising personal influence in free-floating group interactions. Bloor (1980) has observed that this dilemma results from the specific technique of using social relationships therapeutically. This he suggests involves the elevation of the mundane and the routine to a special status, in which staff (and patients too) try to interact in a self-aware rather than an habitual manner. However, this is difficult to sustain since there is a constant tendency to slip back into habitual interaction. Such a tension between the ideal and the real has been exacerbated in some therapeutic communities by the mythologising of the ideal to a point at which it becomes unattainable, and hence by definition a source of failure (Morrice 1972). However, Manning (1976, 1979) suggests that a set of intermediate rules and norms are generated spontaneously to manage this tension and rationalise its intermittent realisation. This is partly achieved through a familiar process already identified by Goffman (1961), and introduced earlier in this chapter, as a moral division of labour.

In the therapeutic community, this occurs as a separation between junior unqualified 'enthusiastic' staff who are employed to be democratic, permissive, and so on, while senior staff, entrenched in conventional career patterns, use the resulting rich community life as a source of therapeutic material for psychological interpretation. However, this solution also has an inherent tendency to break down as junior staff envy senior staff's skills, status and careers (Manning 1976). This is normally resolved by encouraging a high turnover of junior staff, who leave after about a year drained of enthusiasm (a necessary therapeutic raw material) but not, as yet, formulating sufficient demands for crossing this labour division. In the face of these theoretical and practical difficulties, the therapeutic community has not become as important an organising principle for mental hospitals as its practitioners would wish. Like its predecessor, 'moral treatment', it presents a set of values and organisation principles that are difficult for traditional bureaucracies and professionals to absorb. In particular it does not, like 'moral treatment', lend itself to adoption in the manner of a new technology, since it challenges those very social relationships of hierarchy and expertise upon which techno-logical medicine depends. Nevertheless the number of therapeutic communities within the Association of Therapeutic Communities in the United Kingdom exceeds one hundred, perhaps half of which operate within the National Health Service. In addition they have an influence, by way of example, in many mental hospitals, and have spread to many countries throughout the world (Kennard, 1983).

Hospitals and Patients

Since the main period of the critiques of the psychiatric hospital in the 1960s there have been some significant changes which may both reduce the force of those criticisms and at the same time herald the possibility of a future era of neglect. The major change has been a substantial reduction in in-patient numbers, through a marked reduction in the length of stay of most patients. The negative effect of hospital life on patients is thus considerably reduced simply because they are not admitted for so long. In addition some of the critiques have led to changes within hospitals. Most now have a token therapeutic community operating within one or two selected wards, and the old hierarchical structure dominated by a medical director has been broken down into separate sections, coordinated by a committee of the relevant medical consultants. However, the rapid turnover of patients has been accompanied by the built up of a 'new' long-stay group, noticeable for its high average age. Indeed, it may be that the old asylums will become the homes of an increasing number of elderly confused patients, especially as the population structure contains a rapidly growing number of very old people. In the past these people have often been poorly treated in residential homes, not least because they elicit a therapeutic pessimism amongst nursing staff who have been trained for active therapeutic intervention with younger patients.

The processes which sociologists have revealed within psychiatric hospitals have their counterparts in general hospitals, but these have been less debated. This probably reflects the more limited effects of institutional organisation, and is partly because the rationale for medical activities is more likely to be accepted by patients in general hospitals. The extent to which batch processing can occur is also often limited by the mix of patients on a ward, requiring different levels of care, although patient surveys show dissatisfaction about particular aspects of care, linked to the efficient management of large numbers of people, such as the early waking times and lack of privacy (Royal Commission on the NHS, 1979). The effects of institutional care on patients in general hositals are also generally reduced by the relatively brief periods for which most patients remain in hospital. However, for those groups of patients who have extended lengths of stay or who are unable to accept medical rationales, such as children, the elderly and the terminally ill, the analysis and critiques of mental hospitals may have considerable relevance. For many short-term patients under-going treatment for acute conditions an overwhelming experience has been shown to be one of anxiety and stress, especially for those unfamiliar with the hospital organisation and ward routines, or those who have little information about the nature of the investigative tests they are required to undergo, or knowledge of the process of recovery in the post-operative period (Wilson-Barnett, 1979).

168   *The hospital as a social organisation*

References

Albrow, M. (1970) *Bureaucracy*, Macmillan, London
Barton, R. (1959) *Institutional Neurosis*, Wright & Co, Bristol
Baruch, G. and Treacher, A. (1978) *Psychiatry Observed*, Routledge and Kegan Paul, London
Bateman, J.F. and Dunham, H. (1948) 'The state mental hospital as a specialised community experience', *American Journal of Psychiatry*, *103*, 445-8
Belknap, I. (1956) *Human Problems of a State Mental Hospital*, McGraw-Hill, New York
Bittner, E. (1974) 'The concept of organisation', in R. Turner (ed.), *Ethnomethodology*, Penguin Books, Harmondsworth, Middlesex
Bloor, M.J. (1980) 'The nature of therapeutic work in the therapeutic community: some preliminary findings', *International Journal of Therapeutic Communities*, *1*, 80-91
Brown, G.W. (1973) 'The mental hospital as an institution', *Social Science and Medicine*, *7*, 407-24
Bucher, R. and Stelling, J. (1969) 'Characteristics of professional organisations', *Journal of Health and Social Behaviour*, *10*, 2-13
Caudill, W. (1958) *The Psychiatric Hospital as a Small Society*, Harvard University Press, Cambridge, Mass.
Coser, R.L. (1962) *Life in the Ward*, Michigan State University Press, Michigan
Coser, R.L. (1963) 'Alienation and social structure', in E. Freidson (ed.), *The Hospital in Modern Society*, Free Press, New York
Coser, L. (1974) *Greedy Institutions*, Free Press, New York
Cumming, J. and Cumming, E. (1956) 'The locus of power in the large mental hospital', *Psychiatry*, *19*, 361-9
Day, R. and Day, J. (1977) 'A review of the current state of negotiated order theory', *Sociological Quarterly*, *18*, 126-42
Etzioni, A. (1975) *A Comparative Analysis of Complex Organisations* (2nd edn), Collier Macmillan, London
Fairhurst, E. (1977) 'On being a patient in an orthopaedic ward: some thoughts on the definition of the situation', in A. Davis and G. Horobin (eds.), *Medical Encounters*, Croom Helm, London
Goffman, E. (1958) 'Report on a study of St Elizabeth's Hospital, Washington', in *Symposium on Preventive and Social Psychiatry*, Walter Reed Army Institute of Research, US Goverment Printing Office
Goffman, E. (1961) *Asylums*, Penguin Books, Harmondsworth, Middlesex
Goldie, N. (1977) 'The division of labour among the mental health professions: a negotiated or an imposed order?', in M. Stacey, M. Reid, C. Heath and R. Dingwall (eds.), *Health and the Division of Labour*, Croom Helm, London
Gralnick, A. (ed.) (1969) *The Psychiatric Hospital as a Therapeutic Instrument*, Brenner-Mazel, New York
Hall, D.J. (1977) *Social Relations and Innovation*, Routledge and Kegan Paul, London
Hobson, R.F. (1979) 'The messianic community', in R. Hinshelwood and N. Manning (eds.), *Therapeutic Communities*, Routledge and Kegan Paul, London
Hughes, E.C. (1958) *Men and Their Work*, Free Press, Glencoe, Ill.
Jones, K. (1972) *A History of the Mental Health Services*, Routledge and Kegan Paul, London
Kanter, R.M. (1972) *Commitment and Community*, Harvard University Press, Cambridge, Mass.
Kennard, D. (1983) *An Introduction to Therapeutic Communities*, Routledge and Kegan Paul, London

King, R., Raynes, N. and Tizard, J. (1971) *Patterns of Residential Care*, Routledge and Kegan Paul, London

Kushlick, A. (1973) 'Evaluating residential homes for mentally retarded children', in J. Wing and H. Hafner (eds.), *Roots of Evaluation*, Oxford University Press, Oxford

Manning, N.P. (1976) 'Values and practice in the therapeutic community', *Human Relations*, 29, 125-38

Manning, N.P. (1980) 'Collective disturbance in institutions: a sociological view of crisis and collapse', *International Journal of Therapeutic Communities*, 1 147-58

Manning, N.P. and Blake, R. (1979) 'Implementing ideals', in R. Hinshelwood and N. Manning (eds.), *Therapeutic Communities*, Routledge and Kegan Paul, London

McKinlay, J.B. (1975) 'Clients and organisations', in J.B. McKinlay (ed.), *Processing People*, Holt, Rinehart and Winston, New York

Merton, R.K. (1957) *Social Theory and Social Structure*, Free Press, New York

Miller, D.H. (1957) 'The aetiology of an outbreak of delinquency in a group of hospitalised adolescents', in M. Greenblatt, D. Levinson and R. Williams (eds.), *The Patient and the Mental Hospital*, Free Press, New York

Ministry of Health (1966) *Report of the Committee on Senior Nurse Staffing Structure* (Salmon Report) HMSO, London

Morrice, J. (1972) 'Myth and the democratic process', *British Journal of Medical Psychology*, 45, 327-34

Oakley, A. (1979) *Women Confined*, Martin Robinson, London

Parsons, T. (1957) 'The mental hospital as a type of organisation' in M. Greenblatt, D. Levinson and R. Williams (eds.), *The Patient and the Mental Hospital*, Free Press, Chicago

Perrow, C. (1965) 'Hospitals: technology, structure and goals', in J.G. March (ed.), *Handbook of Organizations*, Rand McNally, Chicago

Perry, N. (1974) 'The two cultures of the total institution', *British Journal of Sociology*, 25, 345-55

Punch, M. (1974) 'The sociology of the anti-institution', *British Journal of Sociology*, 25, 312-25

Rapoport, R.N. (1960) *Community as Doctor*, Tavistock, London

Roth, J.A. (1962) *Timetables*, Bobbs Merrill, New York

Royal Commission on the NHS (1979), HMSO, London

Scull, A.T. (1977) *Decarceration*, Prentice Hall, Englewood Cliffs, N.J

Scull, A.T. (1979) *Museums of Madness*, Allen Lane, London

Simon, H.A. (1955) 'Recent advances in organisation theory', in *Research Frontiers in Politics and Government*, Brookings Institute, New York

Stanton, A. and Schwartz, M. (1954) *The Mental Hospital*, Basic Books, New York

Stelling, J. and Bucher, R. (1972) 'Autonomy and monitoring on hospital wards', *Sociological Quarterly*, 13, 431-46

Stotland, E. and Kobler, A.C. (1965) *The Life and Death of a Mental Hospital*, University of Washington Press, Seattle

Strauss, A. *et al.* (1963) 'The hospital and its negotiated order', in E. Freidson (ed.), *The Hospital in Modern Society*, Free Press, New York

Treacher, A. and Baruch, G. (1981) 'Towards a critical history of the psychiatric profession', in D. Ingleby (ed.), *Critical Psychiatry*, Penguin Books, Harmondsworth, Middlesex

Tobin, S. and Lieberman, M. (1976) *Last Home for the Aged*, Jossey-Bass, London

Tuke, S. (1813) *Description of the Retreat*, York

Weber, M. (1949) *The Methodology of the Social Sciences*, Free Press, New York

Wilson-Barnet J. (1979) *Stress in Hospital*, Churchill Livingstone, Edinburgh

Wing, J.K. and Brown, G.W. (1970) *Institutionalism and Schizophrenia*, Cambridge University Press, Cambridge

Whyte, W.E. (1961) 'Parsons' theory applied to organisations', in *The Social Theories of Talcott Parsons*, Prentice Hall, Englewood Cliffs, NJ

6 HEALTH CARE AND THE STATE

The development and legitimation of professional status for doctors rested not only on the development of technology and the attendant mystifications of scientific knowledge, but more importantly on the support and patronage of the state (see Chapter 4). This pattern of state-regulated medical autonomy has been repeated all over the world, even where medicine has been required to forfeit some clinical autonomy to more pressing state imperatives, such as the requirements of labour discipline in the USSR in the 1930s (George and Manning, 1980). In addition to this direct regulation, the state has also been drawn into the finance of medicine in most countries. In some cases, as in Britain and the USSR, this involves the almost complete funding of health care. Elsewhere the state has more modestly supported non-profit social insurance, common in Europe, or merely picked up the bill for the uninsurable, such as the Medicare/Medicaid schemes in the USA. In return, all states have demanded a greater or lesser control over the administration of health care, including the supply of manpower and equipment and the amount of legitimate demand for services.

Two broad approaches to understanding the growth of state involvement in health care can be identified. A liberal reformist approach understands the state as arising from a variety of incidental factors (technology, war, and so on) such that conflicts and problems can be dealt with piecemeal. A radical approach, however, explains the state as arising from requirements necessarily thrown up by general social and economic developments, and the political consequences of this. Thus radicals see the growth of the labour movement, or the employers' demand for a healthy workforce, as fundamentally affecting the role of the state in health care.

This chapter explores the links between health care and the state, their growth and limits, and a variety of criticisms which have been made of the contemporary organisation of health care.

The Growth of State Organised Health Care in England

Health care was organised on a private and voluntary basis up until

171

the nineteenth century in England. During this early period hospitals were developed according to the interests of private entrepreneurs or public philanthropists. Hospital medical practice was supervised by Royal Colleges, set up in the sixteenth century. During the nineteenth century, however, despite a flowering of political theory in favour of a non-interventionist state, there developed a growing state involvement in all of social and economic life. In the health care field this intervention covered both the regulation and funding of hospitals, and the legal control of the medical profession. This can be examined in five key areas.

First was the adoption of the workhouse in 1834 as the cornerstone of the state post-(Napoleonic)war policy to control welfare expenditure. Since this was designed to deter able-bodied paupers from dependence on the state, the workhouse soon began to fill up with non-able-bodied paupers a substantial proportion of whom were ill. Indeed the workhouse was to become unintentionally the major source of residential medical treatment for the poor working class. Towards the end of the century this was so well recognised that the pauperisation (i.e. change in status) normally required as the key workhouse deterrent for the able-bodied was frequently waived for purely medical cases.

The second area of increased state activity was the widespread building of mental asylums in the 1840s and 1850s. Designed initially as rural retreats from the supposedly mad-making bustle of industrial society, these soon became human warehouses for a variety of deviants suffering more often from social dislocation than any identifiable illness. The population housed in these asylums grew tenfold to 100,000 by the end of the century, as a result of a growing incidence of mental illness, and the increasing acceptance of medical treatment (see Chapter 6).

The third key change was the legislation passed in 1858 to grant the medical profession a market monopoly on doctoring. This secured the establishment of a supposedly autonomous profession, responsible only to its individual clients. Although this change of status continues to depend upon the state's legal definition, the profession's autonomy has become a very real achievement which, as Chapter 4 showed, has been resistant to greater state control. However this market monopoly did not always ensure a steady income, and by the latter part of the century many ordinary doctors became dependent on highly cost-conscious friendly societies concerned to secure the best value for money for their working-class contributors. Indeed, it was the doctors' low income as much as their patients' poverty which shaped a fourth area of state intervention in this period — Lloyd George's health insurance legislation of 1911. This gave doctors a better financial deal and pressured the friendly societies to accept closer state control over their activities. The 1911 National Insurance Act provided general medical services to workers earning less than £160 a year for a weekly contribution of fourpence, to which employers added threepence and the state twopence. Dependents were not covered, nor were hospital or consultant services. By 1939 Lloyd George's 'ambulance wagon' (as he called his legislation) covered about half the population.

The fifth notable development of state health care was the organisation of public health in the areas of general sanitation, sewerage 'nuisance' and disease control. While this area is normally associated with Chadwick's sanitary report of 1842 and his time subsequently with the first London Board of Health, most of the legislation appeared later in the 1850s and 1860s, and was finally codified in the 1872 Public Health Act passed to specify that the new local government authorities should employ Medical Officers of Health to supervise their various public health responsibilities.

Although state intervention in health in the nineteenth and early twentieth centuries must have seemed substantial at the time, it was dwarfed by subsequent twentieth-century developments. Of particular significance was the expansion in the provision of existing state health care in the inter-war years. By the later 1930s the state had organised compulsory primary medical care through social insurance societies for most workers. In addition, of a total of one-quarter of a million hospital beds, two-thirds were publicly provided, either in local government hospitals or poor law infirmaries. The Health Ministry, first formed in 1919, also handled public house-building which became the most significant contribution to public health between the wars, starting from the campaign to provide 'homes fit for heroes' after the First World War. What had originated as the removal of 'nuisances' with the Artisans Dwelling Act of 1875 became between the wars a massive intervention by the state into the housing market, such that nearly 40 per cent of all new houses were state-built. There was seen to be as clear a correlation between overcrowding and infant mortality in the twentieth century as between poor sanitation and cholera in the nineteenth.

Before the Second World War, health care was thus not so much chaotic (as is often assumed) as organised by principles which did not always operate in the interests of the patient. Thousands of friendly societies competed for the insurance of primary medical care, made compulsory for workers by Lloyd George. Their level of provision and charges varied widely as did their efficiency. There was enormously wasteful administrative duplication, while many women and children were not covered except by maternity care. The best hospital services (in voluntary hospitals) were available at cost, or through the benevolence of charitable sponsorship by the wealthy for selected poor individuals. The only alternative was the workhouse infirmary, or some local government hospitals as they appeared in the 1930s, with powerful overtones of either the workhouse 'test' of pauperisation or the means test. For the mentally ill (occupying nearly 50 per cent of all hospital beds) treatment consisted of compulsory detention with little expectation of release, and the use of treatments we now know to be ineffective and dangerous (Jones, 1972).

Since the middle of this century public health efforts to prevent illness have been overshadowed by growing support by the state of health care for the already ill. The most significant change was the nationalisation of existing primary and hospital care under the Second World War Emergency Medical Services, and subsequently the creation of the National Health Service (NHS). This involved the nationalisation of 1,000 hospitals owned and run by a large variety of voluntary bodies and 540 hospitals operated by local authorities. The NHS, which formed the 'jewel in the crown of the welfare state', came into existence on 5 July 1948. It was the first health system in any Western society to offer a comprehensive range of free medical care universally, i.e. to the entire population. It also adopted a collectivist principle in that it acknowledged state responsibility for its citizens, with entitlement to health services not being dependent on financial contributions but on a rational provision of services according to need. The aim was to provide 'a comprehensive health service designed to secure improvement in the physical and mental health of the people of England and Wales by the prevention, diagnosis and treatment of illness' (Ministry of Health, 1946).

The NHS offered the immediate and substantial change that existing health care facilities became available free. It also vastly simplified the administration of primary care services. The response of the population was rapid — the release of pent-up demand for a range of treatments particularly of the less severe kind (such as optical and dental problems) which the old system had suppressed. The twin anxieties of the cost of treatment and obtaining access to it were removed. Not surprisingly, then, 'Whatever the statistics about the distribution of resources may say, the perceived equity of the British Health Service appears to make rationing and scarcity acceptable' (Klein, 1983).

The structure of the NHS which emerged (Figure 6.1) has been seen as a classic example of administrative and political compromise (Willcocks, 1967). The rational model would have been one of regional services developed in accordance with local needs, financed by and accountable to local government. However, not only did general practitioners fear local control, but local government was not respected for its financial management or its administrative skill. Consequently primary care services were set up under the control of independent local executive councils — modelled after the existing local insurance committees, set up in 1911. Thus local general practitioners in effect organised their own services. By contrast local governments were to provide through their health committees such community and environmental services as maternal and child welfare, health visiting, home nursing, after care of the mentally ill and health centres. In addition to local government and general practitioner services, which were already in separate structures, a third structure of regional areas was set up to manage hospitals. These areas, based on the distribution of existing teaching hospitals, bore no relationship to the geographical boundaries of primary care services, or the existing public health activities of local government. These three branches of the NHS have come to be known as the 'tripartite' structure of health care in Britain.

Figure 6.1: National Health Service Structure, 1948 (England)

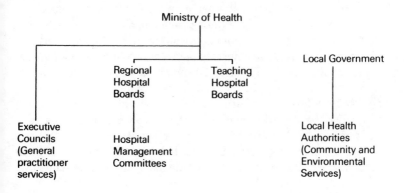

Despite being based on principles of collectivism, comprehensiveness and universality, the principle of professional autonomy was also central to the structure and decision-making in the NHS. Decisions about expenditure within the hospital were to be made by consultants within their specialisms and by GPs in primary health care, while GPs retained an independent contractor status rather than becoming salaried employees. In addition the profession was well represented on the management and decision-making bodies in the NHS. It was hoped that this combination of state support and professional health care would rapidly reduce the pool of sickness which was thought to exist in the general population, so that while health care expenditure might rise initially, the overall cost would shrink in the long run.

The political compromises which shaped the NHS Act in which the interests of general practitioners, teaching hospitals, local government, and the central Ministry of Health were amalgamated, led subsequently to growing dissatisfaction within the NHS, centred around three issues. First, the lack of central financial control combined with rapidly growing demand led to concern about growing costs (Guillebaud Report, 1953). Second, the lack of coordination between the three administrative structures caused difficulties in securing continuity of treatment when patients moved from general practitioner to hospital to local government services, as was the case particularly for the mentally ill after the 1959 Mental Health Act encouraged greater community care (discussed in Chapter 5). Third, the NHS structural compromise failed to tackle two kinds of inequality in medical care, which continued to grow: geographical inequality, and inequality between the development of services for the acute and chronically ill.

These issues stimulated plans to reorganise the health service under local government control (Ministry of Health, 1968), but in the event the new structure that emerged in 1974 was again shaped by compromises (Figure 6.2). Although all three parts of the NHS were now geographically coterminous (local government boundaries had also been changed), and elaborate plans for financial review were set up, the medical profession retained effective autonomy at the primary care level and, through medical advisory committees, at the regional and central levels. Nevertheless the issues of financial control, inequality, coordination and balance between patient groups have been tackled, and are discussed in more detail below.

The administrative structure created in 1974 was itself soon perceived as cumbersome and over-bureaucratised and consequently, in the light of recent public expenditure squeezes and hence the desire to slim down administrative costs, one layer of the 1974 structure (the Area Health Authority) was removed in 1982; and at the same time some autonomy was re-established for general practitioners as Family Practitioner Committees were separated from mainstream NHS administration.

Figure 6.2: National Health Service Structure, 1974 (England)

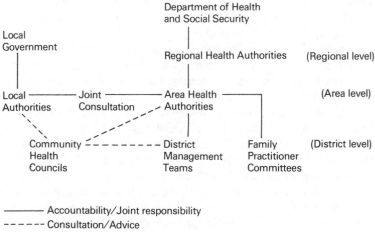

——— Accountability/Joint responsibility
— — — — Consultation/Advice

Explaining State Involvement in Health Care

Rational Problem Solving

This general approach to state intervention has been developed within a functionalist explanation of general social development. It is argued that as industrial societies differentiate their structures during development, functional requirements for the integration of the system lead to specialised structures such as government health services developing. However the precise ways in which such structures develop to meet functional requirements are not clearly spelled out. Therefore sociologists concerned specifically with health care from this perspective have focused on the steady accumulation of knowledge about health needs and medical technology to meet those needs. From this point of view health care developments are the rational solution to the perceived health problems which have been cumulatively identified through research and professional experience.

Thus Titmuss (1968) has suggested that the most significant long term influence on medical care, and the reason that in all countries the state has been drawn into its provision, is the cumulative technological development of medical science. His strongest example to illustrate this thesis is the inability of the voluntary hospitals in the inter-war period to finance the provision of a growing range of technology such as surgery and pharmacology. The government, he argues, was thus obliged to step in to bale out the voluntary sector. The same point could be made in relation to the US government's financial commitment in the 1960s to buy health care for the poor (Medicaid) and the elderly (Medicare), for whom modern medical developments were too expensive.

A particular stimulus to this growth of knowledge has been the experience of war for government policy. For example, the government created the Emergency Medical Services before the Second World War not only to deal with military casualties, but also the expected consequences of mass civilian bombing. Subsequently this experience confirmed that health care had been provided haphazardly and unequally in the pre-existing system, and that this could be much improved through national control. Earlier, in 1914-18 and during the Boer War, it had been discovered that a substantial proportion of working class recruits were physically unfit for fighting. Hence concern about 'national deterioration' led to medical inspection in schools. But more importantly it had been discovered that state mobilisation could sustain great efforts (and large debts) — a capacity potentially available for social reconstruction.

Another traditional rationalist argument for state involvement is the effect of 'market failure'. This includes the argument that some services, such as health care, cannot be regarded as marketable in any normal sense, and hence must be collectively organised outside the market. This point is reinforced by modern demographic trends in which more and more people are surviving healthily to old age, where their medical demands are likely to escalate while their purchasing power shrinks. In addition those younger people who are not so healthy, such as the physically and mentally disabled, are also unlikely to be able to pay for their medical care. Private insurance based on risk ratings cannot solve this problem, and hence the only solution is direct or indirect state provision.

The factors identified as contributing to this rationalist explanation, technology, war and market failure, do not however specify how the changes are actually implemented, nor why they should vary from one time or place to another. This common problem in functionalist analyses of accounting for change is thus the focus of a second approach to explaining state intervention, in which the politics of change is the central focus.

The Micro-politics of Change

This approach to explaining state intervention draws upon an interactionist view of politics in which the views and interests of significant individuals and groups are held to be the key influences on state policy developments. It is argued that whatever the changing health needs and medical technologies, the way in which they affect medical care depends upon the particular political situation prevailing in a society at any time. A traditional argument is that elites determine state activities according to a variety of criteria. In the past this has often been presented as *noblesse oblige*, whereby the elites (or their key representatives such as Chadwick, Rowntree, or Beveridge) expand state activity paternalistically where they perceive social need. Important influences drawing attention to such needs include the evidence gathered by local Medical Officers of Health employed under the 1872 Public Health Act, and the early social surveys of working-class life conducted by Booth and Rowntree. However there were also less altruistic concerns such as the threat of cholera to the middle and upper classes which produced a rapid growth in state activity (local Boards of Health) in the 1830s; while more widespread diseases such as typhus and tuberculosis, confined mostly to poorer people, were ignored (Fraser, 1973).

A related approach has been to adopt a pluralist model and view policies as the outcome of pressure group activity. Particular importance is attached to the activities of the medical profession in its attempts to shape potential legislation (Eckstein 1960). The first example of this was gaining a market monopoly in 1858. However, subsequent legislation has often been fundamentally influenced by medical pressure groups, with both the 1911 National Insurance Act and the 1946 NHS Act being influenced by the demands of the British Medical Association (BMA). In the debate leading up to the NHS during the 1930s the BMA expressed strong views against local government control of health care, and against doctors being salaried employees. Instead the BMA argued for an independent fee-for-service contract with central government. In the post-war debate about the details of the NHS the medical profession succeeded in obtaining a number of concessions, particularly the separate organisation of general practice through local executive councils. However, the state successfully persuaded hospital doctors to accept a salaried arrangement by offering a generous contract. When the structure of the NHS was reorganised in 1974, further attempts to introduce local government control were again successfully resisted by the BMA.

Another factor within the political system that has shaped the NHS has been the way in which centrally determined policies have actually been implemented at the local level. In the early twentieth century the expansion and consolidation of state health care measures such as the school medical service was carried through by administrative momentum rather than central decree (Fraser, 1973). But more recently the relative autonomy of local managers has led in the opposite direction to delays in the implementation of central policies as a result of administrative inertia (Haywood and Alaszewski, 1980).

Critics of this analysis of state intervention point out that the sources of power available to political actors are not discussed. They suggest that the ability of key social reformers, pressure groups or administrative personnel to influence policy is itself constrained by more general developments in the state, and particularly its relationship to the economy. They have suggested, therefore, that a more radical analysis of the economic context of state politics must be developed to complement the insights of micro-political analysis.

Marxist Approaches to State Health Policy

Marxist theories of the state fall into two distinct types. One combines some of the aspects of both the functionalist and interactionist approaches we have already discussed, to suggest that the state in a capitalist society is constrained to fulfil certain functions, but that the way those functions are met is determined by the particular political history and traditions of individuals and groups at any time. An influential model of this type was suggested by O'Connor (1973), in which the state is constrained to maintain capital accumulation and the legitimation of this process by intervening in the market in three ways. It subsidises the costs of production (by providing public utilities, transport, etc.), encourages the reproduction of labour (by supporting family life, providing health care and education), and discourages political disaffection (by providing income security, but also by enforcing the rule of law). However, these activities are developed within the context of political class struggle which shapes the actual outcome at any particular time.

This approach has been used by Scull (1977) with respect to psychiatry to argue that nineteenth-century state intervention resulted from a concern to control deviant behaviour, or rather behaviour that is or might become deviant with respect to prevailing or new cultural and social expectations. Thus he argues that the growth of asylums, prisons and workhouses in the nineteenth century was the institutionalisation of social control necessary to establish the legitimacy of a new dominant social principle, the market — particularly the market in labour. Gough (1979) suggests that ultimately control has to be exercised by one class over another, whatever the appearance of any specific issue. This point is drawn from a model which suggests that the dynamic at the heart of history is class struggle generated by the economic system — in this case capitalism. From this point of view the history of state health care is the history of the gradual extension of services for working-class people as the state (representing ruling class interests) gives way to the growing strength of the organised working class. Indeed politicians were well aware of the potential of social policy to buy off the attractions of revolutionary socialism. Parliamentary debates about Lloyd George's legislation, and the post-Second World War welfare state legislation acknowledge this. From this perspective, the NHS is one of the major working-class victories of this century, and recent policies for its privatisation are regarded as the product of a major realignment of British class forces.

A detailed analysis of the NHS set explicitly in terms of class struggle is provided by Navarro (1978). He traces the twentieth-century history of state health care in relation to the prevailing balance of class forces, and suggests that intervention (such as the health care reforms of 1911 and 1948) tends to take place at moments of crisis in the struggle between classes. However, these crises themselves are shaped by prevailing economic fortunes, and the ability of the state to manage the economy. Navarro follows O'Connor directly to suggest that the nature of health and illness and their treatment are constrained by the state's prior concerns to maintain capital accumulation, and the legitimacy of this economic system. Accumulation in turn requires a sophisticated control of the labour force via a complex division of labour and specialisation, and the creation and circulation of commodities. Both of these are evident in the NHS, where specialisation has continued to develop, and where the commodification of health care can be seen in the aggressive marketing of drugs (both to public and private consumers) and the creation of new disorders requiring drug treatment such as anxiety, depression, pregnancy and hyperactivity in children. Problems of political legitimacy surrounding this area are, as in society as a whole, in danger of breaking out in the sense that people (patients) find that their immediate life experiences are at odds with dominant ideas and values. For example, Navarro argues, much modern illness is created by relations and environment at work (stress, pollution) or the marketing of unhealthy life styles (smoking, private motoring), yet the solution to these is situated in the NHS within individual behavioural change, or problems of rational/ scientific planning. There is consequently a continuing debate about the proper directions of, and limits to, health policy developments.

The second marxist approach to state activities is more thoroughly critical in that it takes issue with the conventional sociological separation of political and economic factors into two distinct spheres which interact and react upon each other. Drawing its inspiration from Marx's later work, in *Capital*, vol. I, it suggests that the apparent separation of politics and economics is an ideological illusion in capitalist society brought about by the fetishism of commodity production. It means by this that the real value of things (as useful objects) gets translated by the market into money values, which become attached to those things and lend them powers which they do not intrinsically have — that is they literally become fetishes. Marx suggests that 'to find an analogy we must take flight into the misty realm of religion. There the products of the human brain appear as autonomous figures endowed with a life of their own' (*Capital*, vol. I, 1976, p. 165).

This second marxist approach suggests that the conventional categories used in state health policies (as well as elsewhere) may be mere ideological illusions disguising a more unitary social reality of class exploitation. In concrete terms, therefore, ideas of health needs, individual responsibility (for a health-related life style), or indeed the very notions of what mental and physical illness are, are heavily infused with assumptions about capitalist concerns for a healthy, productive and docile workforce.

Clearly this approach bears some similarity with the social constructionist views discussed in Chapter 1. However, in this case the theory suggests a definite disguise of an assumed reality, in contrast to the subjective relativism implied in those views. It therefore explains key points of state intervention and policy change as moments of perceptual slip in which an adjustment of perceived social reality is made within the overall totality of capitalist society. For example, the emphasis in government initiatives on prevention, on the individual as arbiter of his or her own fate, or the constraints on expenditure growth required in order to control inflation, are not regarded from this point of view as real, but as the product of state and individual fetishism.

The NHS in Practice

Inequalities in Provision

The NHS began with some gross inequalities in the distribution of resources inherited from the rather chaotic pre-war system. For example, some prosperous regions had almost twice as many hospital beds per person as others, and a similar imbalance existed for primary care. It was hoped that the nationalisation of the health service would soon eliminate these inequalities. Thus Bevan argued that 'we have got to achieve as nearly as possible a uniform standard of service for all — only with a national health service can the state ensure that an equally good service is available to all'. Some planning was set up fairly soon after the establishment of the NHS to achieve this, by increasing and redistributing consultants, and channelling general practitioners to under-doctored areas through a system of negative controls designed to prevent general practitioners from entering practice in the relatively well-provided parts of the country.

Whereas such limited measures were undertaken to reduce prevailing geographical inequalities a number of trends served to increase or maintain these inequalities, particularly the allocation of future resources in proportion to past allocations. For example, the hospital building programme initiated by the 1962 Hospital Plan (Ministry of Health, 1962) resulted in a faster expansion of hospital beds in regions already well supplied (such as the south-east) and slower growth in underserved areas such as the north-east. In the Labour government period of office in the 1960s whereas 39 per cent of the population lived north of the river Trent, only 29 per cent of new building projects of over one million pounds were placed there. Inequality in capital expenditure during the 1960s necessarily had an influence on the distribution of financial resources in the 1970s and 1980s, both because hospitals take a long time to complete (up to 10 years), and because current expenditure is heavily influenced by past capital developments.

Since the early 1970s evidence has accumulated of the continued existence of substantial geographical inequalities in service provision. Hart (1971) drawing on work up to 1970 put forward the inverse care law that 'the availability of good medical care varies inversely with the need for it in the population served'. Recent evidence to support the continued existence of an inverse care law has been provided by analyses of the relationship between the provision of child health services and indicators of need as determined by mortality rates (West and Lowe, 1976). Moreover variations in expenditure and provision of health services tend to be even greater at the sub-regional than regional level (Rickard, 1976).

A major shift in financial policy which aimed to achieve the original principle of geographical equality in service provision was provided by the formula introduced by the Resource Allocation Working Party (RAWP) (DHSS, 1976). This was a development of a formula introduced in 1970 which gave a stronger emphasis to the size and structure of the population being served by the region in the allocation of resources than previously existed. The aim of RAWP in distributing capital and revenue expenditure between regions was stated to be, 'To reduce progressively, and as far as is feasible, the disparities between the different parts of the country in terms of opportunity for access to health care for people at equal risk, taking into account measures of health needs, and social and environmental factors which may affect the need for health care' (DHSS, 1975a). In 1976/7 *per capita* expenditure on health services varied among the 14 regions of England from £91.52 in the West Midlands to £122.38 in North West Thames. The formula used to establish a target budget was to cover the main areas of expenditure including all hospital-based services, ambulance services and community health services, and was based on the size of the population served, weighted by appropriate combinations of age, sex, mortality (as an indicator of morbidity), fertility and marital status (as an indicator of need for in-patient psychiatric care) which were used as measures of need for health services. These were then adjustments for various exceptional costs, such as cross-boundary flows of patients and the costs of supporting teaching hospitals.

The Working Party found that the formula indicated that some regions received revenue allocations 10 per cent below their target share of resources, while others had allocations more than 10 per cent above. In practice the progress in reducing these inequalities is limited by the small real growth rate in NHS expenditure, reflecting the problem of basing redistribution on the use of growing resources. Nevertheless, the gap between the best and worst funded regions narrowed between 1977/8 and 1981/2. Views differ as to the likely long-term impact of RAWP, although some believe that broad equity in the distribution of revenue may be achieved in a further ten years (Social Services Committee, 1980). A number of criticisms have, however, been levelled against RAWP. One major criticism is that standardised mortality ratios (SMRs), which are the actual measure of mortality used and allow for differences in the age/per structure of the population, form an inadequate proxy for morbidity, particularly chronic illness. In addition, no allowance is made for any variation in social deprivations, such as poor housing which may result in more frequent and longer hospital admissions, except in so far as this is reflected in SMRs. Secondly, it is argued that the greatest disparities occur at the sub-regional level, with some pockets of considerable social deprivation occurring in areas which are over-provided for in terms of RAWP, often reflecting the existence of expensive teaching hospitals. Thirdly, RAWP merely allocates resources and does not control the way these resources are spent or ensure that the additional money is spent to satisfy the greater health needs of populations in these areas.

Of particular current concern are the variations in the availability and quality of general practitioner services which are not affected by RAWP. Thus the distribution of GPs per 10,000 population in 1977 varied from 4.54 in Trent to 5.48 in North West Thames. Sub-regional variations may also be significant in some areas, as the Acheson report showed in a survey of primary care in inner London: there were higher rates of infant mortality and deaths from pneumonia, bronchitis, respiratory tuberculosis, accidents and suicide in inner London compared with outer London or England and Wales as a whole. Yet the provision of primary care in inner London was characterised by a high proportion of GPs aged over 65 years (17 per cent compared with 6 per cent for England and Wales), many GPs working alone (39 per cent compared with a national figure of 16 per cent) in inadequate surgeries (75 per cent were below the recommended standard) (DHSS, 1981).

Despite the continued existence of geographical variations in service provision under the NHS, these appear to be considerably less than in most other Western European countries. As Table 6.1 shows, the variations in physicians per 1,000 population in England were much smaller than in France, Germany and the Netherlands.

Table 6.1: Regional Variations in Number of Physicians per Thousand Population: Highest and Lowest Areas

	England	France	Germany	Netherlands
Average	1.06	1.47	1.74	1.36
Highest (H)	1.31 (NW Thames)	2.18 (Paris)	2.97 (W. Berlin)	2.10 (Utrecht)
Lowest (L)	0.91 (Trent)	0.98 (Basse Normandie)	1.41 (Nieder-Sachsen)	0.92 (Friesland)
Ratio (H/L)	1.4	2.2	2.1	2.3

Sources: England, France, Germany: A. Maynard in *Social and Economic Administration*, 1978, *12*, (1); Netherlands: *Compendium Gezondheitsstatistiek Nederland*, Central Bureau voor de Statistiek, 1974. (From Townsend and Davidson, 1982.)

A second form of inequality in service provision is in terms of the distribution of resources between different sectors and client groups, with there being an overwhelming concentration of resources in the acute hospital sector. In England in 1976/7, *per capita* expenditure on hospital services was £61.76 compared with £28.31 on community health and family practitioner services (Royal Commission on the NHS, 1979). In effect, the medical profession has been able to determine its own distribution, particularly through the staunch defence of clinical autonomy in the face of administrative enquiry. In the 1960s the clinical definition of health care encouraged an increasing use of high technology medicine in hospitals, and hence there was a sustained growth in hospital building throughout the decade. However this definition of health, as the product of high technology health care, contained several irresolvable contradictions. First, new technologies such as renal dialysis or heart surgery were developed faster than they could be made available to the general population. Second, successful intervention merely stored up disorders to be tackled later on in an ageing population. Third, as acute disorders were successfully dealt with they gave way to more intermittent and less resolvable problems, such as mental illness, respiratory disorders and so on. In short the harder and more spectacularly the NHS worked, the more overwhelmed it became by insatiable demand.

In addition to these difficulties, others were caused by the planning of medical priorities on the basis of the interests of members of the medical profession. Thus an examination of expenditure on different patient groups shows that the category of general and acute hospitals and maternity services accounts for 39 per cent of current and capital expenditure. By contrast only 12 per cent of expenditure is on the mentally ill and handicapped, and 14 per cent on the elderly and physically handicapped. As a proportion of all cases the old and the mentally ill grew rapidly, but the profession rewarded itself in areas such as surgery, leaving vacant jobs (to be filled by overseas doctors) in those areas where demand was growing. Government policy has been to allocate special funds to improve the so called 'Cinderella services' of psychiatry and geriatrics. For example, in the years following the 1969 Ely Report into the ill-treatment of patients in a large mental handicap hospital in Cardiff, additional money was spent on long-stay services. A number of priority documents such as 'Better Services for the Mentally Ill' (DHSS, 1975b), and 'Priorities for Health and Social Services' (DHSS, 1976), have also set out targets to be achieved. However, government attempts to re-align priorities in favour of patients' needs have been continually frustrated. While establishing national targets, these policy documents do not specify local (i.e. regional) changes and have not included them in mechanisms which have any real effect, such as RAWP. Furthermore, the medical profession's significant influence at the local level continues to divert resources to the popular high technology areas of medicine. Plans for 'Better Services' have not made psychiatry or geriatrics more popular specialisms, and they remain near the bottom of the league table of areas favoured by medical students (Clare, 1976). Consequently overseas doctors are heavily concentrated in areas where no one else wants to work, and ones for which cultural discontinuity is a particular handicap to good medical practice (Royal Commission on NHS, 1979).

Health Service Expenditure and Outcome

In all countries the state is increasingly involved in the provision of health services. However, the NHS continues to be distinctive in the extent to which it depends on funding through taxation (the majority of health care in other Western European countries being funded through public or private insurance schemes), as well as in the small proportion of health care being financed through private fees (Table 6.2). However, whereas there are increasing pressures in the USA to increase public funding of health care and thus improve access for all sectors of the population, in Britain private health care has expanded as a response to unsatisfied demands.

Table 6.2: Public and Private Sources of Health Care Finance (mid 1970s) — percentages

	Britain	Sweden	Germany	France	USA	USSR
General taxes	87.3	78.5	14.6	7.0	31.0	80.0
Public insurance	5.3	13.1	62.5	69.0	11.7	–
Private fees	5.8	8.4	12.5	19.6	27.1	
Private insurance	1.4	–	5.3	3.0	25.6	20.0
Employers	0.4	–	5.2	1.4	4.6	

Sources: Heidenheimer *et al.* (1983); George and Manning (1980).

The NHS exhibits a pattern of expenditure characteristic of all health systems, particularly in the increasing costs of health care.

The expectation when the NHS was introduced was that after the initial backlog of need had been coped with, the cost of the NHS would stabilise or might even fall as the population became healthier. However, this assumption turned out to be false, and, rather than declining, expenditure steadily increased in the years following the establishment of the NHS. In the first full year of operation the service cost £433 million to run, whereas by 1980 expenditure in the UK had risen to £11,800 million. The real cost of the service after allowing for inflation has increased more slowly than these figures suggest, but whatever indicator is employed spending on the NHS has increased substantially. For example, the NHS consumed 3.9 per cent of GNP in 1949 compared with 6.1 per cent in 1980.

The increasing costs of the NHS formed a major early issue of concern and resulted in the setting up of the Guillebaud Committee in 1952. This Committee suggested that fears over the extravagance and inefficiency of the NHS had been exaggerated but nevertheless recommended the retention of prescription charges introduced earlier in 1949, as well as charges for dental treatment and ophthalmic services, in order to limit demand and raise a small amount of money. Whereas concern over costs has been ever present such concern has become particularly acute with the recent cutbacks in public expenditure. A major factor accounting for the general increase in costs is the emphasis on high technology medicine and the availability of new high cost procedures (e.g. hip replacements, kidney transplants and renal dialysis). Moreover, this expansion has been almost entirely located in hospital provision for acute or serious illness. Consequently, the return in terms of improved health for spending more and more money on difficult cases has been far less than was hoped when the NHS was set up. A related cause of cost increases is the fact that the greater availability of health care has stimulated rather than satisfied public demand. As public expectations have risen, the medical profession has been unable or unwilling to limit the expansion of areas of physical or social conditions defined as treatable illnesses, particularly amongst the elderly who form a rapidly increasing proportion of the population.

Despite the increasing costs of the NHS, health service expenditure *per capita*, and as a percentage of GNP, is still relatively low in comparison with other West European countries, Australia and the USA. Since salaries and wages account for over 70 per cent of this expenditure, the relatively low level of staffing shown in Table 6.3 is a major reason for this comparative cheapness. In addition, doctors' earnings in the form of salaries and *per capita* fees in the UK are only 2.7 times the average production worker's gross earnings, compared with 6.1 times for West Germany, 7.0 for France, and 5.6 for the USA, in all of which doctors receive a fee for each item of service provided. The relatively lower level of hospital bed provision, also shown in Table 6.3, is a further factor responsible for this expenditure pattern.

Table 6.3: Manpower and Beds per 10,000 Population, 1980

	Physicians	Nurses	Pharmacists	Hospital Beds (All Hospitals)
England	16.0	39.2	2.7	79
West Germany	22.6	54.3	4.7	115
USA	18.2	51.1	6.3	59
Sweden	22.0	88.2	4.3	147
Netherlands	18.5	n.a.	1.0	125
France	17.2	64.3	6.3	122
Australia	17.9	82.0	3.7	125
Italy	29.0	n.a.	7.6	97
Canada	18.2	n.a.	6.8	78
Switzerland	24.5	n.a.	n.a.	115

Source: Harrison and Gretton (1984).

The underlying reason for these low NHS costs is that, despite the weakness of local control in the original NHS structure, central budgets could be set more economically and firmly through central control of salaries, staffing levels and capital expenditure (on new hospitals for example). However the consequences of central restraint, incremental annual budgeting and local autonomy have been that available services have had to be rationed in a variety of *ad hoc* ways. The commonest method is to place patients in a queue, whether a waiting list for minor surgery or the waiting room in a general practice or out-patient department. Another method is to assign medical priorities for the delivery of limited, high cost procedures, with professionally defined need rather than patients' ability to pay thus forming the rationing mechanism. A study of the choice of patients for renal dialysis and transplantation showed the effects of this rationing process. Recipients were most likely to be between the ages of 15 and 45, without other health problems, married with children rather than single. Others were likely to be refused treatment (Klein, 1975). In addition to these formal rationing mechanisms, health service staff tend to discourage demand for services for conditions they regard as trivial. The success with which the costs of the NHS have been limited by meeting only administratively or medically defined health needs has in turn generated pressure for privately financed health care, especially for minor surgery.

Despite lower relative expenditure on the NHS, Table 6.4 shows that in terms of mortality the UK is about average for Western industrial societies. Since mortality is also influenced by socio-environmental conditions outside the control of the NHS (see Chapter 1), there is no evidence to suggest that a substantial increase in expenditure would yield greatly reduced mortality rates. In terms of more subjective measures of outcome, such as patient satisfaction, the NHS has always been popular. This is closely associated with the ideal of a universally available service, which, despite the inequalities and rationing we have noted, most people feel the NHS comes close to achieving. However, despite this general support for a 'free' health service and a fairly high level of general consumer satisfaction, surveys have uncovered specific complaints. Expressed dissatisfaction relates mainly to waiting times and to the 'hotel' aspects of hospital care, which are of course the aspects most easily judged by the lay person (Royal Commission on the NHS, 1979).

Table 6.4: Health Spending and Mortality Rates

	Health Spending (1975)		Mortality (1975)		Infant Mortality Rate (1980)	
	% GNP	Rank	Standardised Index	Rank	per 1,000 live births	Rank
UK	5.5	10	0.91	4	12.0	6
West Germany	9.4	1	1.23	10	12.6	8
USA	8.6	2	1.18	9	12.5	7
Sweden	8.5	3	0.76	1	6.9	1
Netherlands	8.1	4	0.80	2	8.6	2
France	7.9	5	1.11	8	10.0	3
Australia	7.3	6	1.01	5	10.7	4
Italy	7.1	7=	1.04	6	14.3	9
Canada	7.1	7=	1.08	7	10.9 (1979)	5
Switzerland	6.9	9	0.86	3	?	

Source: Harrison and Gretton (1984).

Consumer Representation

Despite accusations of 'creeping socialism', particularly from the USA, the NHS has never been democratic, and has no elected tiers. The public thus have little chance to participate in the formulation of health policy at a local or national level, with community interest being especially weakly represented at the local level. Nationalisation does not mean socialisation, or as Engels wrote, 'Napoleon and Metternich would rank among the founders of socialism ... The Royal Maritime Company, the Royal Porcelain Manufacturer and even the regimental tailors in the army would be socialist institutions' (George and Manning, 1980, p. 27). This lack of democracy has been an important reason for the unresponsiveness of the NHS to local needs.

Part of the aim of the 1974 reorganisation was to achieve democratic participation, with the assumption being that this would facilitate national priorities and make the service more sensitive to local needs. This was to be achieved in two ways — through increased lay representation within health authorities and by the creation of a new institution, Community Health Coucils, to represent public interests. However, neither has made a significant impact on the direction of health service policies, reflecting their lack of power.

Lay representation on health authorities took the form of the inclusion of appointed nominees from the local authorities, together with representation from the professions and trade unions. However, research studies suggest that the impact of the local authority nominees on health authorities has been small, associated with the lack of an organised power base or a coherent approach to policy. Members therefore tend to act as individuals, with power mainly resting with the professional service providers.

A total of 207 Community Health Councils (CHCs) — one for each district — were set up in 1974. Half of their members were to be nominated by local authorities, one-third by voluntary organisations, and the remainder by regional authorities. The main functions of CHCs were to comment on local services and to be consulted on future plans and intentions of health authorities. However, the only real power given to CHCs was that area health authorities could not close a hospital without CHC approval, and if this was not forthcoming the matter was to be referred to the Secretary of State for the final decision. Because of their clear lack of power and limited budgets, CHCs have made little direct impact on policy, and have been described by Klein (1974) as lap-dogs rather than watchdogs.

To the extent that CHCs have exerted influence this has mainly been through forming a source of information and advice to the public, and particularly in helping to channel complaints. However, despite strenuous efforts, the existence and functions of CHCs are not widely known and need to broadcast to a larger section of the population.

Outside the formal administrative structure of the NHS there are numerous autonomous groups that exist either to serve or represent the consumers of health care, or more commonly combine both service and pressure group functions. These groups range from small self help groups, often organised on a local basis (see Chapter 8) to national organisations with a paid staff, such as Age Concern and the National Association of Mental Health (MIND), which have established close links with the DHSS in their role of representing and campaigning for the interests of their members (Ham, 1977).

Private Health Care

Two aspects of private practice have always existed in the NHS. First, there has always been a right for private treatment by a private doctor, financed by private insurance or direct payment. Second, Bevan agreed at the time the NHS was established to make a small number of beds available in NHS hospitals for private patients ('pay' beds) and allowed consultants to hold part-time contracts within the NHS so that they could maintain some private practice. These are seen as being tactical concessions made by Bevan to the medical profession to ensure that the public sector would acquire the services of the best specialists who, without the option of private practice, might not have participated in the NHS.

Private health care in England is distributed between 2,400 pay beds in NHS hospitals, 3,000 private hospital beds and 30,000 private nursing home beds. Private out-patient facilities are also available in many NHS hospitals, while a minority of GPs have a few private patients each. About half of those who seek private acute hospital treatment are covered by medical insurance, and about 3.6 million people (6.4 per cent of population) currently have some form of private health insurance. These schemes offer what is essentially a narrow package of medical care, often limited to in-patient care for acute conditions. In general, private health insurance is used to cover elective surgical procedures, and enables people to avoid the waiting time for these procedures under the NHS list.

The private sector, although attracting considerable attention, still forms a small proportion of all hospital care in Britain. For example, private hospital beds (pay beds plus beds in private hospitals) currently form less than 2 per cent of NHS hospital beds, and private health care expenditure is about 3 per cent of the total expenditure on health care. It has also been estimated that in 1971/2 private practice added roughly one-fifth to the incomes of hospital consultants engaged in it, although there were wide variations between specialities, and added on average 10 per cent to the incomes of general practitioners with private patients (Klein, 1980).

The past 30 years has seen some expansion of the proportion of the population covered by private health insurance. This reflects both dissatisfaction with waiting times for surgical procedures and other aspects of NHS provision, and the increasing trend for employers to provide health insurance as a 'fringe' benefit for their staff. The other main change has been in the distribution of hospital beds, with a decline in pay beds in NHS hospitals and a corresponding growth in private hospitals. The growth of private hospitals has largely occurred since 1975 (there were 105 private hospitals in 1975 compared with 153 in 1980), as a response to the phasing out of large numbers of pay beds under the Health Services Board introduced by the Labour Party in 1976. Subsequently this policy has been reversed by the Conservative Party, and encouragement given to the growth of the private sector through the tax concessions given to employers who subscribe to private health insurance schemes for their employees.

The existence of the private sector, and particularly of pay beds in NHS hospitals, has formed the main area of political conflict and discord in health policy. The private sector is important despite its limited impact on the day-to-day effectiveness, efficiency or even fairness of the health service, because of its symbolic value. It is seen by its supporters as maintaining individual freedom and choice, and by its critics as challenging the fundamental principles of the NHS by enabling health care to be bought and thus based on one's ability to pay. As the Secretary of State stated in 1976, in her defence of the Labour party's plan to phase out pay beds:

> Intrinsically the NHS is a church. It is the nearest thing to the embodiment of the Good Samaritan that we have in any aspect of our public policy. What would we say of a person who argued that he could only serve God properly if he had pay pews in his church? (quoted in Klein, 1980, p. 12)

Strategies and Policy Options

Health care systems are faced with problems of controlling the costs, quality and distribution of health services. The different explanations considered earlier in this chapter for the growth of state involvement in health care also suggest different approaches to these issues within the NHS. The liberal reformist approach favours a problem-oriented view, in which greater efficiency and control are achievable through sophisticated planning techniques and better information, with specific problems being tackled as they arise. The radical approach, however, suggests these problems may be irresolvable contradictions thrown up by deeper pressures, such as the struggle over the distribution of wages, profits and taxes, or the tension between local autonomy and central state regulation. Nevertheless both approaches are concerned to raise levels of health in the general population and to ensure the rational use of resources.

Liberal Reformist Approaches

Actual solutions adopted to problems in the NHS have employed a liberal reformist approach, concentrating on discrete issues as these arise. This approach can usefully be considered in terms of three broad periods in the history of the NHS; the formative period, 1948-66; the managerial period, 1960-74; and the period of retrenchment from the mid 1970s (Allsop, 1984).

Formative Period. The early period of the NHS was characterised by policy drift, with the general direction of developments in the service stemming from the decisions of key service providers, predominantly the consultants in prestige specialisms, general practitioners in the community and Medical Officers of Health on local authority boards. This was associated with the belief that the original goals of equitable and free access to comprehensive health care would have been reached, through steadily eliminating existing demand to a level at which limited resources would have to be committed, based on the assumption of a finite pool of sickness. When it became evident that costs were rising, an attempt was made to control costs through prescription charges. Limited attempts were also made to direct general practitioners to areas of need through the introduction of financial incentives. However, the most immediate concerns during this period tended to be financial rather than organisational, as the original belief in the levelling off of demands and costs was shown to be mistaken.

Managerial Period. The 1960s began two decades of increased spending on health services and of various managerial techniques designed to commit resources to a totally rational set of operations. The managerialism which characterised this period was based on the assumption that organisational change can be used as a strategy for improving service provision, and that changes in structure would bring about improved access to better quality services because they would be better managed. The better coordination of policies between different sectors of the service is similarly regarded from a managerial perspective as leading to a greater cooperation between the different professionals involved in care, while planning is viewed as a neutral tool, with targets being set and progress made towards them. Indeed, it is this faith in rationality in operation that is one of the hallmarks of the liberal approach to social engineering in the health field.

The decade began with two policy documents, *A Hospital Plan for England and Wales* (Ministry of Health, 1962) and *Health and Welfare: The Development of Community Care* (Ministry of Health, 1963), which both encapsulated this managerial approach. These documents were regarded as providing a 'rational basis' for the development of services, and outlined targets to be achieved in terms of bed norms and community service provision. Revised several times during the 1960s as experience with them accumulated, their targets have nevertheless been missed by a large margin. Central to the Hospital Plan was the belief that beds could be used more efficiently by reducing the average length of stay, while the increased capital expenditure made available for new buildings was regarded as ensuring a better distribution of beds and achievement of the norms established for the target number of beds per 1,000 population in different sectors. The concept of a district general hospital with 600-800 beds serving a population of 100,000 to 150,000 population was also introduced, based on the belief that a larger hospital would bring significant economies of scale.

Another example of this managerial approach is seen in the 1966 Salmon Report (Ministry of Health, 1966) which introduced a hierarchy of nurse managers. A similar attempt to create a managerial consciousness was made at the level of the medical profession through the setting up of the Cogwheel Working Party. Its first report in 1967 (Ministry of Health, 1967) recommended the grouping of clinicians into divisions, with the aim of coordinating decisions in relation to the allocation of medical resources over the hospital as a whole.

The zenith of the managerialist phase is regarded as being reached in the 1974 NHS reorganisation. This aimed to transform the NHS into a more efficient and effective service by changes in its structure, the strengthening of management, the introduction of a planning system and the provision for increased democratic participation. The major structural change was the move away from the original tripartite structure towards a more integrated service, designed to provide greater continuity of care and in this sense a more effective service. The new structure sought to foster links between health and social service departments by making the boundaries of the health and local authorities coterminous and by making collaboration in providing and planning for service provision mandatory, with Joint Consultative Committees established as the means of collaboration between the health and social services. Secondly, the combination of a centralised service and a clear definition of tasks and roles at region, area and district level, with lines of accountability upwards to the DHSS and delegation and responsibility downwards to the health authorities, was regarded as ensuring both a more efficient service and one which was effective in carrying through department policies, particularly in regard to reducing regional inequalities between client groups. This was combined with the introduction of a planning system to ensure the forward planning of service provision to achieve nationally defined goals and priorities at a local level. Greater consumer participation was also provided for, although in a fairly restricted form (see pp. 192-3). Perhaps of greater significance was the introduction of a more democratic structure of decision-making through the principle of consensus management. This involved the representation of the major professional groups as equal members on management teams at regional and area level, with the aim of making services more sensitive to local needs and facilitating the implementation of national policies. In practice, the structure adopted in the 1974 reorganisation was soon criticised for having too many tiers, which led to delays in taking decisions and problems of communication. Following the recommendation of the 1979 Royal Commission, the area level was removed in the 1982 reorganisation.

Post 1974. Soon after the 1974 reorganisation the era of growth and managerialism really ended. The public expenditure crisis of 1976, which marked the beginning of the current general recession, coincided with growing internal criticism of the increased bureau-cratisation of the NHS, and the discontent of workers within it.

Strikes averaged about one a year in the 1960s but grew rapidly in the 1970s to peak at 21 stoppages in 1977 (Royal Commission, 1979). More generally this period has been marked by the appearance of a growing ideological split between the Labour and Conservative parties. Thus the political compromise which characterised the early years of the NHS has been falling apart. Under pressure from the declining rate of economic growth there has been a questioning of the fundamental principles of the NHS and of the assumptions of the post-war period that public expenditure could be manipulated, usually in an upward direction, to achieve economic and social progress. In particular, the Conservative Party, since its election to office in 1979, has attempted to translate monetarist as opposed to Keynesian ideas into public policy. Monetarists see public expenditure as being at the heart of Britain's economic difficulties and argue that growth rates must be improved before welfare services can be improved. As a result the attainment of economic goals is given priority over social goals. This is reflected in the current emphasis on the need to make savings, and cope with only a limited increase in revenue. This is to be achieved by employing health service resources more efficiently (generally taken to refer to the maintenance of a given standard of service at a lower cost or an improved standard at the same cost) and increasing the effectiveness of resource use (referring to an improvement in the quality or outcome of services or procedures). This strategy is taking four forms:

(a) *Organisational.* In 1983 a NHS management enquiry, chaired by Mr Roy Griffiths, was set up to examine the way resources are used in the NHS, with the aim of identifying changes in management necessary to secure the best value for money and the best possible services for the patient. Griffiths identified the NHS as suffering from institutional stagnation, and a lack of clear direction. The main recommendation he put forward to overcome these problems was to appoint general managers at every level of the NHS, from the DHSS downward to the individual unit or hospital. These managers are to be responsible for the services provided and for giving the leadership required to 'stimulate initiative, urgency and stability' in the process of seeking even greater efficiency (DHSS, 1983). This approach constitutes a fundamental departure from the principles of consensus management introduced in 1974, which was regarded by Griffiths as reducing pressures towards efficiency and leading to long delays in the management process (Day and Klein, 1983).

Another organisational change currently being considered is to make doctors budget-holders, with the aim of reducing unnecessary service use. This approach reflects the fact that the demand for services (X-rays, tests, hospital bed use, etc.) is largely doctor-led, and is thus intended to encourage doctors to be more 'cost-conscious'.

(b) *Monitoring and evaluation.* This is occurring at several levels. It includes the development of performance indicators to monitor activity (in terms of throughput, costs per case, etc.), so highlighting major disparities at regional and district levels. A second important component is the increasing emphasis on the need for studies to assess the efficiency and effectiveness of different types of treatment or places of care. Such assessments are however often surrounded by considerable problems (Holland, 1983). For example, the outcome of different types of health service provision or clinical intervention often cannot be judged solely in terms of their impact on life expectation, but rather requires a complex and composite evaluation. This may include outcomes being assessed in terms of the relief of pain and distress, the quality of life experienced by the patient and functioning achieved and the burden on their family. In addition to these various outcomes, which pose considerable problems of measurement, is the fact that they may be valued differently by different age, sex or social class groups, or by patients compared with doctors. Furthermore, the use of Randomised Control Trials, which form the traditional approach to evaluation and are in principle free from confounding factors, is often precluded by organisational ethical problems and thus non-random designs are dictated. Other difficulties relate to problems of cooperation by doctors if the evaluation is seen as disruptive of their clinical routine or as potentially threatening. Despite these difficulties it is likely that increasing priority will be given to assessments of the efficiency and effectiveness of resource use, and especially of new developments in high technology medicine.

(c) *Diverting costs and direct financial control.* Costs to the NHS may be diverted onto consumers through raising prescription charges and other direct costs. The growth of private health insurance, which has been encouraged by the relaxation of controls, also has implications for the demands made on the NHS and possible cost savings. The recent experiments in 'privatising', or contracting out laundry, domestic and other services to commercial firms, have similarly been justified in terms of the financial savings achieved. Another approach to controlling costs is through increasing the involvement and responsibility of the voluntary and informal sector.

A clear step in this direction was taken by the DHSS priorities document, 'Care in Action' (DHSS, 1981), which sees the voluntary and informal sector as the primary source of community care, with statutory and private sources supplementing and supporting this provision. These methods of diverting costs are being accompanied by direct financial control, through the control of the central budget for NHS services and the introduction in 1976/7 of cash limits into health expenditures except in relation to general practitioners. Cash limits mean that any overspending by a health authority is no longer met by the DHSS but is first call on next year's budget.

(d) *Approaches to health.* The increasing costs of medical intervention, together with its limited impact on mortality rates, have been associated with an increasing emphasis on both the prevention of disease (primary prevention) and its detection at an early stage (secondary prevention). Primary prevention has involved measures to improve environmental conditions, notably through the control of industrial waste and restrictions on smoking in public places, and measures to reduce motor vehicle and industrial accidents. In addition there has been considerable emphasis on seeking to promote healthy habits by increasing knowledge. This strategy is clearly presented in the 1977 White Paper on 'Prevention and Health' (DHSS, 1977), which declares:

> Much ill-health in Britain today arises from overindulgence and unwise behaviour . . . The individual can do much to help himself, his family and the community by accepting more direct responsibility for his own health and well-being.

The current approach to health and to perceived problems in the health service is thus broadly in line with the views of McKeown (1979) who drew attention to the importance of personal behaviours as determinants of health, and with the prescriptions of Cochrane who advocated the use of Randomised Control Trials to establish effectiveness, and cost benefit analyses to establish efficiency (see Chapter 1). However, the prevailing approach to health, although broader than at the time the NHS was established, still relies largely on an individual interventionist approach. Similarly, although there has been an increase in the private health sector and some degree of privatisation of health services, the NHS remains as the predominant source of health care for the majority of the population. Whilst liberal reformers may differ in their approaches to particular aspects of the health service, or in the level of funding advocated, they do not question the fundamental assumptions about the nature of health and of the health service.

Radical critiques

A growing movement, which may be termed the radical right, would like to reduce the role of government intervention in health care, on the basis that health care is a good, like any other, and as such should be part of provision in the private rather than the public sector (Allsop, 1984). They see covert rationing, queueing, inertia and resistance to change occurring as a result of public sector management, with professionals being prevented from providing the sort of service they wish to offer. They thus seek to remedy the faults of the NHS through a system of private and state insurance, linked to other measures which encourage the private sector to provide health care facilities. This strategy necessarily carries all the weaknesses of a market approach. These include the problems for consumers of evaluating the health care they receive and thus being able to make informed choices, the problems of provision for those unable to pay and the tendency for this type of approach to focus on curative medicine and to neglect the social and economic determinants of disease. Furthermore, private financiers and providers will ultimately face the same pressures that are generated in a public system, as can be seen in the United States, and will respond by trying to control prices, quantities and quality of health care. There is also no systematic evidence that demonstrates that the private sector is more efficient, while both public and private sectors have failed to evaluate what they do (McLachlan and Maynard, 1982).

In contrast to the critique of the radical right, that of the radical left focuses on the undemocratic nature of the NHS, and its emphasis on individualistic intervention. Although wishing to defend the NHS against public expenditure cuts they thus believe the NHS must be changed. The lack of democracy in the NHS is seen by the radical left as an important reason for its unresponsiveness to local needs and demands. A central strategy is thus to reestablish local democratic control. This has been a common demand by the Socialist Medical Association, the Politics of Health Group and individual authors (e.g. Doyal, 1979). A related but distinct policy is to encourage consumer participation, for while local control would help to shape the NHS to general local needs, there is still the issue of what health care should be provided. The liberal critique of this idea is that market demands may be for trivial treatments (a common complaint by GPs). Clearly, the ultimate response to the consumer might be a private market. However, radicals argue that this merely opens the door to producer manipulation and gross inequalities related to income. The solution to these problems is often seen in terms of breaking down the barriers between professionals and patients. This approach is adopted by Carpenter (1980) who argues that 'A socialist health service . . . will be one where all barriers of hierarchy and mystification between health workers and between them and the sick people they work with are torn down.' The nearest to achieving this in modern industrial countries is probably in some of the health clinics set up by the women's movement, which provide for lay participation in the provision of care (see Chapter 8).

A second clear strategy advocated by the radical left is to redirect resources towards areas which will affect the general health of the population, by moving more firmly away from the current emphasis on curative medicine and an interventionist approach, which is seen as a product of the culture and demands of capitalism, and as having little effect on overall mortality rates (see Chapter 1). Thus, rather than treating the individual with even greater technological sophistication, it is argued that we should be rearranging our social relations to minimise the creation of illnesses which are less and less able to be treated. The specific expression of this line of argument is in the call for stronger policies on prevention, which focus on all aspects of life, including food, housing, transportation and work. This general strategy is clearly described by Deacon (1984):

> This concern with preventing avoidable ill health is a touchstone of socialist policy. It would reach into every corner of working and domestic life. Not only would each work process be evaluated from the standpoint of whether it made workers ill or not, but also such diverse aspects of life as food, housing, transportation and personal relationships would be affected far more than under capitalism by considerations of their health-enhancing potential. Changes in lifestyle in relation to all of these things would be a matter of general public concern and action. (p. 454).

The general strategies advocated by the radical left which encompass the twin concerns of an altered form of curative medicine and a greater emphasis on prevention, are clearly described. What is less clear is the process by which these goals will be attained. In particular there is the question of how far it is possible to achieve radical reforms of the medical system, without equally radical changes in the wider society, for the former can be regarded as a reflection of the wider system of which it forms a part.

Radical solutions are often critisised as being not 'realistic'. However the NHS is also increasingly acknowledged as being less and less 'realistic' towards general health needs. As we have seen, this has led to some strong critiques from both liberal and radical writers about the nature of medical intervention generally, whether state organised or not.

Emerging Trends

Whatever the specific form the health care system takes in each country, issues of distribution, cost, and effectiveness have emerged. A pluralist explanation, as we have seen, would understand this common development as the result of similar pressure group activity by the medical profession, bureaucratic sectors and patients in different countries. A more radical explanation would place these developments in the context of the dynamics of the modern capitalist state, with issues of cost containment and the dominance of the biomedical model seen as resulting from the imperatives of the capitalist economy.

The common problems of health care which characterise modern industrial societies may lead to a gradual convergence of their health care systems, as they adopt reformist measures to deal with these problems. This is clearly illustrated by changes in the financing of health care. Countries with high levels of private insurance are increasing the amount of state funded care and schemes which provide comprehensive coverage based on pre-payment, while in Britain there is a growth of the private sector. A particularly interesting example in the United States of what can be provided by the establishment of Health Maintenance Organisations (HMOs) (Luft, 1983). HMOs differ considerably in their origins, organisation and the comprehensiveness of the services provided. However, the basic characteristic of an HMO is that it comprises a population of voluntary subscribers who, for a fixed subscription, are entitled to a range of services, including out-patient and hospital services. Doctors are generally paid on a *per capita* or salaried basis, linked to the revenue generated by the organisation. HMOs are regarded as attractive in the USA because they provide comprehensive coverage, including ambulatory care, which is often not included under third party insurance schemes. They are also generally seen as a means of cost control, because they alter the usual financial incentives to increase service use inherent in third party reimbursement schemes, through their system of physician renumeration and the need to keep premiums low to attract subscribers. Some writers have considered the possible introduction of HMOs in Britain as one form of cost control, which forms a development of the notion of clinical budget holding. However, the precise impact of HMOs in terms of the nature and quality of services provided still seems unclear, with part of the difficulty of evaluating HMOs stemming from their varied forms.

Attempts to increase democratic control of health services and to address the social and environmental determinants of health are most clearly demonstrated in some of the Third World countries which have adopted the World Health Organization's (WHO) concept of Primary Health Care (PHC). This is enshrined in the Declaration of Alma Alta (WHO, 1978), where the member states of the WHO general assembly committed themselves to the goal of 'health for all by the year 2000'. The Declaration of Alma Ata conceives primary health care as:

> ... essential health care made universally accessible to individuals and families in the community by means acceptable to them, through their full participation and at a cost the community and country can afford. It forms an integral part both of the country's health system of which it is the nucleus and of the overall social and economic development of the community.

The major changes which result from the move to PHCs are (1) that health promotion is seen as involving not only the health sector but also more general social and economic development; (2) a reversal in resource allocation is implied, away from the existing bias towards urban and hospital care towards health education, nutrition, water and sanitation, maternal and child health, immunisation and communicable disease control, basic curative care and essential drug therapy; and (3) in contrast to the emphasis on the training of high level technicians, priority needs to be given to the training of larger numbers of lower level workers with skills appropriate for dealing with common problems in the area.

Success in implementing the PHC concept has been patchy. Some interesting attempts to organise health promotion on these lines have been made in several countries, including Botswana (Hogh and

Petersen, 1984), Mozambique (Jelley and Madeley, 1984), and Tanzania (Gish, 1983). However, PHCs often exist as single, often externally-funded, projects, isolated from the overwhelmingly hospital-based systems which consume a large proportion of health care resources. The problem which exists is therefore the need to bring PHCs into the mainstream of health and health sector development, which in turn is often resisted by professional and other interest groups.

References

Allsop, J. (1984) *Health Policy and the National Health Service*, Longman, London

Carpenter, M. (1980) 'Left wing orthodoxy and the politics of health', *Capital and Class*, *11*, 73-95

Clare, A. (1976) *Psychiatry in Dissent*, Tavistock, London

Cochrane, A. (1972) *Effectiveness and Efficiency*, Nuffield Provincial Hospitals Trust, London

Day, P. and Klein, R. (1983) 'Two views on the Griffiths Report', *British Medical Journal*, *287*, 1813-16

Deacon, B. (1984) 'Medical care and health under state socialism', *International Journal of Health Services*, *14*, 453-80

DHSS (1975a) *First Interim Report of the Resource Allocation Working Party*, HMSO, London

DHSS (1975b) *Better Services for the Mentally Ill*, HMSO, London

DHSS (1976) *Report of the Resource Allocation Working Party: Sharing Resources for Health in England*, HMSO, London

DHSS (1976) *Priorities for Health and Personal Social Services in England*, HMSO, London

DHSS (1977)*Prevention and Health*, HMSO, London

DHSS (1981) *Primary Health Care in Inner London (Acheson Report)*, HMSO, London

DHSS (1981) *Care in Action. A Handbook of Policies and Priorities for the Health and Personal Social Services in England*, HMSO, London

DHSS (1983) *NHS Management Inquiry Report (Griffiths Report)*, HMSO, London

Doyal, L. with Pennel, I. (1979) *The Political Economy of Health*, Pluto Press, London

Eckstein, H. (1960) *Pressure Group Politics*, Allen and Unwin, London

Fraser, D. (1973) *The Evolution of the British Welfare State*, Macmillan, London

Gish, O. (1983) 'Some observations about health development in three African Socialist countries: Ethiopia, Mozambique and Tanzania', *Social Science and Medicine*, *17*, 1961-70

George, V. and Manning, N. (1980) *Socialism, Social Welfare and the Soviet Union*, Routledge and Kegan Paul, London

Gough, I. (1979) *The Political Economy of the Welfare State*, Macmillan, London

Guillebaud Committee (1956) *Report of the Committee of Enquiry into the Cost of the National Health Service*, HMSO, London

Ham, C. (1977) 'Power, patients and pluralism', in K. Barnard and K. Lee (eds.),

Conflicts in the NHS, Croom Helm, London

Ham, C. (1981) *Policy Making in the National Health Service*, Macmillan, London

Harrison, A. and Gretton, J. (eds.) (1984) *Health Care in the United Kingdom, 1984*, CIPFA, London

Hart, J. (1971) 'The 'Inverse Care Law'', *The Lancet*, 27 Feb. 1971, 405–12

Haywood, S. and Alazewski, A. (1980) *Crisis in the National Health Service*, Croom Helm, London

Heidenheimer, A., Heclo, H. and Adams, C. (1983) *Comparative Public Policy* (2nd ed.), Macmillan, London

Hogh, B. and Petersen, E. (1984) 'The basic health care system in Botswana: a study of the distribution and cost in the period 1973-1979', *Social Science and Medicine*, *19*, 783-92

Holland, W.W. (ed.) (1983) *Evaluation of Health Care*, Oxford University Press, Oxford

Jelley, D. and Madeley, R.. (1984) 'Primary health care in practice: a study in Mozambique', *Social Science and Medicine*, *19*, 773-82

Jones, K. (1972) *A History of the Mental Health Services*, Routledge and Kegan Paul, London

Klein, R. (1974) 'NHS brokers or activists', *New Society*, 28 Nov., 1974

Klein, R. (1975) 'The National Health Service', in R. Klein (ed.), *Inflation and Priorities: Social Policy and Public Expenditure*, Policy Studies Institute, London

Klein, R. (1980) 'Ideology, Class and the National Health Service', *Kings Fund Project Paper*, Kings Fund Centre, London

Klein, R. (1983) *The Politics of the NHS*, Longman, London

Luft, H. (1983) 'Health-Maintenance Organisations', in D. Mechanic (ed.), *Handbook of Health. Health Care and the Health Professions*, Free Press, New York

MacLachlan, G. and Maynard, A. (eds.) (1982) *The Public/Private Mix for Health*, Nuffield Provincial Hospitals Trust, London

Marx, K. (repr. 1976) *Capital*, vol. I, Penguin Books, Harmondsworth, Middlesex

McKeown, T. (1979) *The Role of Medicine*, Nuffield Provincial Hospitals Trust, London

Ministry of Health (1946) *NHS Bill. Summary of the Proposed New Service* (Cmnd 6761), HMSO, London

Ministry of Health (1962) *Hospital Plan for England and Wales*, HMSO, London

Ministry of Health (1963) *Health and Welfare: The Development of Community Care*, HMSO, London

Ministry of Health (1967) *First Report of the Joint Working Party on the Organisation of Medical Work in Hospitals* (Cogwheel Report), HMSO, London

Ministry of Health (1968) *The Administrative Structure of Medical and Related Services in England and Wales*, HMSO, London

Ministry of Health and Scottish Home and Health Department (1966) *Report of the Committee on Senior Nursing Staff Structure* (Chairman, Brian Salmon), HMSO, London

Navarro, V. (1976) *Medicine Under Capitalism*, Neale Watson Academic Publications Inc., New York

Navarro, V. (1978) *Class Struggle, the State and Medicine*, Martin Robertson, London

OECD (1977) *Public Expenditure on Health*, OECD, Paris

O'Connor, J. (1973) *The Fiscal Crisis of the State*, St James Press, London

Rickard, J.H. (1976) *'Per capita* expenditure of the English Area Health Authorities', *British Medical Journal*, 31 Jan. 1976, 299-300

Royal Commission on the National Health Service (1979), HMSO, London

Scull, A. (1977) *Decarceration*, Prentice Hall, Englewood Cliffs, NJ

Social Services Committee (1980) *The Government's White Papers on Public Expenditure: The Social Services*, Third Report from the Social Services Committee, vol. I, Report, HMSO, London

Titmuss, R.M. (1968) *Commitment to Welfare*, Allen and Unwin, London

Townsend, P. and Davidson, N. (1982) *Inequalities in Health*, Penguin Books, Harmondsworth, Middlesex

West, R.R. and Lowe, C.R. (1976) 'Regional variations in need for, and provision and use of child health services in England and Wales', *British Medical Journal*, 9 Oct. 1976, 843-6

WHO (1978) *Primary Health Care*, Report of the International Conference on Primary Health Care, Alma Ata, USSR, WHO, Geneva

Willcocks, A. (1967) *The Creation of the National Health Service*, Routledge and Kegan Paul, London

7 INEQUALITIES IN HEALTH

A fundamental aim underlying the creation of the National Health Service in 1948 was to provide equality of access to health services for those in need by removing the financial barrier to service use. This was regarded not only as fulfilling notions of social justice, but also as leading to the elimination of, or at least substantial reduction in, the mortality differentials of social class groups. In contrast to these expectations a recent review by the Working Group on Inequalities in Health suggests that the social class differentials in health may be as great as in the early years of the NHS (DHSS, 1980). Their report, commonly referred to as the Black Report (after the Chairman, Sir Douglas Black), has provoked considerable debate concerning the nature and causes of social class inequalities in health, and the changes required to reduce these differentials.

Whereas attention has traditionally focused on differences in the health experience of social class groups, inequalities in health also occur between geographical areas and among sex, marital and racial groups. Furthermore, the inequalities in health which occur among social groups within a country, although significant, are relatively small when contrasted with the dramatic inequalities in health which exist between today's advanced industrial countries and countries of the Third World. For example, the crude death rate in England and Wales is 12 per 1,000 population, compared with 17 per 1,000 in India, and 22 per 1,000 in Zaire.

This chapter focuses particularly on the inequalities in health experienced by social classes and by men and women. It seeks to explain their differential rates of mortality and morbidity using a social causation model, which focuses on the differential distribution of risk factors, and in social constructionist terms. Taking the latter approach, attention is paid to the way in which the observed inequalities in health may reflect differences in lay perceptions and responses to illness or form a product of the social construction and application of diagnostic labels. Although focusing on the experience of particular social groupings, the different types of explanations put forward to account for their inequalities in health can also be employed to explain the inequalities in health of other social groups.

Social Class and Health

In Britain the most widely used measure of social class is the Registrar General's (RG's) social class classification which was introduced in 1911 to analyse infant mortality rates (Leete and Fox, 1977). This classification has since undergone substantial revisions to take account of changes in the occupational structure. Despite these changes both the familiar Roman numerals designating social classes and the basic aim remain, with occupations being allocated to social class groups on the basis of the degree of skill involved and the social position implied. An alternative, but fairly similar, classification frequently employed in government surveys is a system of six hierarchically ranked socio-economic groups (SEGs) which aim to group together people with a similar social and economic status. The six SEGs are not identical with the RG's social classes, although a comparison of the two classifications using 1971 census data showed the only marked divergence occurred in the RG's social class II (Morgan, 1983).

The RG's social class classification and the classification by SEGs are valuable in identifying groups which differ in their material resources, life styles and behaviour. However, there are problems regarding the applicability of occupational measures to elderly people for whom previous occupation is likely to be of decreasing significance. There is also the question of the validity of the traditional practice of classifying married women by their husband's occupation. A large proportion of married women are now themselves gainfully employed, while many would fall into a different social class from their husband if classified by their own occupation (Reid, 1981). Furthermore, there is the question of whether a single occupation can accurately reflect the life style of a two-earner family. Other fundamental issues concern the extent to which the RG's classification achieves its stated aim of ranking occupations in terms of skill or prestige, and whether prestige and status should form the main criteria of classification rather than other criteria reflecting different conceptions of class. Despite these problems, the RG's classification continues to be the most widely used measure of social inequality in Britain.

Social classes, as measured by the RG's classification, exhibit differences in mortality rates at all stages of the life cycle. As Table 7.1 shows, the chances of being stillborn are about twice as great for babies whose fathers were classified as social class V as for those with social class I fathers. This difference widens during the next eleven months of life, with the chances of survival during infancy being just over two and a half times as great for infants with a social class I father as for those with a social class V father. The most marked social class gradients in mortality during infancy are for deaths from accidents and respiratory disease, whereas other causes associated with birth itself and with congenital disabilty have significantly less steep class gradients.

During childhood (1 to 14 years) the class differences in mortality rates narrow but there is still an inverse mortality gradient. Accidents, which form the biggest single cause of childhood death (30 per cent of total), continue to show the sharpest class gradient. However, marked class differences are also found for infectious and parasitic diseases and pneumonia. Class differences in mortality among adults of working age (15 to 64 years) are less marked than in childhood, but this conceals an important variation by age. The class differential is much greater among adults in their twenties and thirties than for those approaching retirement age, while after retirement social class is less closely associated with mortality rates than at any other stage in the life cycle.

An examination of the causes of death giving rise to the social class mortality differential among adults (15-64 years) shows that accidents and infectious disease continue to display a steep class gradient, as do rates of heart disease, lung cancer and stroke, which form the three leading causes of death among the adult population. However, a remarkable feature of the mortality rates of the adult population is the extraordinary variety of diseases that show marked class differences (see Figure 7.1). An analysis of 92 causes of death in 1970-2 among men aged 15-64 showed the mortality ratios for both social classes IV and V to be higher than for social classes I and II for 68 conditions, and for only four causes were the mortality ratios for I and II higher than for IV and V. Despite this general pattern, in many cases the cause-specific mortality rate among men was lower for III manual than for III non-manual (OPCS, 1978).

The General Household Survey (GHS) forms the main source of information on the morbidity experience of social groups. This is a continuous national survey based on interviews with all adult members of about 15,000 households in Great Britain. Data collected in the GHS on chronic health problems in the two weeks prior to the survey shows the rate of such problems to increase fairly consistently with declining socio-economic position. There is a less

Table 7.1: Social Class and Death from All Causes (1970-72)

Social class	Stillbirth rate[a]		Infant mortality rate[b]		SMR 1-14 years[c]		SMR 15-64 years[c]	
	Male	Female	Male	Female	Male	Female	Male	Female
I Professional	9	9	14	10	74	89	77	82
II Intermediate	10	10	15	12	79	34	81	87
III Skilled non-manual	11	12	17	12	95	93	99	92
III Skilled manual	12	13	19	15	98	93	106	115
IV Semi-skilled	13	13	22	17	112	120	114	119
V Unskilled	17	18	35	27	162	156	137	135
Ratio V to I	1.9	2.0	2.5	2.7				

Notes: a. Number of deaths per 1,000 live and dead births
b. Number of deaths in first year of life per 1,000 births
c. Ratio of the observed mortality rate in a sub-population to the mortality rate expected from the total population, multiplied by 100.

Figure 7.1: Social Class and Mortality in Adult Life (Men and Married Women 15-64 by Husband's Occupation)

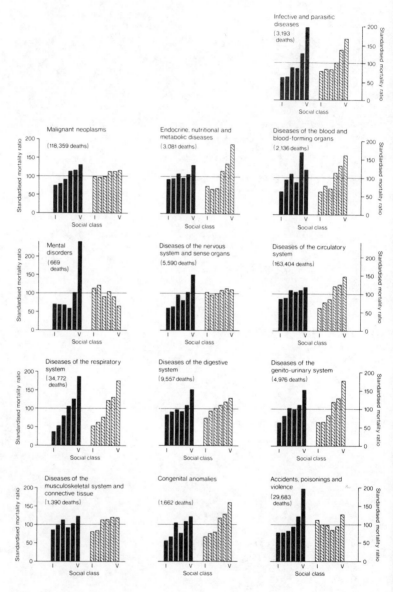

Source: DHSS (1980).

consistent class difference in reported rates of acute illness in a two-week period, with a notable feature being the fairly high rates reported by men and women in the highest socio-economic group (OPCS, 1982). This poses the question of whether differences in the perception and reporting of symptoms are being reflected, rather than in the incidence of acute clinical conditions.

Information on mental illness derived from rates of hospital admissions and community surveys, although again difficult to interpret, suggests that psychiatric illness is also closely related to social class. Underlying this broad pattern, the neurotic disorders have sometimes been found to vary directly with socio-economic status, whereas an inverse relationship is more often reported for psychotic disorders (Liem and Liem, 1978).

Explaining the Association between Social Class and Health

The association between social class and health is traditionally explained in terms of the health risks associated with particular aspects of the life circumstances, health beliefs and behaviour of social class groups. Alternative approaches are to view the apparent differences in morbidity and mortality rates from particular diseases as forming a product of social labelling, reflecting differences in doctors' readiness to apply specific disease labels to different social class groups, or as forming a product of the selective effects of health on social class membership.

Social Class and Labelling. The labelling approach is concerned with the way in which disease labels are socially constructed, and with the influence of social processes on their application to particular groups in the population. For example, Scheff (1975) suggests that people who possess the least power and fewest resources are most likely to be officially labelled as mentally ill, thus contributing to the higher incidence of officially designated mental disorders among the lower social classes (see Chapter 2).

The notion of the differential labelling of social class groups has mainly been applied to mental illness. However, differences in diagnosis may also contribute to the apparent differences in the incidence of physical disorders between social classes. An example is provided by the diagnosis of coronary heart disease. During the 1930s the death rate for coronary heart disease among men appeared to be highest in the higher social classes, and came to be regarded as a 'disease of affluence'. In contrast, by the 1960s the rates appeared to be inversely related to social class, with social classes IV and V having higher rates of coronary heart disease than social classes I and II. Another important change which occurred over this period, and may have contributed to the relative rise in deaths from coronary heart disease in social classes IV and V, was the decline in deaths attributed to myocardial degeneration and rheumatic heart disease. It was found that whereas in the 1930s mortality from coronary heart disease and angina increased with rising social class, mortality from all heart disease, including myocardial degeneration and rheumatic heart disease, showed the opposite pattern (see Table 7.2). This indicates that the apparently higher rate of coronary heart disease in the 1930s among men in the higher social classes was largely due to their being less often recorded as dying from myocardial degeneration (Marmot, Booth and Beral, 1981). This may have been due to differences in the knowledge of doctors working in predominantly middle-class and working-class areas, or to the effects of the image of coronary heart disease as a disease of affluence on doctors' readiness to attach this label to working-class patients.

Table 7.2: Heart Disease Mortality (SMRs) by Social Class

| | Social Class | | | | |
	I	II	III	IV	V
Coronary disease and angina	237	147	96	67	67
All heart disease	98	101	95	102	109

Source: Marmot, Booth and Beral (1981).

In many cases social class may interact with other characteristics, such as sex or racial group, to influence medical responses. For example, the relatively high rates of psychiatric diagnoses and admissions among ethnic minorities may reflect a greater readiness among doctors to diagnose their behaviour as a sign of mental illness. This may be due to the low social position of ethnic minorities and the influence of moral and political prejudices, or to the tendency to misinterpret cultural beliefs and modes of expression (Littlewood and Lipsedge, 1982).

Social Selection. The social selection hypothesis suggests that the concentration of ill health among the lower social classes reflects the effects of health on social mobility, and thus in determining the individual's place in the class structure. An early statement drawing attention to this process is provided by Jarvis, who explained the findings from his 1855 study which showed the highest rates of 'insanity' were in the 'pauper' class, in the following way:

> Men of unbalanced mind and uncertain judgement do not see the true nature and relation of things, and they manifest this in mismanagement of their common affairs... Hence they are unsuccessful in life: their plans for obtaining subsistence for themselves or their families, or of accumulating property, often fail; and they are consequently poor, and often paupers ... the cause of ... their mental derangement lies behind, and is anterior to, their outward poverty (Jarvis, 1855).

Subsequently the social selection hypothesis has been formalised to include both the downward social drift of previously ill persons and the effects of poor health in preventing upward social mobility. Several studies documenting a downward occupational drift of schizophrenic patients have been cited as evidence for the social selection hypothesis. In one study of the social class distribution of schizophrenic patients and their fathers in England and Wales, there were found to be over twice as many patients in social class V at admission than would be expected by chance. In contrast, when patients were categorised by their father's occupation at the time of the patient's birth they were not overrepresented at all in social class V, thus pointing to the effects of health in determining social class position (Goldberg and Morrison, 1963).

Whereas attention has traditionally focused on the effects of mental illness on occupational position, chronic physical conditions have been shown to have a similar selective effect. Evidence pointing to a downward occupational drift among men with physical disorders is provided by a comparison of the occupational histories of male hospital patients aged 45 to 64 with chronic bronchitis with a control group matched for age (Meadows, 1961). The occupational distribution of the group of men with chronic bronchitis was shown to have dropped compared with their position twenty years earlier, whereas no such drop had taken place in the control group. A more extensive study drawing attention to the effects of health on both upward mobility and downward social drift is provided by Illsley's research on mobility at marriage (Illsley, 1980). Data for married women having a first pregnancy in Aberdeen, 1951-4, showed that women who were born into social classes IV and V and who married into a higher social class (upwardly mobile) differed in a number of important characteristics from women born into social classes IV and V and who stayed there on marriage (stable), and from downwardly mobile women who married into social classes IV and V from a higher social class. Compared with these last two groups, upwardly mobile women had higher scores on IQ tests, left school later, entered more prestigious occupations, were taller with a better physique and had a lower perinatal death rate in their first pregnancies. Data for first pregnancies to married women in Aberdeen districts, 1969-75, indicated that the same processes were operating twenty years later, with upwardly mobile women being most healthy and having the highest educational achievements, and the downward mobile having the least favourable characteristics (Illsley, 1980).

The limited data available on the extent and nature of social mobility makes it difficult to assess its impact and contribution to the social class differentials in mortality and morbidity rates. The Black Report considered this question in seeking to account for the apparent maintenance, or even slight widening, of the social class mortality differentials over the last thirty years. As the Report showed, the decline in infant mortality rates between 1949-53 and 1970-2 was slightly greater in social classes I and II than in IV and V, thus increasing the differential. During childhood, social differences in mortality rates appear to have remained fairly constant over this period. However, for adult men aged 15 to 64 a widening of the gap appears to have occurred between 1949-53 and 1959-63 (see Table 7.3). One possibility is that changes in the occupational structure, and hence the effects of occupational mobility, contributed to the maintenance or apparent widening of social class mortality rates. This hypothesis was examined by re-classifying occupations in 1959-63 and 1960-72 by the 1950 classification. This approach aimed to take into account the substantial revisions to the RG's classification carried out in 1960, when 26 per cent of occupations were allocated to a different social class compared with their 1950 allocation. The adjusted figures based on the 1950 classification still suggested there has been some widening of the gap (see Table 7.3). Thus, while the Report accepts that the selective effects of health may have played a small role in the maintenance of social class differences in mortality through its effect on occupational mobility, such mobility is not regarded as forming a major factor contributing to the maintenance of social class inequalities in health. The Report therefore concludes that there has been little real reduction in social class inequalities in health in the postwar period.

Table 7.3: Standardised Mortality Ratios for Men Aged 15-64 by Social Class (1931-71)

Social class		1930-32	1949-53	1959-63	1970-72
I	Professional	90	86	76 (75)[a]	77 (75)[a]
II	Intermediate	94	92	81	91
III	Skilled (manual and non-manual)	97	101	100	104
IV	Semi-skilled	102	104	103	114
V	Unskilled	111	118	143 (127)[a]	137 (121)[a]

Note: a. Adjusted rate based on the 1950 Classifications of Occupations.
Source: Townsend and Davidson (1982).

Stern (1983) suggests that the influence of social mobility may in fact be greater than the Black Report allows for. He points out that there has been a considerable change in the occupational structure with the decline in semi-skilled and unskilled occupations and the increase in skilled manual and non-manual occupations; 16 per cent of men aged 16 to 44 were in social class V in 1931 compared with only 6 per cent in 1971. Stern argues that in a period of such net upward movement in the occupational and class structure the conventional methods of comparing social class mortality rates by achieved social class may be insufficient. This is because the correlation of social mobility with health may result in producing constant or widening social class differentials by achieved social class, even if the differentials have narrowed when measured by social class of origin. Stern believes this process may explain why the observed social class mortality differentials as measured by achieved social class have not fallen in Britain during the post-1945 period, despite the existence of the National Health Service. He suggests that to test whether mortality rates over time have been equalised or not requires that mortality rates by achieved social class be supplemented, if not replaced, by rates according to social class of origin.

Social Causation Theories. Both social mobility and the differential labelling of conditions appear to contribute to the observed differences in the patterns and rates of mortality among social classes. The main determinants of inequalities in health are, however, generally viewed as lying in the material circumstances, life styles and behaviours of social classes, which produce differences in exposure and resistance to disease (see Table 7.4).

Table 7.4: From Social Structure to Health Outcomes

(1)	(2)	(3)	(4)	(5)
Aspects of social structure	Everyday life experience of individuals	Health beliefs and orientation to health	Health related behaviour	Health outcome
Political	Income	Concepts of health	Eating	Growth
Economic	Expenditure	Health as a value	Drinking	Physique
Cultural	Work	Knowledge about health	Smoking	Illness
Medical	Education	Planning	Exercise	Disease
Religious	Family life	Risk taking	Exposure	Stress
Familial	Social relationship	Prevention	Service use	Handicap
Environmental	Physical and cultural milieu		Family planning	Well-being
			Child rearing	

Source: Illsley (1980).

One determinant of health which has received considerable emphasis is the differences in the provision and use of services by social classes. Despite the removal of the financial barrier to health care with the introduction of the NHS, the manual classes continue to make less use of a wide range of preventive health services, including antenatal care, cervical screening and childhood immunisations (DHSS, 1980). In contrast, the manual classes appear to have fairly high rates of general practitioner consultations, with the possible exception of consultations for children (OPCS, 1982). However, a question which has been the subject of much debate is whether the higher rate of GP consultations among the lower social classes matches their greater need for care. In other words, is there equity in service use?

Forster (1977) examined this question of the relationship between the need for and the use of general practitioners' services by social classes using data from the 1972 GHS. The method he adopted was to calculate use/need ratios for each social class based on their rates of self-reported consultations (use) and self-reported morbidity (need). This led him to conclude that when morbidity or 'need' is considered, the apparently higher consultation rates of the lower social classes are eliminated or even reversed. This approach of calculating overall use/need ratios has been criticised by Collins and

Klein (1980), who pointed out that people who report morbidity and those who report service use are not necessarily identical populations. In an attempt to overcome this problem, they analysed the 1974 GHS data relating reported use of primary care services to morbidity classified in terms of four health categories: (1) the not sick; (2) the acutely sick; (3) the chronically sick without activity restrictions; and (4) the chronically sick with activity restrictions. In view of the association between age and service use and the differences in the age composition of SEGs, they compared the actual rates of use in each SEG with the predicted rate expected from the age composition of SEGs.

The main differences Collins and Klein comment on are the higher actual-to-predicted rates of use by the unskilled among men classified as 'acutely sick', and the relatively high use by professional men among the 'not ill', possibly reflecting their more frequent consultations for preventive health checks. Collins and Klein conclude that there is little evidence of systematic social class differences in the use of medical care and that 'If there are continuing social inequalities in health there was no similar inequality in access to primary care.' Their critics point out that although Collins and Klein classify people into four health categories, they are still relating need and use among broad groups, rather than matching the use and need of individuals within groups. Furthermore, as Collins and Klein acknowledge, their use of GHS data means they cannot allow for possible differences in reporting or in the reasons for consultation. Other criticisms relate to the lack of attention paid to the relatively low consultation rate of unskilled men among the chronically sick with activity restrictions, and the much higher percentage of partly skilled and unskilled manual workers who were in the categories of chronic sick. In view of such limitations and deficiencies, Le Grand (1980) challenges the conclusions drawn by Collins and Klein that the NHS is operating in an equitable manner. In contrast he states: 'The conclusion derived from earlier evidence remains intact: the better-off appeared to receive more health care under the NHS relative to need than the less well off.'

A second way in which the use of health services appears to vary between social classes is in terms of the quality of health care provision. For example, referrals to specialist care have been found to be highest amongst patients in social class I and lowest in social class V, despite the inverse relationship between social class and mortality rates (Blaxter, 1984). Working class patients have also been shown to have shorter GP consultations and receive less information about their condition than middle-class patients, even when attending the same practice. The main factor responsible for this situation appears to be the greater readiness of middle-class patients to express their desire for information (Cartwright and O'Brien, 1976). Similarly, in the hospital setting middle-class patients appear to be more able to obtain information about their children that satisfies them (Earthrowl and Stacey, 1977). However, while differences in the use of health services and care received have important implications for patient satisfaction, anxiety, pain and suffering, their contribution to the overall mortality rates of social classes is likely to be considerably less. This is because although there are some conditions for which mortality is potentially preventible with timely and appropriate intervention, there are few effective cures for the major killer diseases. This suggests that differences in mortality rates must be largely explained in terms of the non-health-service determinants of health.

Epidemiological research has identified a number of risk factors which are differentially distributed among social classes, and which may both increase exposure to specific diseases and affect individuals' resistance or susceptibility to diseases in general. One aspect of the life style of social classes which has received particular attention is the differences in consumption patterns. The high sugar and low fibre content of diets of social classes IV and V compared with those of I and II have, for example, been identified as contributing to the higher rates of coronary heart disease among the manual classes (Marmot *et al.*, 1981). Alcohol consumption also increases with declining social class, especially among men, and is associated with increased risks of cirrhosis of the liver, cardiovascular disease and death from accidents. The prevalence of smoking is also higher among manual workers. In 1980, only 21 per cent of professional men and women (SEG 1) aged 16 and over in Great Britain were current smokers compared with 57 per cent of men and 41 per cent of women in SEG 6 (OPCS, 1982). Smoking has in turn been linked to increased risks of a large number of conditions, including lung cancer, respiratory and cardiovascular disease.

A second group of risk factors are those which arise directly from the individual's living and working conditions, comprising various types of environmental hazards. These include the overcrowding of homes and high levels of air pollution in the area of residence, which appear to contribute to the higher rates of respiratory disease among working class children. Those at particular risk are children made susceptible through other factors, such as a parental history of respiratory problems and poor physical development (DHSS, 1980). Living conditions, and especially the lack of gardens to play in and less safe forms of heating and furnishing, have been identified as contributing to the class gradient in childhood accidents. Other factors thought to be responsible for childhood accidents are differences in the socialisation of middle- and working-class children and the extent of parental supervision. The other group particularly affected by their living conditions are elderly people, with poor housing conditions and inadequate heating contributing to increased risks of death from bronchitis, pneumonia and hypothermia.

Occupational health risks form a major factor contributing to the higher mortality rates among manual workers. The 1972 Report of The Committee on Safety and Health at Work (the Robens Report) suggested that every year something like 1,000 people are killed at work in the UK and about half a million suffer injuries of varying degrees of severity, although this figure may, like other official statistics, underestimate the real numbers involved due to the underreporting of accidents. A second form of physical hazard associated with many mining and manufacturing industries is the risk of exposure to dust and other toxic substances, which give rise to cancers of various sites, other skin disorders and respiratory conditions. The incidence of industrial disease is again difficult to determine. This is partly owing to the problems in identifying the role of industrial hazards in conditions which only become apparent after a number of years or have multiple causes. Doctors may also sometimes be reluctant to identify a condition as industrially related, in view of the implications for compensation and possible pressures to modify industrial processes. A further problem in quantifying the extent of industrial-related diseases is that hazards associated with industrial production may often spread outside the workplace. Workers may, for example, unknowingly bring dangerous substances, such as lead or asbestos, into their homes on their clothing, thus increasing the health risks for their families. Similarly, the spreading of industrial waste in the air or water also exposes the wider community to increased health risks (Doyal, 1980). Epidemiologists and government bodies in the UK generally accept an estimate of between 1 and 5 per cent of cancer being of occupational origin. However, a recent report suggests that in the near future 20 to 38 per cent of cancer in the USA will be occupational, and some bodies tend to apply this higher figure to cancer in this country (Davies, 1982).

Another type of risk factor regarded as contributing to the higher rates of depressive illness and increasing risks of a wide range of physical disorders among the lower social classes is their greater experience of stress. Sources of stress include the monotony of work and fears of unemployment, housing problems, problems associated with poverty and family crises. One view is to regard people in the lower social classes as experiencing greater stress because of their greater exposure to stressful situations. An alternative hypothesis is that the main difference between social classes lies not so much in the differential distribution of stressors, as in differences in their ability to cope with stress, due to their lack of the material resources and psychological support which assist coping behaviour. For example, Brown and Harris (1979) suggest that the higher rates of depression among working-class than among middle-class women in their study could be explained not so much by the differences in their experience of life events as by differences in the availability of support, which in turn helps to promote coping by increasing self esteem (see Chapter 8).

Links between Structural Position and Health Risks

So far the emphasis has been to identify aspects of the life styles and working and living conditions of social classes that form risk factors in disease. A further sociological question concerns the determinants of the differences in health related behaviours, health beliefs and life experiences of social classes, which in turn produce inequalities in health. This involves tracing the links across the columns of Table 7.4 from the social structure to health outcomes.

One view is to regard differences in the health related behaviours of social classes as forming a product of cultural patterns, rather than arising directly from differences in their social circumstances (pp. 87-91). For example, the lower rate of uptake of preventive health services among the manual classes has been explained in terms of their general orientation towards the present and unwillingness to engage in activities which have only long-term and uncertain benefits. Similarly, differences in attitude to and use of family planning and in patterns of childhood socialisation is seen as reflecting broad cultural differences between middle-class and working-class people.

The notion of the existence of cultural differences in beliefs and behaviours has also been applied by Lewis (1967) in more restricted terms to refer to the existence of a distinct 'culture of poverty' among the poorest sections of the population. Lewis' cultural hypothesis was derived from studies of poor communities in Central America. He described these communities as characterised by a set of attitudes and beliefs which are at variance with those of the wider society, including a fatalistic attitude towards life, which serves to reduce people's capacity to take advantage of any opportunities made available to them. This culture is regarded as largely self-perpetuating, surviving even when the conditions from which it arose have changed. This occurs through its influence on children who, by the time they are 6 or 7 years of age, have usually absorbed the basic attitudes and values of the sub-culture. As a result, they are not psychologically geared to take full advantage of the changing conditions which may occur in their lifetime, thus leading to the perpetuation of disadvantage.

This notion of the existence of a distinct and self-perpetuating sub-culture among the poorest section of the population has recently been reinvoked to explain the existence of multiply deprived groups in the population, despite the general increase in economic prosperity. The size of the group identified as being in poverty necessarily depends on the definition and measures employed. Using the Supplementary Benefit standard, which forms the state's current definition of the poverty line, just over 5 million people were in poverty in the United Kingdom in 1980. This group with its multiple disadvantages and associated health risks may make a major contribution to the overall health experience of the lowest social class. As Blaxter (1984) notes:

> Some of the evidence of the British Longitudinal studies suggests that much of what appears to be a social class 'trend', with the families of unskilled workers being in a particularly unfavourable position, may be the effect of specially deprived groups included in that class. (p. 217)

Sir Keith Joseph, when Secretary of State at the Department of Health and Social Security, suggested in a series of speeches delivered in 1972–4, that the existence and perpetuation of deprived groups in the population are likely to be a product of economic and environmental factors as well as personal and emotional ones. However he identified an important cause of the continued existence of deprivation as being the transmission of disadvantage by families to successive generations. He described this 'cycle of deprivation' as occurring through the direct transmission of genetic endowment and through patterns of childbearing and socialisation which fail to instil in children the motivation, skills and capacities necessary to avail themselves of educational and job opportunities. The children of deprived parents thus themselves experience failure at school and in employment, and an unsatisfactory marriage and family life, so continuing the perpetuation of disadvantage (see Figure 7.2).

Figure 7.2: Cycle of Deprivation

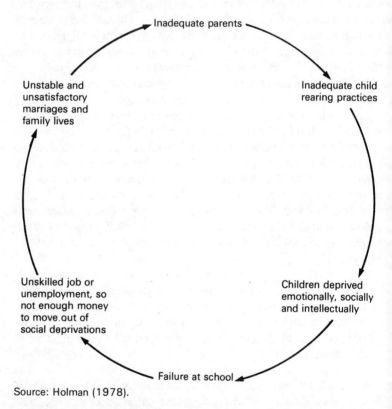

Source: Holman (1978).

Research to assess the validity of the cycle of deprivation thesis in contemporary Britain has provided evidence of some continuity of disadvantage over generations. However it also suggests that continuities over more than two generations are rare, with large numbers of people managing to break out of the cycle of deprivation. As Madge (1983) notes in a recent review of the evidence:

Some children may grow up seemingly unscathed by their background, while deprivation may arise quite spontaneously, and without earlier precedent, in other families. This variety of pathways to deprivation makes it essential to look beyond family history when assessing the life chances of individuals. (p. 201)

To the extent that a continuity of disadvantage does occur between generations, there is the further question of the reasons for this continuity. The accumulating evidence suggests this may be explained not so much by cultural patterns as by the influence of structural opportunities. This is illustrated by a study of parents and children in the inner city which showed that working-class parents resorted to child care methods they themselves did not approve of because of poor housing and a lack of play facilities (Wilson and Herbert, 1978). The influence of both cultural and structural factors in producing continuities in behaviour was also demonstrated in Blaxter and Paterson's (1982) study based on interviews with mothers and their married daughters living in Aberdeen. The sample was selected with the aim of identifying families most likely to demonstrate an intergenerational transmission of attitudes and beliefs. The interviews revealed some continuity in health beliefs between generations among this group, including ideas about infant feeding and the fear of chest complaints, a low value placed on health and the belief that 'lying down to illness' was a moral weakness. Important differences were, however, also evident. Whereas almost all of the older generation presented themselves as reluctant to use medical services, most of the younger generation displayed little reluctance to use medical services, especially curative services, viewing such services as a 'right'. The main reason for inappropriate service use among the younger generation was their lack of ability to cope with the increasing complexities of the health care system, associated with their low educational levels and skills. Similar patterns of behaviour could therefore not be entirely explained by the intergenerational transmission of attitudes and beliefs. Instead it reflected their low educational levels (however caused), together with the prevailing structural organisation of the health care system.

The identification of structural factors as a major determinant of differences in life styles and health related behaviours of social groups raises questions as to the causes of these socially structured inequalities. The causes of inequalities in health service provision are considered in Chapter 6. This chapter focuses more broadly on the determinants of the economic position and life experience of social classes.

The functionalist approach regards the existence of inequalities in the rewards accruing to different occupations as contributing to the efficient functioning of society as a whole. It explains the universal presence of social stratification in terms both of the requirement faced by any society of ensuring that the most important positions are filled by the most qualified persons, and the need to ensure that their holders are motivated to perform the duties attached to these positions. Society is, therefore, concerned with motivating individuals at two levels. As Davis and Moore (1945) explained:

> Inevitably, then, a society must have, first, some kinds of rewards that it can use as inducements, and second, some way of distributing these rewards differentially, according to positions. The rewards and their distribution become a part of the social order, and thus give rise to stratification.

The acceptance of a functionalist belief in the need for differences in rewards associated with occupational position is generally accompanied by a concern to ensure that 'poverty' is eliminated, that health service resources and other benefits are equitably distributed and that health hazards at work are controlled. The existence of what is regarded as a maldistribution of resources is in turn explained in historical terms, or as forming a product of the peripheral malfunctioning of society. Such inequalities are thus viewed as remediable within the existing system, through, for example, the provision of financial aid to the unemployed or to poor families, and policies to improve housing and working conditions and to reduce the uneven distribution of health services.

The conflict perspective, rather than emphasising the functionality of the differential distribution of rewards for society as a whole, encompasses a number of traditions which emphasise the role of competing interests in contributing to the prevailing distribution of resources between social groups. One approach is to regard the formation of contending groups as based on differences in life style associated with cultural traditions or political interests, and to see the distribution of resources as influenced by the power of various competing groups. A second major approach is provided by the marxist conception of class, which views social classes as groups characterised by an antagonistic relationship based on their relative positions in the social relations of production. The two main divisions are between capitalists who own their own means of production and purchase the labour powers of others, and workers who do not own their own means of production and, therefore, sell their labour power to others. To this basic two-fold distinction can be added a third class, the petty bourgeoisie who own their own means of production but do not, except perhaps in the most limited way, purchase the labour power of others. A fourth class which expresses the development of late capitalism is managers, who form wage labourers, who do not own their own means of production and do not formally employ workers, but who do control or supervise labour power (Wright and Perrone, 1977). Marxist analyses regard the distribution of resources between social classes as serving the interests of the ruling class. The reduction of disadvantage, including the existence of groups in poverty and the health hazards associated with industrial production, is thus seen to require a fundamental change in power relationships. This perspective is illustrated by Holman (1973) who suggests that the presence of a group in poverty is essential to the continuation of wealth in capitalist society. This is because it has the effect of persuading the working class that their lot in terms of resources and power is acceptable, which reduces the possibility that they will strive to challenge the position of the elite. The existence of a group in poverty also serves to demonstrate the fate of those who do not conform to prevailing work and social standards, and acts as a vulnerable group on whom the blame for social problems can be placed. Since the causes of poverty are seen from this perspective as residing in the social structures of society, rather than in the personal characteristics of the poor or their immediate environment, it follows that poverty can only be removed through structural changes which enlarge access to resources and widen the opportunity structure. Furthermore, reformist measures are regarded as often having a negative effect in terms of limiting possibilities of more fundamental change. For example, the provision of financial benefits to the poorest groups may serve to limit any major redistribution of income.

Just as the existence of poverty is viewed as directly linked to the needs of capitalist society, so the health risks associated with manual occupations are explained from a marxist perspective as resulting from an overriding concern with the maximisation of profit. This leads to the use of toxic substances and dangerous procedures, despite their health risks to workers, and to a work situation which forms a major source of stress. Eyer's (1977a and b) analysis of the adverse effects of work in capitalist society on the health experience of the population, and particularly of manual workers and their families, provides an example of the application of this perspective. In a review of data for the United States since 1870 Eyer identified 24 death rate peaks. Of these, 12 occurred at the height of employment in the business cycle, 5 in the year following the high, 5 just before the high while employment levels were rising, and only 2 occurred at the peak of unemployment. Eyer argues that the death rate is low during periods of recession because solidarity develops among the workers which has a protective effect on health. However, as the boom develops this solidarity disintegrates. Migration destroys solidarity by enhancing labour market competition among strangers. Divorce occurs partly as a result of the divergent pulls of high demands on male and female labour, with overwork depriving people of the time necessary to form cooperative social bonds. Eyer regards the effects of solidarity and disintegration/overwork as accounting for 72 per cent of the business cycle variation in death rate, of which the major component is the adverse effects of the loss of solidarity between workers (see Table 7.5). He also views social stress as having an indirect effect through increased consumption of tobacco and alcohol, accounting for 17 per cent of the variation in the death rate. Eyer regards material conditions as playing only a small role in determining mortality rates this century, but as probably forming the major effects of the economic booms in the nineteenth century prior to the widespread social stresses introduced with the development and demands of capitalist production.

Writers adopting a marxist perspective differ in the importance attached to stress, alienation and the physical hazards associated with capitalist production. Thus, Eyer's emphasis on stress as the disease-producing mechanism of capitalism has been criticised by Cooper (1979) who attributes greater importance to the materials insults of diet, carcinogens and physical injury. Navarro (1982) has also questioned the role of stress in increasing consumption of products harmful to health. He suggests that consumption patterns reflect instead the alienation experienced by manual workers engaged in production in capitalist society, as a result of the increasing specialisation and deskilling of labour. Lacking control over their work, workers thus look for self-realisation in the sphere of consumption. Such consumption is encouraged, being intrinsically necessary for the survival of the capitalist economic system (see Chapter 1).

The main alternative to Eyer's theoretical analysis of the links between economic cycles and health has been put forward by Brenner

Table 7.5: Causal Relations Accounting for the Business Cycle
Variation of the Death Rate, United States, 1949-75

MATERIAL CONDITIONS (8%)	
Housing	(2%)
Nutrition	(6%)

SOCIAL RELATIONS IN CLASS STRUGGLE (89%)

SOCIAL SOLIDARITY (19%)	
Strikes	(17%)
Marriage	(2%)

SOCIAL DISINTEGRATION AND OVERWORK (53%)	
Overwork	(34%)
Migration	(9%)
Divorce	(8%)
Unemployment	(2%)

DRUG CONSUMPTION (17%)	
Alcohol	(11%)
Tobacco	(6%)

Source: Eyer (1977b).

(1977a, b). Brenner, like Eyer, identifies social stress as providing the
link between economic cycles and health. However, in contrast to
Eyer, he does not attribute stress specifically to the capitalist
economic system, and regards the greatest stress as occurring during
periods of recession rather than during economic boom. Brenner
describes economic recessions as forming periods of particular stress
due not only to the effect of unemployment in depriving the population
of part of its income but also to the loss of a sense of achievement, and
of friends and a pattern of life associated with work, which may lead to
a disruption and breakdown of family relationships and community
life. Brenner viewed the lower social classes as most vulnerable in
recessions, as semi-skilled and unskilled workers are the first
employees to be released and the last to be rehired. In addition, in
periods of rapid economic growth unskilled workers and those whose
skills are no longer required as a result of technological change are
least likely to benefit from the increased economic prosperity. They
thus become relatively deprived. The social class differential in
mortality rates is, therefore, maintained through the concentration of
the adverse effects of economic cycles among the lower social classes,
which serves to reduce the trend of declining mortality in these
classes. Brenner explained the association between the peak in the

death rate and the peak in the employment rate and business boom by introducing the notion of a lag between the experience of recession and its effects on death rates. He suggested that the length of lag is likely to be approximately three years for heart disease, approximately two years for cirrhosis, and one to two years for mental hospitalisation.

Eyer, in criticising Brenner's analysis, argues that the lagged impact of life events, such as unemployment, is shorter than Brenner allows for, and is generally not more than twelve months. In support of this he cites a study by Kasl and Cobb (1970) which shows that the elevation of mortality risk factors often occured in anticipation of unemployment rather than forming the lagged effect of unemployment. Eyer therefore claims that the association between economic booms and peaks in the death rate must be explained in terms of the adverse effects of rapid economic growth, rather than as the lagged effects of the preceding period of unemployment. Furthermore, for Eyer, the adverse effects of economic booms are an inherent feature of the capitalist economic system. Thus whereas stress is identified as a major health risk which is differentially distributed among social classes, views differ as to its links with the economic system. Similarly, as we have seen, views differ as to the extent to which other health risks associated with work are seen as an inevitable feature of industrial production under capitalism and whose elimination thus requires a change in the economic structure, or alternatively form a more general feature of industrial production, requiring the introduction of various controls and safety measures to safeguard the health of workers.

Reducing Social Class Inequalities in Health

This chapter has shown how the observed social class inequalities in health are likely to be partly due to the selective processes influencing social class membership, and to the differential labelling of conditions among social classes. However, the major cause of the observed differences in the mortality rates of social classes is generally regarded as being the differences in the behaviours, and living and working conditions of social groups. Differences in health related behaviours have been attributed to cultural values, but also viewed as a direct product of differences in the socially structured opportunities and circumstances of social class groups.

To the extent that differences in health related behaviours, and more broadly the persistence of deprivation between generations, reflect the knowledge, attitudes and cultural values of these groups, measures to increase knowledge and change attitudes (including health education campaigns, nursery school provision, etc.) will have an important effect on levels of health. Reliance on this approach will, however, be ineffective in reducing social class differences in smoking, dietary patterns, etc. to the extent that such behaviours form a response to, or are constrained by, differences in their social or material circumstances.

Approaches to promoting health through measures which directly affect the socially structured opportunities and circumstances of social classes will necessarily be influenced by views of the nature and functions of social inequality. Those adopting a reformist approach generally accept the existence of inequalities in terms of wealth, but seek to reduce what are seen as gross inequalities and deprivations, to improve access to and use of health services and to control environmental hazards. However, the emphasis is on ameliorating problems and controlling health hazards, rather than engaging in more fundamental change and challenging the nature of the prevailing socio-economic system.

Traditionally, particular attention has been given to reducing social class inequalities in health by measures to ensure that health services are more equitably distributed. These include the designated area schemes designed to influence the distribution of general prac-titioners, and the recent incorporation of standardised mortality ratios and marital status as measures of health need in the formula employed to allocate resources between regions (see Chapter 6). Likewise, attention has been paid to increasing the take-up of preventive services through health education programmes and measures to increase the availability and attractiveness of services. This broad approach is reflected by Brotherston (1976) when he describes the unequal facts of morbidity and mortality as forming a 'challenge' to the health planner of how best 'to bring the services to groups who cannot or will not use them to their best advantage'. However, as shown in Chapter 6, this approach does not question the appropriate-ness of health service provision in relation to the needs of the population, and tends to overlook the more fundamental social causes of ill health and its distribution among social groups.

At a broader level, reformist measures have sought to compensate for disadvantage through providing financial benefits for the low paid and unemployed, and to reduce health risks by introducing controls on industry which aim to reduce environmental pollution and health hazards to workers. However, emphasis is often placed on education, persuasion and incentives to achieve these aims, rather than more direct controls. Thus, in the industrial sector there has been a considerable reliance on voluntary agreements between government and industry, while the main approach to the manufacture of tobacco products has been to require that health warnings be printed on cigarette packets, to place restrictions on advertising, and to increase the duty levied on cigarettes (thus increasing the cost and possible financial barrier for the consumer) rather than to restrict the production of cigarettes and other tobacco products.

An important contribution of the Black Report was to acknowledge that many of the determinants of social class inequalities in health lie outside the health care system. Thus in addition to proposals to increase the quality of primary medical care and to encourage the uptake of preventive services, it put forward a series of measures to improve living and working conditions. This included a comprehensive anti-poverty programme to reduce poverty through increasing maternity and child benefits, and introducing an infant care allowance and comprehensive disability allowance, as well as measures to increase and improve the housing stock, to discourage smoking and to improve working conditions. As the Secretary of State for Social Services noted, the authors of the Report had 'reached the view that the causes of health and inequalities are so deep-rooted that only a major and wide-ranging programme of public expenditure is capable of altering the pattern'. However, he went on to state that

> additional expenditure on the scale which could result from the Report's recommendations — the amount involved could be upwards of £2 billion a year — is quite unrealistic in present in present or any forseeable economic circumstances, quite apart from any judgement that may be formed of the effectiveness of such expenditure in dealing with the problems identified. (Townsend and Davidson, 1982, p. 336)

The measures proposed by the Black Report, although far-reaching, largely aimed to ameliorate and reduce prevailing social inequalities and to control specific health hazards through reformist measures. In this way they form a continuation of traditional approaches to health, and have been criticised by the radical left for failing to alter the fundamental economic and socio-structural factors which determine prevailing social inequalities and the distribution of health risks. In particular measures which conflict with vested interests are seen as likely to have only a limited impact in the absence of a more fundamental change in power relationships. Such measures include the Black Report's proposal that government departments, together with representatives of business and trade unions, should 'draw up minimally acceptable and desirable standards of work, security, conditions and amenities; pay and welfare or fringe benefits'. In contrast to the reformist approach, the radical left emphasises the need for a transformation of the social and economic system, with a view to changing the distribution of power and eventually eliminating inequalities in wealth and health.

Just as the previous chapter considered the reformist and radical options in terms of the nature of health service provision, this chapter similarly poses questions of the extent to which a society is prepared to accept the existence of inequalities in terms of health or wealth, and to give priority to health considerations in relation to industrial policies and public expenditure decisions, and thus raises issues which go far beyond the health system. Although the trend among all social class groups in Western industrial societies is towards improved health and a greater expectation of life, to the extent that large and far-reaching social class inequalities continue to exist they may be expected to give rise to inequalities in health. This is because the distribution of health among social groups is largely a product of the differences in their life situations and thus reflects the priorities and nature of the wider socio-economic system. The nature and pattern of social inequalities identified and which become the focus of attention, can itself also be viewed from a social constructionist perspective as reflecting broader concerns and values. Traditionally, the Registrar General's social class classification, which reflects a functionalist approach to stratification with its emphasis on the skill and status attached to occupations, has formed the basis of discussion and policy regarding the existence of social class inequalities in health. However, increasingly attention is being focused on the health needs and circumstances of multiply deprived groups in the population, as evidenced by recent interest in the cycle of deprivation thesis and proposals to target services and make more adequate financial provision for these groups. The questions surrounding the validity and applicability of the RG's classification suggest there may also be renewed attempts to develop alternative measures based on different conceptions of class. This will in turn have the effect of introducing changes in the composition of the classes identified and should provide new insights concerning the distribution and causes of disease.

Sex, Gender and Health

Differences in the health and expectation of life of men and women, although receiving rather less attention than social class differences in health, are nevertheless quite marked. These differences in health are in turn associated with differences between the sexes in reproductive capacity, in social roles and power and in assumed personality traits, with dominance, aggression and objectivity in our culture being regarded as characteristics of men, and passiveness, tenderness and subjectivity of women. However, there are questions of the extent to which such differences between the sexes are biologically or socially determined and of the precise ways in which they contribute to the observed differences in health.

Mortality Rates

In all contemporary industrial countries men have higher death rates and a shorter life expectation than women, although these sex differences vary in magnitude. For example, in the 1970s the difference in life expectancy was 8.5 years in Finland but only 5.3 years in Japan, and 3.5 years in Greece (Waldron, 1983). In England and Wales, 1979, the expectation of life at birth was 70 years for men and 76 for women and was associated with higher male death rates at all ages (see Table 7.6). The higher death rates among men occur from a wide variety of causes, including heart disease, lung cancer, stroke, bronchitis, accidents and other violence, which are each responsible for large numbers of deaths. With the exception of breast cancer, women tend to experience higher mortality rates from conditions which cause relatively small numbers of deaths.

In developing countries, men also generally have higher mortality rates than women, although the sex differences in mortality rates are generally smaller. In contrast to this general pattern there are a few countries where males have lower mortality rates than females. For example, in India life expectancy was 3 years shorter for females than males in the early 1970s.

A small component of the higher male mortality rates is probably directly attributable to physiological sex differences. This includes the slightly higher risk of birth injury and asphyxia owing to male

Table 7.6: Death Rates per Thousand Population by Sex and Age (England and Wales, 1981)

Age group	Men	Women
Under 1 year	12.67	9.37
1-4	0.53	0.45
5-14	0.28	0.19
15-24	0.84	0.34
25-34	0.90	0.52
35-44	1.82	1.25
45-54	6.06	3.76
55-64	17.47	9.33
65-74	45.52	23.94
75-84	104.90	66.27
85 and over	227.06	179.86
All ages	11.98	11.34

Source: Office of Population and Surveys (1983).

babies being on average slightly larger. Males also have rather higher rates of malformations and of genetically transmitted disorders (Roberts, 1976). The contribution of these factors to overall mortality rates is however likely to be small. Although there are more than 50 pathological conditions which occur almost exclusively in males, associated with X-linked recessive mutations, most of these patho-logies are not common and the few common ones are rarely lethal. Similarly, although there is some evidence that women's sex hormones may reduce risks of ischaemic heart disease, such inherent sex differences are regarded as playing only a small role in contributing to the overall sex differences in mortality rates.

The differences in the mortality rates of men and women are mainly attributed to differences in life styles and behaviour. Men experience greater hazards at work, are more likely to engage in risk-taking activities leading to higher rates of accidents and have higher rates of tobacco and alcohol consumption. Although the main causes of sex differences in mortality rates can easily be identified, what is less clear is the extent to which differences in roles and behaviours reflect innate differences between the sexes or form a product of learned differences in behaviour and socially structured differences in opportunities and expectations.

The social roles, social positions and life styles of men and women are viewed from a biological determinist perspective as being directly due to physiological sex differences. One approach is to explain differences in innate aggression, in physical strength and in mental capacities as associated with differences in the size and presumed organisation of the male and female brains. Other approaches attribute differences in the roles and positions of the sexes to differences in their reproductive capacities, or to men's greater physical strength and aggressiveness which allow them to achieve a dominant position.

Feminists have challenged approaches which emphasise the prevailing divisions between the sexes as rooted in nature, and instead regard these differences as socially constructed. The radical feminist approach can, however, be regarded as adopting a biological determinist position to the extent that it emphasises the importance of women's role in reproduction and men's greater physical strength in determining women's subordinate position. This version of radical feminism has, to some extent, now been replaced by 'cultural feminism' which asserts that it is not so much the biological fact that women bear children, as the psychological construction of this fact, that leads men to control women and subordinate them (Sayers, 1982).

Theories which explain differences in the social positions and social characteristics of men and women, or what are often referred to as gender differences, in terms of the way in which biological differences are interpreted and responded to within a given society, are described as social constructionist theories. An example of the social constructionist approach is provided by liberal feminism, which argues that the dominant position and greater aggressiveness and competitiveness of men, and emotionally dependent behaviour of women, largely reflect learned behaviours associated with differences in the socialisation and education of men and women. A problem surrounding liberal feminism, which limits its contribution, is that it does not provide a basis for explaining sex differences in socialisation or sex discrimination in adult life. The development of marxist and other radical analyses of the women's position have thus been important in providing an explanation of the origins of sex differences in socialisation. Marxist feminists suggest that sex differences in roles and patterns of behaviour can be explained in terms of their function in reproducing the existing sexual divisions in society, which are important to and encouraged under capitalism. In explaining the importance of the division of labour between the sexes for capitalism, particular attention has been paid by marxist feminists to women as unproductive workers. Women are regarded as contributing in this capacity to the process of commodity production and capital accumulation through their role in reproducing and maintaining the labour force. A second approach emphasises the role of women in contributing to capitalist production through serving as a reserve army of labour. This is seen not only as serving to meet additional requirements for labour but also by its constant availability as keeping wages in the semi-skilled and unskilled sectors of the labour market to a minimum. The implications of the sexual division of labour are that it not only provides an economic underpinning to the capitalist system but also makes women economically dependent on their husbands for support. Women's economic dependence has in turn been viewed as affecting their personality structure giving rise to emotional dependence, passivity and other 'typical' personality traits.

Biological determinist and social constructionist approaches are generally presented as involving distinct and opposing theories. Nevertheless, what are presented as purely biological accounts of sex roles are often rooted in social rather than biological considerations. Similarly, social constructionist theories, although stressing the socio-economic determinants of inequality, often include a consideration of the influence of biology in determining women's social status. For example, Marx and Engels in their analysis of the development of the social positions of men and women acknowledged the role of biology in the basic sexual division of labour which occurred with the domestication of cattle. This led to the surplus wealth being produced in the sphere of men's rather than women's work and hence to their dominant economic position. Sayers thus argues that sexual inequality is determined through the interaction of biological, social and historical factors.

Just as differences in behaviour and roles may be socially determined, so the effects on mortality rates of inherent sex differences in reproductive physiology and anatomy may also depend on prevailing customs and social and economic conditions. For example, pregnancy-related mortality makes a major contribution to sex differences in mortality in conditions of inadequate nutrition and medical care but plays only a minor role in modern industrial societies. As Waldron (1983) concludes:

> current evidence indicates that sex differences in human mortality reflect the interacting effects of a considerable variety of genetic and environmental factors. (p. 330)

Morbidity Rates

Whereas men have higher mortality rates, health surveys consistently show that women tend to report more illness, leading to the observation that 'women get sick and men die'. For example, Verbrugge (1976) in an analysis of US Health Interview Survey data for 1957-72 showed that over this period women consistently had higher age standardised rates of reported acute conditions compared to men, and that female excess morbidity for acute conditions persisted when 'disorders of pregnancy and the puerperium' were removed. Women were also more likely to report a chronic condition, but men reporting a chronic condition were more likely to report an associated limitation of activity. The General Household Survey provides a similar picture of higher reported rates of acute illness among women, although the differential is less consistent for chronic illness, with the relative rates varying between age groups (OPCS, 1982).

One factor identified as contributing to a greater amount of morbidity among women, despite their lower mortality rate, is the differences in the conditions experienced by men and women. Women appear to experience more psychological problems and disabling conditions, while men experience a greater number of conditions which result in fairly sudden death, such as accidents and ischaemic heart disease. This poses the question of why women experience more psychological problems, which has been explained both in terms of a social causation model and as forming a product of the social construction of illness. Explanations involving a social causation model have taken a number of forms. These include:

(1) Women's reproductive systems, and in particular the hormonal changes experienced after childbirth and at menopause, may give rise to higher rates of depressive illness. This response to biological changes may, however, be partly socially determined and represent a response to external as well as internal events. For example, a women may have good reason to react emotionally to all major reproductive events since they represent her main avenue of achievement and self-expression.

(2) Women may be more at risk of depressive illness through being less able to cope with problematic and stressful situations. Following Seligman's (1975) theory of learned helplessness, this can be attributed to women's gender role socialisation, which

emphasises passivity, helplessness and dependence as appropriate feminine behaviour and attitudes. Such responses have also been attributed to women's dependent economic position, or explained in biological terms.

(3) Differences in the social roles of men and women may give rise to differences in morbidity. Gove and Tudor (1973) have identified several ways in which the nature of women's social role increases risks of psychiatric illness. Firstly, women are often restricted to the role of housewife and thus, unlike men, have no major alternative source of gratification. Secondly, the role of housewife is one of low prestige and technically undemanding, which is not consonant with the intellectual and educational attainment of a large number of women. Thirdly, the role of housewife is relatively unstructured and invisible, which allows one to brood over troubles. Fourthly, even when a married woman works, she is typically in a less satisfactory position than the married man. In particular, married women are often under greater strain as they typically also perform most of the household chores. Fifthly, the expectations confronting women are unclear and diffuse, which may form a source of stress and uncertainty. Gove and Tudor claim that their hypothesis concerning the importance of women's social roles in contributing to their higher rates of mental illness is supported by the differences in rate of mental illness among marital groups. Thus they point out that the major difference in social roles and in rates of mental illness occurs between married men and married women. In contrast, both the rates of mental illness and the nature of the social roles between unmarried men and women are fairly similar.

Gove and Tudor's notion of the positive effects of work in providing a source of self-esteem and support corresponds with Brown and Harris' (1979) hypothesis that the greater susceptibility to depression of working-class women compared with middle-class is partly due to their exclusive dependence on wife and mother roles for a sense of accomplishment. However, the literature on the adverse effects of work is vast, and draws attention both to specific occupational hazards and to the adverse effects of more general working conditions and occupational demands. This illustrates the problems of generalising about the health effects of labour force participation, and suggests that the effects of paid employment on the health both of men and women are likely to vary according to the nature of their work and their wider social circumstances, including their other roles and sources of support.

In contrast to explanations which seek to account for 'real' differences in morbidity between men and women is the view that the apparent differences in morbidity reflect differences in illness behaviour and the reporting of symptoms by men and women.*

One explanation for differences in reported morbidity is that this forms a product of the design of health surveys. A specific feature of health surveys which may influence responses is that the interviewers are generally women, which may produce an underreporting of symptoms by men. Some surveys also allow proxy responses by women for other family members, which may result in an under-reporting of the morbidity of absent persons. A second explanation for differences in the readiness of men and women to report illness is that it may reflect differences in their psychological and personality characteristics and expected behaviour. Whereas men are expected to be self reliant and tolerant of pain, women learn that it is acceptable to be expressive about discomfort and to be dependent on others. This in turn may influence their readiness to acknowledge illness and seek professional medical advice. Thirdly, differences in responses to illness have been attributed to differences in the social roles of men and women. Women's greater involvement in family health matters may make them more sensitive to symptoms of illness. Women's social role may also provide greater flexibility, thus encouraging the use of health services and influencing rates of officially defined morbidity.

Views are still sharply divided as to whether sex differences in reported morbidity reflect differences in the incidence of clinical morbidity (Gove and Hughes, 1979) or differences in illness behaviour (Verbrugge, 1980; Mechanic, 1980). A third explanation is that the apparent differences in morbidity between men and women may reflect the social construction of health and illness and the social processes underlying medical diagnosis. A good example of the influence of definitions of disease in producing apparent sex differences in health is provided by the debate concerning the

---

*The dominant emphasis has traditionally been to explain a generalised tendency among women to report more symptoms. In contrast, recent evidence suggests that sex differences in reporting symptoms are smallest or non-existent with regard to the most tangible and observable symptoms, and greatest for vague symptoms, such as headaches, dizziness, sleep disturbance and lack of energy.

relative rates of mental illness among men and women. Gove and Tudor (1973) claim women have higher rates of mental illness than men. They base this claim on the following definition of mental illness which relates primarily to neurotic disorders and functional psychoses:

A disorder which involves personal discomfort (as indicated by distress, anxiety etc.) and/or mental disorganisation (as indicated by confusion, thought blockage, motor retardation and, in the more extreme cases, by hallucination and delusions) that is not covered by an organic or toxic condition.

In contrast, Dohrenwend and Dohrenwend (1976) found no sex differences in rates of mental illness. This appears to reflect their use of a broader definition, which encompasses not only neurotic disorders and functional psychoses but also personality disorders, which are more common among men. With regard to physical conditions, the social construction of 'health problems' may similarly result in conditions for which male rates are far larger than female rates, such as accidents, alcoholism and cigarette addiction, being excluded from reports of symptoms in health surveys. Nevertheless, these conditions are 'illness' in the sense that they are immediately tied to physiological malfunctioning in the body and may even lead to death (Clarke, 1983).

A second way in which definitions of illness may increase apparent rates among women is through the doctors' greater readiness to apply the label of 'sick' to women, and through the medicalisation of pregnancy and childbirth which has led to a great deal of doctoring of women. The image of women as emotional and suffering from psychogenic symptoms has been shown to be conveyed in drug advertisements in several prestigious and widely circulated medical journals. In contrast, men tend to be presented as non-emotional, rational and stoic, and suffering from organic illness (Prather and Fidell, 1975). Thus it is suggested that the higher rate of admission of women to psychiatric hospital care, and the greater proportion of women receiving psychotropic drugs, may be a consequence of the greater readiness of doctors to diagnose women as suffering from emotional and depressive disorders. Furthermore, once diagnosed as suffering from a psychiatric disorder, the labelling approach suggests this in itself may lead to attitudes and behaviour which confirm the diagnosis, particularly if it results in hospitalisation.

Ehrenreich and English (1973), adopting a radical feminist approach, regard the attitudes and practices of the medical profession towards female patients as reflecting the dominant interests of men. They describe the view of women held by the medical profession in the latter part of the nineteenth century as postulating innate differences between men and women of different social classes: 'Poor women were innately robust and in need of almost no medical care; affluent women were innately sick and in need of almost constant medical attention.' They describe these beliefs as serving the economic interests of doctors. Firstly, by establishing middle and upper-class women as a kind of 'client caste' to the medical profession, they ensured a supply of wealthy patients. Secondly, these beliefs helped to discredit women as healers and thus protected the male monopoly. Ehrenreich and English note that at present the majority of doctors is still male and argue that their view of women is dominated by the belief that 'women are vain, silly, ignorant creatures, best suited for the "trivia" of homemaking under the firm guidance of husband and, of course, doctor'. Thus, just as nineteenth-century doctors traced all female ills to the erratic and diseased womb (or ovaries), today's doctors are viewed as tracing women's ills to the frivolous female brain, and as treating their presented conditions as psychosomatic. This in turn has the effect of increasing recorded rates of depressive disorders among women.

Whereas Ehrenreich and English regarded the attitudes and practices of the medical profession as reflecting and serving the dominant interests of men, who form the majority of doctors, marxist feminists emphasise the way in which the medical profession and medical institutions serve the interest of the capitalist economic system. As Verbrugge (1975) comments, 'Like class and social hierarchies, sexism is a vehicle, not a motive power, in the structure of American capitalism.' Doctors are thus viewed as exercising social control functions which serve to maintain existing sexual divisions. This occurs through treating conditions, such as depression, as individual problems, rather than as arising from women's socially defined roles. Similarly, the existence of unnecessary surgery, as indicated by the high rates of hysterectomy and mastectomy in privately funded health care systems, can be viewed as one aspect of a larger process in which institutions seek to create new markets under capitalism, thus contributing to the survival of capitalism itself.

Despite the substantial differences in mortality and morbidity rates between men and women, these differences have received relatively little attention in health policy. This may reflect a belief in the biological determinants, and thus inevitability, of differences in the roles and behaviour of men and women, with their consequent health risks. Alternatively, it may reflect the belief that social class divisions form the fundamental source of inequality. This view is implicit both in functionalist analyses of social stratification, and in marxist feminist writings, and is reflected in the treatment of women's place in the class structure as merely a derived or shared class based on their husbands' occupational position.

Social Groups and Health Inequalities

This chapter has drawn attention to important similarities in the analysis of social class and sexual inequalities in health. In both cases, epidemiological research has sought to identify aspects of the life styles, environment and behaviour of these social groups which contribute directly to the observed variations in rates of morbidity and mortality. In contrast, these differences have also been viewed as forming a product of underlying social processes which influence prevailing definitions of health and illness and the application of medical labels.

Whereas the inequalities in health of social class groups and of men and women have been considered separately, the various subgroups in the population which differ in their experience of health and illness necessarily overlap. For example, the mortality rates both of men and women vary by marital group, with married people of both sexes having lower mortality rates than single and widowed people. This may in turn be due to the selective effects of health on marriage and remarriage, to differences in exposure to risks of illness associated with the differences in the economic resources and life styles of marital groups, or to differences in the responses of the medical profession and the health care received (Morgan, 1980). The relative health experiences of men and women may also vary for different social classes and racial groups, and in some cases compound the disadvantage experienced. For example, it has been suggested that sex role stereotyping may have its most profound effects on physicians' judgements and diagnoses when linked with other patient characteristics, such as age, social class, ethnicity, education, and various personality and behaviour patterns (McCranie, Horowitz and Martin, 1978). Similarly, the problems experienced in using the health service are particularly great for ethnic minorities with low levels of education and semi- and unskilled occupations, while these groups are most likely to experience poverty and its associated health risks.

References

Blaxter, M. (1984) 'Equity and consultation rates in general practice', *British Medical Journal*, no. 6345: 1963-6

Blaxter, M. and Paterson, E. (1982) *Mothers and Daughters: A Three Generation Study of Health Attitudes and Behaviour*, Heinemann Educational Books, London

Brenner, H. (1977a) 'Mortality and the national economy: a review of the experience of England and Wales 1936-1976', *Lancet*, 15 Sept., pp. 568-73

Brenner, H. (1977b) 'Health costs and benefits of economic policy', *International Journal of Health Services*, 7, 585-623

Brotherston, J. (1976) 'Inequality: is it inevitable?', in C.O. Carter and J. Peel (eds.), *Inequalities in Health*, Academic Press, London

Brown, G.W. and Harris, T. (1979) *The Social Origins of Depression*, Tavistock, London

Cartwright, A. and O'Brien, M. (1976) 'Social class variations in health care', in *The Sociology of the NHS*, Sociological Review (Monogr); 22

Clarke, J. (1983) 'Sexism, feminism and medicalisation — a decade review of literature on gender and illness', *Sociology of Health and Illness*, 5, 62-82

Collins, E. and Klein, R. (1980) 'Equity and the NHS: self reported morbidity, access and primary care', *British Medical Journal*, 281, 1111-5

Cooper, R. (1979) 'Prosperity — of the capitalist variety — as a cause of death', *International Journal of Health Services*, 9, 155-9

Davies, J. (1982) 'The prevention of industrial cancer', in M. Alderson (ed.), *Prevention of Cancer*, Edward Arnold, London

Davis, K. and Moore, W. (1945) 'Some principles of stratification', *American Sociological Review*, 2, 242-9

Department of Employment (1972) *Safety and Health at Work: Report of the Committee, 1970-1972* (Robens Report), HMSO, London

Department of Health and Social Security (1980) *Report of the Working Group on Inequalities in Health* (Black Report), HMSO, London

Dohrenwend, B.P. and Dohrenwend, B.S. (1976) 'Sex differences and psychiatric disorders'. *American Journal of Sociology*, 81, 1447-54

Doyal, L. (1980) *The Political Economy of Health*, Pluto Press, London

Earthrowl, B. and Stacey, M. (1977) 'Social class and children in hospital', *Social Science and Medicine*, 11, 83-8

Ehrenreich, B. and English, D. (1973) *Complaints and Disorders: the Sexual Politics of Sickness*, Feminist Press, New York

Eyer, J. (1977a) 'Does employment cause the death rate peak in each business cycle?', *International Journal of Health Services*, 7, 625-62

Eyer, J. (1977b) 'Prosperity as a cause of death', *International Journal of Health Services*, 7, 625-62

Forster, D.P. (1976) 'Social class differences in sickness and general practitioner consultations', *Health Trends*, 8, 29-32

Goldberg, E. and Morrison, S. (1963) 'Schizophrenia and social class', *British Journal of Psychiatry*, 22, 123-42

Gove, W. and Hughes, M. (1979) 'Possible causes of the apparent sex differences in health: an empirical investigation', *American Sociological Review*, *44*, 126-46

Gove, W. and Tudor, M. (1973) 'Adult sex roles and mental illness', *American Journal of Sociology*, *77*, 812-35

Holman, R. (1978) *Poverty: Explanations of Social Deprivation*, Martin Robertson, London

Illsley, R. (1980) *Professional or Public Health?*, Nuffield Provincial Hospitals Trust, London

Kasl, S. and Cobb, S. (1970) 'Blood pressure changes in men undergoing job less', *Psychosomatic Medicine*, *32*, 19-38

Leete, R. and Fox, A.J. (1977) 'The registrar general's social classes: origins and uses', *Population Trends*, *8*, 1-7

Le Grand, J. (1980) *The Strategy of Equality*, Allen and Unwin, London

Lewis, O. (1967) *The Children of Sanchez*, Random House, New York

Liem, R. and Liem, J. (1978) 'Social class and mental illness reconsidered', *Journal of Health and Social Behaviour*, *19*, 139-56

Littlewood, R. and Lipsedge, M. (1982) *Aliens and Alienists*, Penguin Books, Harmondsworth, Middlesex

Madge, N. (1983) 'Identifying families at risk', in N. Madge (ed.), *Families at Risk*, Heinemann Educational Books, London

Marmot, M., Booth, M. and Beral, V. (1981) 'Changes in heart disease mortality in England and Wales', *Health Trends*, *13*, 33-8

McCranie, E., Horowitz, A. and Martin, R. (1978) 'Alleged sex role stereotyping in the assessment of women's physical complaints', *Social Science and Medicine*, *12*, 111-16

Meadows, S. (1961) 'Social class migration and chronic bronchitis', *British Journal of Preventive and Social Medicine*, *15*, 171-6

Mechanic, D. (1978) 'Sex, illness behaviour and the use of health services', *Social Science and Medicine*, *12*, 207-14

Mechanic, D. (1980) 'Comment on Gove and Hughes', *American Sociological Review*, *45*, 513-14

Morgan, M. (1983) 'Measuring social inequality: occupational measures and their alternatives', *Community Medicine*, *5*, 116-24

Morgan, M. (1980) 'Marital status, health, illness and service use', *Social Science and Medicine*, *14*, 633-43

Navarro, V. (1982) 'The labour process and health: an historical materialist interpretation', *International Journal of Health Services*, *12*, 5-29

Office of Population Censuses and Surveys (1978) *Occupational Mortality, 1970-1972*, HMSO, London

Office of Population Censuses and Surveys (1982) *General Household Survey*, HMSO, London

Office of Population Censuses and Surveys (1983) *Mortality Statistics: England and Wales*, HMSO, London

Prather, J. and Fidell, C. (1975) 'Sex differences in the content and style of medical advertisements', *Social Science and Medicine*, *9*, 23-6

Reid, I. (1981) *Social Class Differences in Britain*, Grant McIntyre, London

Roberts, D.F. (1976) 'Sex differences in disease and mortality', in C.O. Carter and J. Peel (eds.), *Equalities and Inequalities in Health*, Academic Press, London

Sayers, J. (1982) *Biological Politics: Feminist and Antifeminist Perspectives*, Tavistock, London

Scheff, T. (1975) *Labelling Madness*, Prentice Hall, Englewood Cliffs, N.J.

Seligman, M. (1975) *Helplessness: On Depression, Development and Death*, W.H. Freeman, San Francisco

Stern, J. (1983) 'Social mobility and interpretation of social class mortality differentials', *Journal of Social Policy*, *12*, 27-49

Townsend, P. and Davidson, N. (1982) *Inequalities in Health: The Black Report*, Penguin Books, Harmondsworth, Middlesex

Verbrugge, L. (1975) 'Historical complaints and disorders: a review of Ehrenreich and English's study of medical ideas about women', *International Journal of Health Services*, 5, 323-33

Verbrugge, L. (1976) 'Females and illness: recent trends in sex differences in the United States', *Journal of Health and Social Behaviour*, 17, 387-403

Verbrugge, L. (1980) 'Comment on Walter R. Gove and Michael Hughes, 'Possible causes of the apparent sex differences in physical health'', *American Sociological Review*, 45, 507-13

Waldron, I. (1983) 'Sex differences in human mortality: the role of genetic factors', *Social Science and Medicine*, 17, 321-33

Wilson, H. and Herbert, G. (1978) *Parents and Children in the Inner City*, Routledge and Kegan Paul, London

Wright, E. and Perrone, L. (1977) 'Marxist class categories and income inequality', *American Sociological Review*, 42, 32-55

8 INFORMAL SUPPORT AND HEALTH

Whereas emphasis has so far been given to the professional health care system, much of the care for sick people, and especially for those with chronic conditions, is provided outside the formal sector. The main sources of informal of lay support are generally the individual's nuclear family, together with their wider kin, friends and neighbours. In addition to, or sometimes in the absence of, these informal support systems, people may band together into more formally organised self-help groups to assist each other in coping with a common problem or common condition.

Functionalism has traditionally formed the dominant perspective in the study of the family and wider social network of relatives and friends. This has been associated with an emphasis on the positive functions of the family both for the individual and for the social system, and a concern that the family in modern industrial society may be opting out of its responsibilities, including the care of its elderly and sick members. The recent rise of the feminist movement and of radical analyses of the family have been important in drawing attention to largely neglected issues relating to the dysfunctions of 'contradictions' of the family. This has focused attention on the adverse effects of family roles and relationships on health, and the wider implications for the status of women of their assumed responsibility in providing a caring role. These two distinct emphases in the analysis of the family are also apparent in the analysis of the growing numbers of self-help groups. Such groups have been praised and encouraged as a means of supplementing formal service provision and providing assistance and care which is superior in many ways to professional care. However, they have also been criticised for their effect in reducing pressures for changes in the professional health care system and promoting a victim-blaming ideology.

Social Ties and Informal Support

One main focus of attention in the study of the family and wider social network of relatives and friends has been their influence on professional help seeking and compliance with medical regimens. A notable attempt to develop theoretical links between the characteristics of social networks and individuals' health behaviour was provided by Freidson (see Chapter 3). Other issues which have received particular attention are policy oriented questions regarding the provision of informal care and its implications in terms of needs for formal services, and epidemiological questions of the effects of social ties on the onset and course of illness.

Caring for the Elderly and Chronically Sick

Concern that the family was losing its functions, including responsibility for the care of elderly and sick people, was prominent in functionalist writings of the 1950s and 1960s (Fletcher, 1966). This reflected the general belief in the decreasing importance of primary groups in modern industrial society conveyed by Durkheim (1893). Parsons (1943), and other classical theorists, as well as the increasing divorce rate and the growth of the welfare state. This belief in the loss of functions of the family has also formed a recurrent theme in government policy documents. As far back as 1832 the Report of the Royal Commission stated:

> The duty of supporting parents and children in old age or infirmity is so strongly enforced by our natural feelings, that it is well performed, even among savages, and almost always so in a nation deserving the name of civilised. We believed that England is the only European country in which it is neglected. (Report of the Royal Commission of 1832, Cmd 2728, 1905, p. 43 – quoted in Moroney, 1976)

In contrast to analyses which emphasise the changing nature and functions of primary groups, historical research based on parish records and census enumerators' books has suggested that the family structure characteristic of modern industrial society is remarkably similar to pre-industrial patterns. Contrary to popular belief, the isolated nuclear family, defined in terms of the nuclear family living apart from its wider kin, appears to have formed the dominant family pattern in pre-industrial England. Only about 10 per cent of households over the period between the sixteenth and nineteenth centuries included kin, although households were more likely to be extended to include kin and lodgers in the early industrial period (Anderson, 1971). The nuclear family household characteristic of modern industrial society thus appears to form a continuation of pre-industrial patterns, with the demands of the early industrial period causing a temporary change in household patterns. The major changes appear to have occurred not so much in the household group, as in the wider family network. Of particular significance is the decline in family size which has resulted in a smaller 'pool' of relatives, and the demands of industrialisation which have led to a greater geographical dispersion of households containing related people. Thus in general, networks have become more differentiated, including both kin and non-kin and extending over a considerable geographical area (Wellman, 1979). Nevertheless, local kinship ties are still evident, especially in relatively stable communities with low rates of mobility, such as mining communities, and among recently established ethnic minorities.

The question of the relative roles of the family and the state in the provision of care for the elderly and chronically sick has been examined by looking at the proportion of the population in institutional care. This appears to have been fairly stable over the course of the century, despite the growth of the welfare state. Since 1911 less than 5 per cent of elderly people in England and Wales have been resident in institutions at the time of the decennial census, and the rate of institutionalisation in the general population has consistently been under 2 per cent (Moroney, 1976). In the case of mentally handicapped people, there has been some increase in residential care compared with earlier this century. Even so, substantial numbers of severely mentally handicapped people are being cared for at home. In England and Wales, 1970, 52 per cent of severely mentally handicapped people (IQ less than 50) were living outside institutions, many of whom had a severe handicap or behaviour difficulty and required considerable supervision and assistance (Moroney, 1976). Similarly, Harris' National Survey carried out in Britain, 1968-69, showed that approximately 116,000 elderly people living in private households were severely handicapped, requiring help with most tasks. Despite their high level of dependency, 37 per cent of these people were not receiving any community services (Harris, 1971). The picture which emerges is thus of a fairly stable institutional population, with large numbers of dependent people being cared for at home.

The substantial numbers of people being cared for outside institutions reflects the outcome of social policies, which since the 1950s have promoted the principle of community care. The policy of caring for elderly and chronically ill people outside institutions was endorsed as a positive principle in the 1962 Hospital Plan (Ministry of Health, 1962) and in subsequent policy statements concerning the care of mentally ill and mentally handicapped people (see Chapter 6). Considerable confusion and uncertainty has however surrounded the meaning and aims of 'community care'. The term community care is often used by health authorities to refer to care, however provided, outside hospitals. However, a distinction which is frequently drawn is between care *in* the community by formal services, including in some cases residential provision, and care *by* the community in terms of the family and voluntary groups. In general, the shortage of formal services has meant that community care has largely consisted of care by the community. The recent statement on the policies and priorities for the health and social services in England (DHSS, 1981) confirmed community care as the major policy objective for the elderly, mentally ill, mentally handicapped and disabled people and children, as well as emphasising the role of the voluntary sector in the provision of such care.

The limited provision of services in the community for the care of dependency groups, means that priorities have to be assigned. As a result, those in receipt of community services, such as home-helps and meals-on-wheels, are overwhelmingly concentrated among people who live alone and who lack relatives, groups which consists largely of elderly single and childless widowed people. Besides relying more on domiciliary services, these groups are also heavily represented among people admitted to residential homes and among patients retained in hospital because of a lack of people to provide care at home (Morgan, 1980). Although current policy emphasises the care of dependency groups outside institutions and the role of the voluntary sector, it is acknowledged that there will always be a core of people who require long-term residential care, because of a combination of dependency, frailty and social circumstances (DHSS, 1981). Nevertheless, estimates of the size of the group requiring formal services, including institutional care, are likely to vary according to the interests and concerns of the parties involved. A recent study of public preferences for the care of dependency groups showed that the majority favoured a range of services involving various degrees of professional involvement, with only a minority advocating family and informal care alone (West *et al.*, 1984).

The 'Costs' of Family Based Care

Advocates of the extension of informal care generally emphasise the qualitative superiority of such care compared with professional services, and particularly institutional care. Although generally justified in humanitarian terms, the emphasis on family based care can also be viewed as a means of reducing the costs of care to the state (see Chapter 5). The provision of caring services by the state is necessarily costly in economic terms, while family and neighbourhood care is very cheap. However, the social costs to the family of caring for a chronically ill person on a continuing basis can be considerable. Also, in some instances the expectations of family members and the stresses and tensions within the family unit can have adverse consequences for the sick person.

In contrast to general notions of the functionality of family based care, the costs both to the sick person and to the family unit of caring for a chronically sick person at home were identified in an early paper by Parsons and Fox (1951). They pointed out that handling sickness outside the family serves to discourage illness in the first place. This is because family based care allows the sick person to enjoy his/her position in the family without having to fulfil normal role obligations. Furthermore, once ill, family based care may have an adverse effect on recovery because the intensive emotional involvement characteristic of family relationships may result in family members being more sympathetic and supportive of the sick person than they ought, thus encouraging the sick person to perpetuate his/her illness. Alternatively, family members may display an excessive intolerance with respect to the disabling features of illness, regarding them as signs of weakness and imposing overly harsh disciplinary sanctions. This in turn is as unfavourable to full and rapid recovery as over-permissiveness. Parsons and Fox also emphasised the adverse effects of family care for the family unit arising from altered role relationships and the effects of the claims of the sick members, which may give rise to jealousies and rivalries. Despite their emphasis on the fit between the nuclear family and the needs of industrial society, Parsons and Fox thus concluded that on the whole extra familial care of the sick person is positively functional for society.

The effects of the expectations and responses of the family on the sick person have since been demonstrated by a number of empirical studies. These have shown that a hostile environment and unrealistically high or low expectations of the sick person can have adverse effects on recovery, confirming Parsons' and Fox's theoretical analysis, although positive attitudes and support can exert a beneficial effect on health (see pp. 250–5). Other studies have drawn attention to the variety of social costs experienced by family members, and especially by the main carer, who tends to be the mother, or daughter in the case of an elderly widowed parent, with elderly spouses of both sexes forming important sources of mutual assistance and care. Some of the costs experienced by families caring for a mentally ill relative are shown in Table 1, while a more detailed study of the tensions and strains experienced by families caring for an elderly relative has been carried out by Nissel and Bonnerjea (1982).

Table 8.1: The Burden of the Family of Treating the Mentally Ill at Home

Effect on	Some disturbance	% of families Severe disturbance	Total burden
Health of closest relatives:			
mental	40	20	60
physical	28	—	28
Social and leisure activities of family	14	21	35
Children	24	10	34
Domestic routine	13	16	29
Income of family	14	9	23
Employment of others than the patient	17	6	23

Source: Sainsbury and Grad de Alarcon (1974).

Critiques of the family and of family based care have also extended beyond those offered by Parsons and Fox. In particular, whereas Parsons questioned the belief in the functionality of family based care for the social system, he did not question the prevailing division of labour between the sexes which assumes that women will perform the caring role. Parsons and Bales (1956) viewed the division of labour between the sexes as representing the natural outcome of biological differences. Women were seen as better suited to provide affective support because of their early biological tie with children, and men to perform the instrumental role in relating the family to society. The sexual division of labour was seen as ensuring family survival by establishing a mutual dependency between family members. They thus stressed the importance of family members being clear about their roles. However, even if smooth group functioning requires both instrumental and expressive role performance, the sex casting of roles is only one way of achieving this. Other analytical possibilities are: (a) both functions can be performed by the same person, as in the case of single-parent families; (b) tasks may be a mixture of both functions; (c) tasks may be performed by different people at different times according to the demands of the situation, as when two members share household tasks (Morgan, 1975). The allocation of women to the expressive caring role is viewed by feminist writers as justified in terms of biological differences rather than forming an inevitable product of biological differences. Radical feminists regard the division of labour between the sexes and the subordinate position of women as serving the interest of men, and as arising from, or at least justified in terms of, men's greater physical strength and women's role in reproduction. They differ from functionalists in that they regard these biological differences as problems to be overcome rather than a natural and inevitable difference in roles. In contrast to approaches which regard women's social role as determined by biology, marxist feminists explain women's position in economic terms. The division of labour within the nuclear family and the subordinate position of women is seen from this perspective as reflecting class interests and serving the needs of the capitalist economic system (pp. 230-1).

Informal Care: Pressures and Priorities

Policies toward the care of dependent people are currently surrounded by considerable pressures and constraints. The control of expenditure on health and personal social services, together with the increasing emphasis on personal responsibility, suggest there will be little overall increase in formal service provision, although there will be a greater emphasis on evaluating the cost and benefits of different forms of care. Demographic changes will produce increasing needs for care, with the numbers of very elderly people aged 85 and over expected to increase by a quarter of a million over the next twenty years. However, the large proportion of married women who are now gainfully employed (61 per cent of married women aged 45-59 were economically active in 1979, compared with only 33 per cent in 1961), together with the increasing pressure from the women's movement, are serving to question the traditional division of labour which is reflected in social policies. For example, there is currently considerable pressure to amend the Invalid Care Allowance introduced in 1976. This provides financial benefits to men and single women who give up paid employment, defined as earning less than £9 per week, in order to care for a sick or elderly relative. Married or cohabiting women are, however, not eligible for this benefit, although often having to give up their job to care for an elderly relative (Finch and Groves, 1982). Thus, on the one hand, the increasing numbers of dependent people and the limited resources devoted to the provision of formal services are likely to increase pressures on lay people to undertake a caring role. On the other hand, current trends suggest there will be a greater emphasis on the need to ensure that men and women do not suffer financially, or in the labour market, by taking time out to perform a caring role. Thus, whereas there has traditionally been a marked separation between the formal and informal sectors, there may be renewed attempts towards a greater integration to provide a solution to the 'problems of care'. An interesting example is the Kent Community Care Project which aims to provide a cost-effective package of care based on the interweaving of paid volunteers and statutory help (Davies and Challis, 1980).

Social Ties and Health

Attention has so far focused on one form of support, namely the provision of care for the elderly and long-term sick. The assistance, advice and emotional support provided by social ties may however also have more direct and wide-ranging effects on health. Research concerning the effects of social ties on health reflects a number of concerns and disciplinary perspectives, including epidemiology, clinical medicine, sociology and psychology. Some of this work draws attention to the adverse effects of social ties on health and well-being, and especially of close family relationships, although the dominant emphasis has recently been on the protective effects of social ties.

Critiques of the Family. The adverse effects of the family on individual health are often overlooked, associated with an unquestioning belief in the positive features of the family and of family life. However, the psychoanalytic tradition has drawn attention to the disharmonies of 'normal' family life and its implications for the individual. Rather than allowing the free expression of creativity, the family is seen from this perspective as constraining invididual choice and forming the most total of total institutions (Cooper, 1976). The potential consequences of such an environment are seen in a number of case studies presented by Laign and Esterson (1970), which suggest that many of the apparently bizarre and meaningless aspects of schizophrenic behaviour can be understood as meaningful in the context of the individual's family experiences and form a normal response to an oppressive environment.

Radical feminist analyses similarly draw attention to the adverse effects of the family for the individual. In particular, women's role within the family being identified not only as the source of their subordinate position and economic dependence but also as contributing to high rates of depressive conditions. The setting up of women's refuges as part of the women's movement has also highlighted the extent of domestic violence through enabling battered women to leave home, as well as having the effects of making the existence of battered women more socially visible (Binney, 1981).

Studies of Hospital Patients. These studies have examined the influence of the family environment and family attitudes on the course of illness. They suggest that family members may exert either a positive or negative effect on compliance with treatment regimens, postoperative recovery and adjustment to the psychological effects of surgery. The varying effects that social ties may have on the course of illness were illustrated by Litman's (1966) study of 100 orthopaedic patients undergoing rehabilitation. This showed that whereas positive family attitudes were associated with success in rehabilitation, negative attitudes were associated with poor response. This is reminiscent of Parsons' concern that the family may be overly protective and keep a person in a dependent sick role rather than encouraging normal functioning.

Particular aspects of the family environment which may have an adverse effect on the course of schizophrenic illness were identified in a study by Brown, Birley and Wing (1972) based on schizophrenic patients discharged from hospital. The family environment in the homes of these patients was measured using an index of expressed emotion based on five indicators: (a) number of critical comments made about someone else in the family; (b) presence or absence of hostility; (c) expressions of dissatisfaction; (d) warmth demonstrated towards the patient; and (e) emotional over-involvement with the patient.

A high level of expressed emotion as measured on this index was found to be significantly associated with the likelihood of relapse (see Table 8.2). This association held even when each of the indices of expressed emotion was examined separately. The asssociation between level of expressed emotion and rate of relapse was not explained by the age or sex of the patient, their previous occupational record, length of clinical history or type of illness. This suggests that the level of relatives' expressed emotion formed an independent factor contributing to relapse. Furthermore, the rate of relapse among patients with a high level of expressed emotion was found to be greater if they spent more than 35 hours per week in close contact with the family than if they had less contact. The researchers explain the observed relationship between expressed emotion and rate of relapse as being due to the adverse effects on schizophrenic patients of both over-stimulating and understimulating conditions.

Table 8.2: Relationship of Relatives' Emotion to Relapse in the Nine Months after Discharge from Hospital

Expressed emotion	Relapse		% Relapse
of relatives	No	Yes	
High	19	26	58
Low	47	9	16

Source: Brown, Birley and Wing (1972).

Community-based Studies of the Protective Effects of Social Ties. One of the earliest statistical analyses of the association between social ties and health is Durkheim's (1897) classic study of suicide. Durkheim drew attention to the relationship between people's degree of social integration and the suicide rate, and suggested that both social isolation and extremely tight social bonds increased risks of suicide. Subsequently, ecological studies provided evidence of an association between social disorganisation and rates of mental illness. A notable early study adopting an ecological approach to the study of mental illness was carried out by R. Faris and H.W. Dunham (1939). This study demonstrated a close association between type of social area and rates of mental hospital admission in Chicago. The higher rates of admission were in the deteriorated areas in and around the city. The authors originally discounted the drift process as forming a major cause for this concentration in rates, and instead adopted a social causation model. They proposed the hypothesis that:

> extended isolation of the person produces the abnormal traits of behaviour and mentality. If the various types of unconventional behaviours observed in different schizophrenic patients can be said to result from one condition, it appears that extreme seclusiveness may be that condition. The hallucinations, delusions, inappropriate action, illness and deterioration may all result from the fact that the

seclusive person is completely freed from the social control that enforces normality in other people. (pp. 173-4)

Recently, the general relationship between social ties and health has come to form a major area of epidemiological research. This is associated with an increasing acceptance of the general susceptibility model of disease, and in particular of the notion that stress may raise people's susceptibility to disease in general, while the support provided by social ties may modify the effects of stress. Groups frequently cited as having fewer social ties and relatively high mortality rates from a wide variety of conditions are unmarried compared with married people, and recent migrants compared with non-migrant populations. There is of course the problem of the direction of this relationship, for just as social ties may affect health, so health may also have a selective effect and influence the availability of social ties. For example, health may affect the chances of marriage or migration, while the experience of illness may restrict an individual's ability to create and maintain social ties, or even the desire for large numbers of ties and participation in social groups.

Longitudinal studies help overcome problems of establishing the direction of the relationship between social ties and health. The most notable survival study to examine this relationship is Berkman and Syme's (1979) nine-year follow-up of a random sample of nearly 5,000 adults, aged between 30 and 69. Information was obtained for this group on four sources of social contacts: marriage, contacts with close friends and relatives, church membership and informal and group associations. A low score on each of these measures at the beginning of the nine-year period was found to be associated with relatively high mortality rates, suggesting that a low level of social ties increased mortality risks. When the four separate measures were combined to form a Social Network Index (SNI), the mortality risks associated with a low score on the SNI were greater than for any single measure of support including marital status. The most isolated group of men, as measured on the SNI, had an age adjusted mortality rate 2.3 times higher than for men with the most connections, and for women it was 2.8 times higher than for those with most connections. The question of whether physical illness itself accounted for the relationship between the SNI and mortality rates was examined in two ways. Firstly, the relationship between the SNI and self reported health status at the baseline year of the study was examined. This showed the SNI to be associated with mortality rates for each of four health status groups. Similar percentages of people with most and least social connections were also found to have died in the first two years, suggesting physical illness was not responsible for the amount of social disconnection reported during the baseline survey. Secondly, an examination of the relationship between level of social connections and health practices (e.g. smoking, dietary habits, obesity, physical activities and use of preventive health services) showed at each health practice level the mortality gradient persisted among social network categories, although the magnitude of the differences was somewhat reduced. As the authors point out, if these two analyses employed valid and accurate indices of health status, they provide important evidence that the relationship between support and mortality is not merely a reflection of underlying poor health.

A second large group of studies has provided evidence of the protective effects of social ties among people experiencing life events, such as widowhood, unemployment, retirement and pregnancy. They have suggested that among people experiencing such events, those who are classified as 'supported' suffer fewer adverse health effects than the 'unsupported'. In one such study, Gore (1978) examined the health experience of men who had recently experienced involuntary redundancy in relation to their level of informal support. Support was measured on a 13-item index which focused on their relationships and social activities with their wife (if present), relatives and friends. Men in the lowest population tertile on this measure were designated as 'unsupported', and the others as 'supported'. Examination of the experiences of these groups over a two-year period showed there to be no differences with respect to weeks unemployed or actual economic deprivation. The main differences were that the unsupported group while unemployed reported more physical complaints, had higher scores on an index of depression and also showed physiological changes, such as higher serum cholesterol levels.

The question of whether support exerts a protective effect on health in the absence as well as in the presence of life events has been examined, based on samples selected without reference to their experience of life events. Respondents are then classified by level of support and the experience of life events, and the health of the different groups compared. These studies have generally shown a small but positive association between level of support and health (usually psychiatric symptoms) both in the presence and absence of life events. (Kasl, 1982) Precise comparisons between the results of the large number of studies examining this association between support and health are however difficult, due to differences not only in the populations studied and measures of health employed but also in the measurement of life events and support. In some cases life events are restricted to what are generally viewed as undesirable events, such as divorce, bereavement and job loss. In other cases, life events are defined in terms of life change and both desirable and undesirable changes included, on the assumption that all life changes is stressful and requires adjustment. The measures of support employed also take various forms but tend to emphasize either the quantity and sources of the individual's social contacts, or more qualitative aspects of support, in terms of the availability of people to confide in or turn to for assistance. However, little attempt is generally made to set these measures in a theoretical context and to hypothesize precise links between the specific measures of support employed and health outcomes.

A further methodological limitation of many epidemiological studies is the use of standard definitions of high and low levels of support which assume that individuals have similar needs for support. Likewise, it is assumed that life events have the same meaning for different people. Life event scores are thus calculated on the basis of the number of events experienced and the amount of adjustment they require (or their undesirability), with the degree of adjustment/undesirability associated with specific events being determined by prior experimental studies and expressed as standard weights. One widely used life event weighting scale is the Holmes-Rathe. Social readjustment Rating Scale (1967). This was constructed by asking a large number of people to score each of a list of life events according to the amount of readjustment they required on a scale from 0 to 100. Marriage with a score of 50 was given as a reference point for rating the other 41 events. The authors reported a high degree of consensus among respondents as to the relative influence of life events and so used the respondents' scores to produce a scale.

A second problem which characterises this approach is the tendency for variables to be confounded. For example, poor health may in itself give rise to other life changes which thus form a consequence rather than a cause of health problems. A large number of life events are also indicators of the loss of potential support resources through death, morbidity or role change, which in turn poses problems for the timing of the measurement of support (Thoits, 1982). In addition the experience of health problems may influence people's assessment of the availability of support, or cause a retrospective over-reporting of life events prior to the onset of illness so as to justify or 'make sense' of their illness.

A major contribution to research on the links between social ties and health has been made by Brown and Harris (1979) who pioneered new methods of measuring life events and support. In contrast to traditional epidemiological approaches which have assumed that social relationships and life events have a similar significance for all individuals and groups, Brown and Harris attempted to assess the meaning of social ties and life events for the individual. Information on respondents' social relationships, experience of life events, and other life circumstances, was obtained through in-depth interviews. Using this interview material raters then scored the respondents' degree of emotional intimacy, which formed the measure of support employed, and the experience of life events in terms of their duration, threat posed, etc., using standard criteria. This approach to eliciting the meaning of social ties and life events for the individual overcomes the problems of much qualitative research of not knowing the basis on which individual assessments have been made, as well as the problems of retrospective distortion.

Brown and Harris' (1979) study examined the effects of life events and support on risks of depression among a sample of women in Camberwell, of whom 16 per cent were found to be clinically depressed. They found that only life events rated as having long-term threatening implications were significantly related to depression. Such events generally involved a major potential or actual loss to the person, such as discovering a life threatening illness in someone close, finding our about a spouse's unfaithfulness or experiencing redundancy at work. They found that women who had experienced a severe life event were four times more likely to develop depression if they had no confidant or saw their confidants less than weekly, than if they had a close, intimate and confiding relationship with a husband or boyfriend (see Table 8.3). The lack of a confiding relationship was not however in itself associated with depression. This suggests that support only exerted a protective effect in the presence of life events, at least over the particular time period considered and in terms of the measure of health state employed. In contrast, other studies have indicated that support is also protective in the absence of life events. The question of whether support is protective only in the presence of specific life events or also serves to reduce the adverse health effects of long-term life stresses is thus still unclear. However, the observed relationship between support, stress and health is likely to be strongly influenced by the measures of support and health outcomes employed. A strong confiding relationship may be of particular importance in protecting people from depression on following a severe life event, whereas other forms of support may be of considerable importance on a longer-term basis.

Table 8.3: Percentage of Women in Camberwell who Suffered Onset of Depression By Whether They Had a Severe Event or Major Difficulty and Intimacy Context

	Intimacy		
	'a' (high)	'b'	'c' or 'd' (low)
	%	%	%
Severe event or major difficulty	10 (9/88)	26 (12/47)	14 (12/29)
No severe event or major difficulty	1 (2/193)	3 (1/39)	4 (1/23)

Source: Brown and Harris (1979).
'a' presence of a close, intimate, and confiding relationship with a husband or boyfriend.
'b' presence of a confiding relationship with someone else.
'c' all other women reporting a confidant who was seen less than weekly.
'd' those who mentioned none of the above.

Social Ties and Coping

Despite the large number of studies examining the association between social ties and health, relatively little attention has been given to explaining this association. This probably reflects the positivist, quantitative orientation of much of the work in this area. However, the concept of coping is most often identified as the mechanism by which support exerts a protective effect. Coping may be either adaptive, involving attitudes and behaviour which promote positive responses to changed circumstances, or maladaptive, giving rise to feelings of worthlessness, psychological distress and excessive dependence.

One way in which social ties may influence adaptive coping at a psychological level is through strengthening the individual's internal resources. The interactionist tradition suggests that this occurs through the effect of social ties on the individual's self concept, which is viewed as originating and sustained in social interaction. A second sociological tradition which links social ties to psychological well-being is provided by Durkheim's (1897) anomie theory. This suggests that the traditional and stable rules of conduct of socially cohesive groups give members a sense of certainty and purpose in living. Social integration is thus viewed as protecting a person against the uncertainty and despair that may itself lead to disordered functioning, as well as increasing the individual's ability to cope with crises.

Brown and Harris (1979), emphasising the psychological aspects of support, identified self esteem as the mechanism by which social ties exert a protective effect on coping ability. They identified three factors apart from the presence of a close, intimate and confiding relationship which are likely to influence self esteem and thus have a protective effect (or in their absence constitute a vulnerability factor) in determining risks of depression. These are: (1) employment, which affects self esteem by providing the role identity of worker, and by serving as a source of extra social contacts, which in turn may provide new personal identities; (2) having less than three children under 14 years at home, which is likely both to enable a woman to perform successfully in the role of mother and make it easier to spend time outside the home building new role identities; and (3) losing one's mother before the age of eleven. This may lead to enduring changes in the personality of the woman herself, and, in particular, may impart a greater risk of undergoing life experiences (such as having only a low level of intimacy) which increase vulnerability to illness.

A second way in which the psychological support provided by social ties may promote coping is through helping to modify the meaning of the problem or loss event in a manner that reduces its perceived threat. This occurs through talking things over with others, which helps to normalise situations and makes life events appear less unacceptable and more understandable. An example is the experience of 'grief work' which allows bereaved people to work through their grief, come to accept their loss and look forward towards new goals (Gerhardt, 1979). Such support may also exert a positive effect on adjustment and coping with chronic illness through reassuring the individual that their changed self is valued by others.

At a social level the coping resources provided by social ties consist of the provision of instrumental support and problem solving, with the aim of changing the situation rather than changing the meaning of the situation. This may involve finding new accommodation for a young mother living in overcrowded conditions, or assisting a widowed person in establishing a new pattern of life and gaining entry into new social groups. Whereas a few close ties providing strong emotional support may best facilitate coping at a psychological level, a large diverse network may best facilitate coping at a social level by providing access to many sources of information and a diversity of skills, thus drawing attention to what Granovetter (1973) has described as the strength of weak ties. In many cases people have high and low levels of different forms of support and may for example possess a few strong supportive ties but have a small network and low level of social contact (Morgan *et al.*, 1984). These people may differ in their ability to cope with different types of situations or stages of illness, although the precise influence of social ties and the differing needs of individuals for support are unclear.

It is often suggested that the onset of disease following life change is consequent on the absence of coping, and the absence of disease on the presence of coping. However, Gerhardt (1979) point out that this may not be the case, because coping is only effective in preventing disease (or promoting recovery) if it is adaptive, promoting positive responses. However coping responses may also be maladaptive in terms of their effect on health and functioning. They may, for example, discourage a return to normal role performances following illness or the formation of new social contacts and roles by the bereaved. The support provided by social ties may also have little impact in either direction if it is not compatible with the problem experienced. For example, emotional support may make little impact if what is needed is practical or financial assistance. Gerhardt also notes that opportunities for social coping may be limited not merely by the absence of social ties but also by the lack of economic resources. Differences in coping responses among social classes may, therefore, be due to differences in their material resources and living conditions, rather than to differences in the availability of psychological support. Gerhardt thus suggests that the low self esteem among women in Camberwell, which Brown and Harris (1979) identified as forming a product of a lack of intimate ties, may in fact represent a realistic response to their situation. In other words, working-class women may experience feelings of low self-esteem and an absence of psychological coping as a result of their lack of the material resources necessary to promote effective coping at a social level.

A third variable in addition to the social and psychological resources provided by social ties and the individual's material resources, which is frequently identified as promoting effective coping is the general psychological disposition of the individual. This is frequently conceptualised in terms of locus of control beliefs, or the extent to which individuals define events in their lives as under their control (an internal orientation) or are determined by forces outside themselves by luck, fate or chance (external orientation). The prevailing view is to regard people with an external orientation as less able to cope effectively with stress and therefore as more likely to experience physical and psychological distress than people with internal locus of control beliefs.

Promoting Health through Social Ties

The considerable attention paid to the association between social ties and health reflects the belief that one way of improving health may be to strengthen or increase supportive social ties. This may involve attempts to influence the quality of existing social ties. For example, patients' families may be 'educated' to ensure they hold realistic attitudes and expectations which will promote recovery and assist normal functioning, and services provided to reduce the strains and tensions experienced by families caring for a dependent person. An alternative approach is to increase opportunities for social contacts, through reducing barriers to general social participation, and encouraging the setting up of clubs and organisations to cater for specific needs, such as home visiting schemes, self help groups, and counselling services. Although such measures may create a situation which provides an opportunity for the development of new social ties, this will not in itself ensure that such ties are developed or maintained. In many cases people may not desire to extend their social ties. For example, disengagement theory postulates a mutual withdrawal of the elderly person and society, during which process the individual may enter a new state of equilibrium and maintain a high level of morale (Lowenthal and Boler, 1965). In other cases an individual's personality disposition or health state may reduce his/her desire or ability to create new social ties.

The approach of promoting health through strengthening and increasing social ties forms an individualistic response and can be criticised for diverting attention from stressors, such as the experience of unemployment, financial or housing problems, and role dissatisfaction, which form the underlying risk factors. Emphasis on the importance of social supports may also divert attention from the importance of material resources in promoting adaptive coping. In many cases informal support may only be effective in conjunction with the ability to marshal material resources. Thus, differences between social groups in their susceptibility to illness may reflect not only a lack of supportive ties but also a greater exposure to stressors, differences in internal coping resources, and differences in material resources. The possibility of promoting health through extending people's social ties and the criticisms of this approach are considered further in the next section in relation to the characteristics and functions of self help groups.

Self Help Health Groups

Self help groups, based on the principle of mutual aid, often supplement and complement the informal support provided by relatives and friends. These groups have seen a rapid expansion over the last thirty years, with one of the earliest and most influential being Alcoholics Anonymous, which began with two members in 1935 and now reports over 30,000 branches throughout the world with more than 600,000 members. It is difficult to obtain precise figures on the total numbers and membership of self help groups because of the fluctuations in membership as groups become established or decline and the problems of determining whether particular groups come within the category of a self help group. However it is estimated that over one million individuals are actively involved in self help groups in the United States, and a directory published in 1977 lists 233 different types of self help groups in Britain concerned with health problems and health related conditions (Robinson and Robinson, 1979). These include groups for people with various types of addictions, such as gamblers, smokers and drug addicts; groups for people with various physically disabling conditions, as well as for people with abnormal mental attitudes, such as feelings of chronic depression, guilt or fear; and groups for those with socially deviant behaviour such as homosexuals and child batterers. There are also groups for those whose problems stem from other people's problems, such as the families of alcoholics and gamblers, and for those with an abnormal personal situation, such as being divorced or a single parent, and many more besides.

Characteristics of Self Help Groups

Self help groups are characterised by considerable diversity in terms of their origins, activities, philosophies and organisational structures, as well as catering for people with a wide variety of needs. As Robinson and Henry (1977) observed, 'self help is not a unitary phenomenon with a universally agreed definition, arising from a simple set of circumstances for particular kinds of people, in readily identified situations. Self help is merely a phrase that has conveniently come to stand for a very loose collection of ideas, organisations and activities.' Research into self help groups, as with early work on the professions, has placed considerable emphasis on defining self help groups and identifying their key characteristics or attributes. The great number and diversity of self help groups has however led to a situation in which there have been almost as many attempts to define self help groups as there are groups.

Killilea (1976) attempted to draw together the main features of self help groups which appeared to be most commonly stressed in the literature and identified seven features of self help groups and their processes to which researchers have given particular emphasis. These she lists as:

(1) Common experience of members: the belief that the care giver has the same disability as the care receiver.

(2) Mutual help and support: the fact that the individual is a member of a group that meets regularly in order to provide mutual aid.

(3) The helper principle: this draws attention to the fact that in a situation in which people help others with a common problem it may be the helper who benefits most from the exchange.

(4) Differential association: this emphasises the reinforcement of self concepts of normality, which hastens the individuals' separation from their previous deviant identities.

(5) Collective willpower and belief: the tendency of each person to look to others in the group for validation of his/her feelings and attitudes.

(6) Importance of information: the promotion of greater factual understanding of the problem condition.

(7) Constructive action toward shared goals: the notion that groups are action oriented, their philosophy being that members learn by doing and are changed by doing.

Some combination of these seven characteristics is generally identified as forming the essence of a self help group, with primary emphasis often being given to the fact that the groups are run wholly or largely by their own members who provide each other with mutual help and support. However, not all groups are completely self run, with many having particular functions allocated to non-members and professionals. As a result, difficulties often arise in determining the dividing line between a self help group and a professional organisation or agency. How many paid counsellors and staff, for example, can be employed for a group still to be regarded as a self help group? Killilea (1976) restricts her discussion of self help groups to the 'more or less formal, more or less structured, non-professional mutual aid groups which are problems or predicament focused', and thus excludes formal voluntary associations. In contrast, Tracy and Gussow (1976) adopt a broader definition and include not only groups which provide direct services to sufferers and their relatives through mutual assistance but also organisations such as the National Association for Mental Health and the Association for Vaccine Damaged Children, which emphasise the promotion of research, fund raising and public or professional campaigns and pressure group activities.

The difficulty in determining what is and what is not a self help group appears to be shared by the groups themselves. Over 150 groups and organisations described as 'self help' by various directories, information agencies, newspapers and magazines were sent a short letter with a request for information. In response many explained that they did not view themselves as a self help group and a small number of groups were unsure what they were. As the researchers commented, 'Many organisations, then, appear to be doing things that other groups would certainly take to be self help and yet were reluctant to describe themselves as self help groups' (Robinson and Henry, 1977). Of groups who regarded themselves as self help groups the one feature given almost universal emphasis was that the group was run wholly or largely by its own members.

Systems of classification have been developed for ordering the vast number and types of self help groups. Like definitions, classifications of self help groups are many and varied. Writers typically organise the range of groups and organisations falling under their definition of self help around a small number of selected criteria, so as to produce anything between two and five types. The criterion most commonly emphasised is the primary focus of the group or the kind of problem the group handles. Two examples of such systems of classification are those put forward by Levy (1976), who distinguishes four types of groups, and Katz and Bender's (1976) fivefold classification (Figure 8.1). One problem of such classifications is that many groups do not fit neatly into one particular category, for systems of classification are abstractions which may not exist in pure form. Recognising this problem Katz and Bender (1976) included in their classification a 'mixed' category to cater for groups which did not have the predominant focus of any of their other types of groups. In a more recent paper Katz (1979) adopted a different approach and identified a continuum along which groups may be placed, and which he believes affects, or even determines, their structural properties (Figure 8.1).

Figure 8.1: Examples of typologies of self help groups

Author: Levy (1976)   Katz and Bender (1976)
Criteria: Purposes & composition of group.
Types of groups

1. Groups that aim to manage a problem   1. Self fulfilment or personal
   behaviour (e.g. alcoholism, drug   growth.
   addiction)
2. Groups whose members share a   2. Social advocacy
   common situation and who want to
   ameliorate the stress of this (e.g.
   single parent families)
3. Groups comprised of people labelled   3. Alternative living
   as deviant (e.g. homosexuals, dwarfs)
4. Groups whose members share the goal   4. Outcasts or people at 'rock
   of 'personal growth, self actualisation   bottom'
   and enhanced effectiveness in living
   and loving, (e.g. some of the women's   5. Mixed types — shares
   groups, various collectivess and   characteristics of two or
   communes)   more groups

Author: Katz (1979)
Criteria: Characteristics that significantly affect (or even determine) the struc-
          tural properties of groups.
Dimensions of groups:
1. The nature and intensity of the group's ideology — continuum from groups
   with a rigidly enforced belief system about the problem they deal with, to
   groups with a variety of ideologies, to those with little or no ideology.
2. Attitude toward professional help givers and agencies — continuum from
   outright rejection, to limited acceptance, to complete acceptance and
   cooperation.
3. Degree of identification with or rejection of the dominant society and its
   values — continuum as for (2) above
4. Degree to which it employs such democratic practices as the rotation of
   leadership and the division of labour, as contrasted with the centralisation of
   power.

Growth of Self Help Groups

Groups based on the principle of mutual aid have probably existed throughout history. From the Middle Ages onwards they have been shown to have provided for a wide variety of needs and not merely physical survival, while during the early industrial period the Friendly Societies were of particular importance in providing for the elderly, the sick and the infirm (Katz and Bender, 1976). Although self help groups are not new they have enjoyed an unprecedented growth during the last thirty years, a period which has also seen the proliferation of the helping professions and of social welfare legislation.

One explanation for the recent expansion of self help groups is that they form part of a more general protest against the dominant values and institutions in our society. A small number of groups, particularly the self help groups organised by the women's movement, and some of the groups established by the gay liberation movement and by disabled people, clearly come within this category.

A more common functionalist explanation of the expansion of self help groups, which focuses on their role in social provision, is to view these groups as arising to meet needs which are not catered for by the existing institutions. One type of need arises from the inadequacies of existing medical services. Two groups of people especially neglected by these services are those suffering from alcoholism, obesity and other conditions, which have never come fully within the medical sphere, and the increasing numbers of people with chronic conditions who often receive little assistance in adapting to and coping with their disability once the acute phase of the illness has passed. The creation of self help groups as a direct response to gaps in service provision is illustrated by the formation of groups to cater for people with new types of chronic conditions. For example, ostomy clubs sprang up simultaneously in a number of American cities in the early 1950s within a few years after ileostomy surgery began to be performed regularly, to help cope with rehabilitation and with the management of daily problems made necessary by the surgery. Today there are over one hundred ostomy clubs in North America and branches on four other continents, while groups for patients who have undergone heart surgery and laryngectomy have a similar history (Robinson and Henry, 1977). A second type of need regarded as explaining the rise of self help groups is the feeling of isolation, loss of identity and rootlessness associated with the process of industrialisation and the growth of bureaucracy. Groups for those who share a similar situation, such as being a lone parent, the wife of a prisoner, the parents of a handicapped child or a person with a stigmatised condition such as epilepsy or dwarfism, are seen as providing an alternative form of coping and security to that offered by the traditional support systems. Thus self help groups have been described as 'the emerging church of the twenty-first century' (Mowrer, 1971).

Two points need to be borne in mind in relation to the types of explanations of the expansion of self help groups outlined above. Firstly, although a conceptual distinction can be drawn between self help groups that form part of and arise from a general protest movement and groups whose development and activities can be explained in terms of the gaps in existing institutions, in reality groups often encompass both goals, although differing in their relative emphasis. On occasions individual group members may even be found to differ in their perceptions of the primary function of the group. This is illustrated by a study of a women's refuge which showed there to be no consensus as to the primary aim of the Centre. Some voluntary workers, the 'radicals', saw it as part of a social movement to help change the position of women in society, while other workers, the 'reformers', saw it as a social provision, being one of several possible types of accommodation which might be provided for battered women and their children (Pahl, 1979). Secondly, although the expansion of self help groups can be explained as the response to a common situation or common problem, it is also necessary to explain why the response took the form of setting up a self help group rather than some other course of action. Reasons given for the self help response in the health care field are the increasing emphasis on individual responsibility for health, and the growing consumer movement. This movement developed in the 1960s and was formally acknowledged in the setting-up of organisations such as the Patients' Association in 1963, and the Community Health Councils, following the reorganisation of the NHS in April 1974. Another factor regarded as stimulating a self help response is the increasing recognition of the limits to the knowledge and expertise of the medical profession and their ability to help people to cope with their everyday lives.

The question of why self help groups are more prevalent in the United States than in Western Europe has been explained in terms of the differences in attitudes and values between the two societies. These include the greater emphasis on the individual's responsibility for their own destiny and development in the USA, together with differences in health and welfare provision. Social service provision in the United States is also more punitive in nature and carries a heavier stigma, while long-term medical care often involves the individual in considerable personal expense. As a result, self help groups may be a more favourable alternative to professional services in the USA than in Western Europe and are also more likely to remain apart from the state. Differences in the activities of the women's health movement between the two countries, particularly the fact that women's health clinics are largely confined to the USA, can also be explained in terms of differences in their health care systems and thus in the context in which responses occur. In Britain, where health treatment is free at the time of consumption, alternative services always run the risk of appearing to promote private medicine. Thus an important aspect of the women's health movement in Britain has been the defence of the NHS, and particularly the provision of services for women under the NHS, whereas the establishing of women's health clinics in the USA merely adds to the varied provision which already exists.

Development of Self Help Groups

On the basis of a study of the self help origins of several professionally staffed associations, Katz (1970) identified five phases of the development of self help groups: (1) origins by disadvantaged persons and relatives; (2) informal organisation spread through friends and acquaintances; (3) emergence of leaders; (4) formal organisation through rules and by-laws; and (5) the use of professional methods and staff. However he notes that not all self help groups develop to the point of a formal organisation and professionalisation and that many are able to maintain their original characteristics. An important determinant of whether groups do maintain their original structure and emphasis on mutual aid, which involves the helper being one of the helped, or whether they drift towards professionalisation and bureaucratisation, appears to be whether they embrace mainstream social values or seek to challenge prevailing values. This is associated with differences in the extent to which professional bodies seek to promote their activities and provide funding. The acceptance of outside funding in turn forms one of the main pressures to professionalise.

A study of the Fellowship, a self help group for alcoholics, demonstrated how the acceptance of outside funds led to a need to budget, document activities and expenditures and conform with tax laws, which in turn led to the employment of full-time administrators and personnel (Lusky and Ingram, 1979). This gave rise to a division between expert and client and to the identification of core members as 'counsellors' and newcomers as 'clients'. Such clients were the largely passive recipients of counsellor expertise rather than participants in a collective search for solutions to common problems. Secondly, a process of goal displacement was apparent, characterised by an increased concern with the quantity of services delivered to clients in the programme rather than with the quality of the content of the programme. This was associated with what Goffman (1961) has called 'institutional display' — the tendency to make use of facilities, open-houses or cultivated inmates or clients to project a satisfactory public image. Recognising the danger that the fundamental characteristics and effectiveness of self help groups will be lost with the acceptance of formal funding and all this entails, the Alcoholics Anonymous groups have a fairly strict policy about the acceptance of funds. An important question is whether the increasing professionalisation and formalisation described by Lusky and Ingram in relation to the Fellowship necessarily accompanies the acceptance of outside funds. It may be that this process can be avoided by groups categorised as socially conforming through practices such as deliberate leadership rotation.

Whereas Katz (1970) depicted the process of development of self help groups from their inital origin to professionalisation, a pronounced feature of self help groups is often their short life. This is associated with the important role of a few individuals who often display charismatic leadership in the creation and early stages of the group. After the departure of such a leader difficulties often occur in the group. Unless new leaders with similar qualities emerge, the group may disintegrate, or possibly continue in a changed form. In many cases the spontaneous commitment to a cause is replaced by 'the routinisation of charisma', characterised by a tendency for organisations to become goals in themselves (Gerth and Wright Mills, 1964).

Functions for Individual Members

Most self help groups perform four main functions for their members, although the ways these are achieved and the broader aims of groups vary widely. These functions are: (1) the provision of emotional support both to the individual sufferer and to their family; (2) the provision of information and services; (3) the provision of opportunities for forming friendships and becoming involved in activities which contribute to the running of the group; (4) changing attitudes and values which involves attempts at the individual level to destigmatise a problem by changing members' self conception, as well as attempts to change wider social attitudes and possibly influence social provision by pressing for changes in legislation, financial benefits and services.

Few self help groups have been subject to evaluative studies, while their effectiveness in controlling alcoholism or other addictions or phobias is frequently questioned by the medical profession. The value and success of self help groups ought not, however, to be judged solely in conventional medical terms, for other important functions are to enhance people's feelings of self worth and reduce their sense of isolation and alienation. It is also important to consider the effectiveness of self help groups in a wider context, with the criteria of success being not only the quality and effectiveness of their provision for individual members but also their implications for the wider society and health care system.

Self Help Groups as Agents of Change

Some self help groups actively seek to promote social change and can be regarded as forming a social movement, in that they share a common ideology, and are organised and act to achieve their goals. The women's health movement is generally viewed as the prime example of a social movement in the health field. This forms an extension of the women's liberation struggle into the area of health and medicine and shares its ideological base. As Ehrenreich and English (1976) explain:

> The medical system is strategic for women's liberation. It is the guardian of reproductive technology — birth control, abortion and the means of safe childbirth. It holds the promise of freedom from hundreds of unspoken fears and complaints that have handicapped women throughout history.

The women's health movement exhibits a considerable sense of common purpose, with the varied targets of the women's movement, including the restriction of abortion, the conventional gynaecological examination, childbirth procedures and increasing surgery, serving to unite large numbers of women. The women's health movement has also been successful in attaining recognition as a distinct movement and in influencing professional programmes and attitudes. Specific activities of the women's health movement include the setting up of small self help groups teaching self examination, sharing knowledge, and in some cases challenging so-called 'objective' clinical knowledge. Other activities, particularly in the United States, have been the setting up of women's health clinics which seek to redefine roles in medicine and provide a different type of service from that of the conventional medical system. The doctor's role in feminist clinics is confined to specifically medical tasks, such as prescribing drugs and performing abortions. Much of the patients' contact is with lay women who administer the clinics and provide counselling. The patients themselves are also encouraged to participate in the non-medical tasks involved in medical practice, as well as playing an active role in their own treatment. The effects of the women's health movement in modifying the wider health care system is still unclear and will depend on the extent to which it can maintain its momentum. Few other self help groups which actively seek to promote change have as solid an ideological base, or as fully developed a structure and organisation as the women's health movement, although they may possess the essential conditions for the development of such a movement (Schiller and Levin, 1983).

The question of the effects of the vast number of self help groups, whose primary aim is one of social provision, in promoting change in the health care system is subject to competing interpretations. Sidel and Sidel (1977), Crawford (1977) and other writers adopting a conflict perspective view such groups as serving to maintain the status quo and of limiting possibilities for fundamental change. The Sidels (1977) identify three main ways in which self help groups may inhibit change. Firstly, medical self help groups may help to perpetuate the basic inequalities which characterise society and its health care system. This arises through their effect in relieving some of the pressure on society to provide preventive services, which in turn may help perpetuate the disparities between resources devoted to care and prevention. In addition, through involving only those who are most actively interested, drawn predominantly from the middle classes, rather those hardest to reach, self help groups may expand areas of inequality of access to care. A second feature of self help groups is their emphasis on individual symptoms and problems. The Sidels claim that this has the effect of further fragmenting individuals, families and communities, by encouraging people to seek help from those with whom they have little in common apart from a shared problem, and that it also serves to promote the medicalisation of life by emphasising problems, rather than regarding them as an integral part of total human and community life. A third feature of self help groups identified as a major factor limiting possibilities for change is their focus on individual deviance from the norm. This is viewed as placing the burden increasingly on the individual to modify his or her response rather than on society to modify the conditions which create the response. The Sidels conclude that, 'This can turn into simply another way of society's "blaming the victim" rather that attempting to change the conditions which have vitimized him'.

An alternative approach has been to welcome the reforms initiated by self help groups to a system which is viewed as in need of modification, rather than requiring a fundamental change in power relations. Katz (1979), who adopts this view, emphasises the way in which self help groups have influenced public policy, through, for example, the lobbying for public funding of dialysis or chronic renal patients in the United States and the adoption of mass screening of infants. While agreeing that members of self help groups are recruited mainly from the middle class, he thus argues that the effects of group activities extend more widely. Katz also takes issue with the notion of self help groups as adopting a 'victim blaming' ideology, pointing to the many different ideologies and approaches characterising self help groups. In particular Katz and Levin (1980) argue that one of the most pervasive components of these self help ideologies is the possibility of increasing individual awareness of the threats arising from external sources, as well as from individual behaviour patterns. This they believe is likely to lead to remedial actions to reduce threats of both kinds. Katz and Levin thus argue that, rather than diverting attention away from important struggles as critics of self help groups suggest, 'Participation in self care and self help groups becomes a specific antidote to passivity, apathy and dependency in the health care area' (Katz and Levin, 1980). Although acknowledging that there are dangers surrounding the self care and self help movement, they therefore conclude that it is likely to exert a beneficial effect on the health care system.

In general the medical profession appears to view self-help groups in reformist terms as a valuable complement to the formal health-care system. Thus many have been influential in encouraging and assisting the development of individual groups, to the extent that such groups may come to be viewed as posing a challenge to the existing health-care system, following the example of the feminist clinics in the USA. The medical profession may however exert its authority as the recognised experts, and insist on supervising and controlling their activities, thus limiting their scope for forming an effective vehicle of radical change.

The increasing financial strategy in the health sector and rising demands for care will continue to produce pressures for the greater involvement of lay people, in the provision of informal assistance and care, whether to family members or a neighbourhood or on self-help basis. However, critics of this approach are likely to become increasingly vocal in drawing attention to the social costs of such care and its effects in limiting pressures towards more adequate formal provision or in promoting a victim blaming approach to health problems.

References

Anderson, M. (1971) 'Family, household and the industrial revolution', in M. Anderson (ed.), *Sociology of the Family*, Penguin Books, Harmondsworth, Middlesex

Berkman, L. and Syme, L. (1979) 'Social networks, host resistance and mortality: a nine year follow-up study of Alameda county residents', *American Journal of Epidemiology*, *109*, 186–204

Binney, V. (1981) 'Domestic violence: battered women in Britain in the 1970s', in the Cambridge Women's Studies Group, *Women in Society: Interdisciplinary Essays*, Virago Press, London

Brown, G.W., Birley, J. and Wing, A. (1972) 'The influence of family life on the course of schizophrenic disorders: a replication', *British Journal of Psychiatry*, *121*, 241-58

Brown, G.W. and Harris, T. (1979) *The Social Origins of Depression*, Tavistock, London

Cooper, D. (1976) *The Death of the Family*, Penguin Books, Harmondsworth, Middlesex

Crawford, R. (1977) 'You are dangerous to your health: the ideology and politics of victim blaming', *International Journal of Health Services*, *7*, 663-79

Davies, B. and Challis, D. (1980) 'Experimenting with new roles in domiciliary service', *The Geronotologist*, *20*, 287

DHSS (1981) *Care in Action: A Handbook of Policies and Priorities for the Health and Personal Social Services in England*, HMSO, London

Durkheim, E. (1983) *The Division of Labour in Society*, Macmillan, London (1934)

Durkheim, E. (1897) *Suicide*, Free Press, New York (1951)

Ehrenreich, B. and English, D. (1976) *Complaints and Disorders*, Feminist Press, New York

Faris, R. and Dunham, H.W. (1939) *Mental Disorders in Urban Areas*, University Press, Chicago

Finch, J. and Grove, D. (1982) 'Community care and the family: a case for equal opportunities', *Journal of Social Policy*, *9*, 487-511

Fletcher, R. (1966) *The Family and Marriage in Britain*, Penguin Books, Harmondsworth, Middlesex

Gerhardt, V. (1979) 'Coping and social action: theoretical reconstuction of the life event approach', *Sociology of Health and Illness*, *1*, 195-225

Gerth, H.H. and Wright Mills, C. (1964) in Max Weber (ed.), *Essays in Sociology*, Routledge and Kegan Paul, London

Goffman, E. (1961) *Asylums: Essays on the Social Situation of Mental Patients and Other Inmates*, Doubleday and Co., New York

Gore, S. (1978) 'The effect of social support in moderating the health consequences of unemployment', *Journal of Health and Social Behaviour*, *19*, 157-65

Granovetter, M. (1973) 'The strength of weak ties', *American Journal of Sociology*, *78*, 13-60

Harris, A. (1971) *Handicapped and Impaired in Great Britain* (OPCS Social Survey Division, HMSO, London

Holmes, T.H. and Rahe, R.H. (1967) 'The social readjustment rating scale', *Journal of Psychosomatic Research*, *11*, 213-17

Hunt, A. (1978) *The Elderly at Home* (OPCS Social Survey Division, HMSO, London

Kaplan, B., Cassel, J. and Gore, S. (1977) 'Social support and health', *Medical Care*, *15*, 47-58

Kasl, S. (1982) 'Social and psychological factors affecting the course of disease: an epidemiological perspective', in D. Mechanic (ed.), *The Handbook of Health: Health Care and the Health Professions*, Free Press, Riverside, N.J.

Katz, A. (1970) 'Self help organisations and volunteer participation in social welfare', *Social Work*, *15*, 551-60

Katz, A. (1979) 'Self help groups: some clarifications', *Social Science and Medicine*, *13a*, 491-4

Katz, A. and Bender, E.I. (1976) *The Strength in Us: Mutual Aid Groups in the Modern World*, Franklin Watts, New York

Katz, A. and Levin, L. (1980) 'Self care is not a solipsistic trap: a reply to critics', *International Journal of Health Services*, *10*, 329-36

Killilea, M. (1976) 'Mutual help organisations: interpretations in the literature', in G. Caplan and M. Killilea (eds.), *Support Systems and Mutual Help*, Grune and Stratton Inc., New York

Laign, R. and Esterson, A. (1970) *Sanity, Madness and the Family*, Penguin Books, Harmondsworth, Middlesex

Levy, L. (1976) 'Self help groups: types and psychological processes', *Journal of Applied Behavioural Science*, *12*, 310-22

Litman, T.J. (1966) 'The family and physical rehabilitation', *Journal of Chronic Diseases*, *19*, 211-17

Lowenthal, M. and Boler, D. (1965) 'Voluntary vs involuntary social withdrawal', *Journal of Gerontology*, *20*, 363-7

Lusky, R. and Ingram, R. (1979) 'The pros, cons and pitfalls of self help rehabilitation programs', *Social Science and Medicine*, *13a*, 113-21

Ministry of Health (1962) *Hospital Plan for England and Wales*, HMSO, London

Morgan, D. (1975) *Social Theory and the Family*, Routledge and Kegan Paul, London

Morgan, M. (1980) 'Marital status, health, illness and service use', *Social Science and Medicine*, *14a*, 633-43

Morgan, M., Patrick, D. and Charlton, J. (1984) 'Social networks and psychological support among disabled people', *Social Science and Medicine*, *19*, 489-97

Moroney, R. (1976) *The Family and the State*, Longman, London

Mowrer, O. (1971) 'Peer groups in medication: the best "therapy" for laymen and professionals alike', *Psychotherapy: Theory, Research and Practice*, *8*, 44-54

Nissel, M. and Bonnerjea, L. (1982) *Family Care of the Handicapped Elderly: Who Pays*? Policy Studies Institute, London

Pahl, J. (1979) 'Refuges for battered women: social provision or social movement?', *Journal of Voluntary Action Research*, *8*, 25-35

Parsons, T. (1943) 'The kinship system of the contemporary United States', reprinted in Parsons, *Essays in Sociological Theory*, (rev. edn.), Free Press, New York (1964)

Parsons, T. and Bales, R. (1956) *The Family, Socialisation and Interaction Process*, Routledge and Kegan Paul, London

Parsons, T. and Fox, R. (1951) 'Illness, therapy and the modern urban family', *Journal of Social Issues, 8*, 31-44

Robinson, D. and Henry, S. (1977) *Self Help and Health: Mutual Aid for Modern Problems*, Martin Robertson, London

Robinson, D. and Robinson, Y. (1979) *From Self Help to Health*, Concord Books, London

Sainsbury, P. and Grad de Alarcon, J. (1974) 'The cost of community care and the burden on the family of treating the mentally ill at home', in D. Lees and S. Shaw (eds.), *Impairment, Disability and Handicap*, Heinemann, London

Schiller, P. and Levin, L. (1983) 'Is self care a social movement?', *Social Science and Medicine, 17*, 1343-82

Seebohm Report (1968) *Report of the Committee on Local Authority and Allied Personal Social Services*, HMSO, London

Sidel, V. and Sidel, R. (1977) 'Primary care in relation to socio-political structure', *Social Science and Medicine, 11*, 415-19

Thoits, P. (1982) 'Conceptual, methodological and theoretical problems in studying social support as a buffer against life stress', *Journal of Health and Social Behaviour, 23*, 145-59

Tracey, G. and Gussow, Z. (1976) 'Self help groups: a grass roots response to a need for services', *Journal of Applied Behavioural Science, 12*, 381-96

Wellman, B. (1979) 'The community question: the intimate networks of East Yorkers', *American Journal of Sociology, 84*, 1201-31

West, P., Illsley, R. and Kelman, H. (1984) 'Public preferences for the care of dependency groups', *Social Science and Medicine, 18*, 287-95

9 FUTURE DIRECTIONS

Attempts to speculate as to the future directions of sociological research in the field of health and medicine, as in other areas of enquiry, must necessarily examine the variety of forces which affect the nature and direction of research. One major influence is the perception of 'problems' by doctors and policy makers and the prevailing policies and approaches to health, which affect the priorities identified for research and the allocation of funds by policy oriented organisations. A second major influence derives from more general sociological concerns and the interests and orientations of sociologists themselves, which determines the nature of theoretical developments, as well as influencing the general approaches and perspectives employed.

In Britain the Department of Health and Social Security and the Scottish Home and Health Department form the major sources of funding for 'health services' research. In line with other government departments they have increasingly sought to mould research more closely to the needs of policy makers, and in the early 1970s adopted the system of research organisation advocated by the influential Rothschild Report (1971). This Report introduced the customer-client principle as a means by which research could be linked more closely to policy. It stated that for applied research to be funded it must have a named customer (a government department or one of its divisions), and in essence, 'the customer says what he wants, the contractor does it (if he can), and the customer pays'. In practice, however, proposals for funded research have often been put forward by researchers, and policy divisions then sought as a customer, rather than research being commissioned directly by the policy divisions.

The cut-backs in research funding which appear to be a feature of the 1980s compared with the 'golden years' of the 1970s, together with the current emphasis on the efficient allocation of resources, suggests that research funding may become even more closely tied to the perceived needs of policy makers over the next decade. New mechanisms of research commissioning and review may possibly contribute to this process. In view of the responsive role of much research, some indication of future areas of research activity can be gained by examining what appear to be the perceived problems and

279

approaches that currently characterise the health field. However, it is important to remember that changes in a government's philosophy, the spread of new diseases, changes in the economy and other external factors may produce unanticipated changes in perceptions of the main problems and priorities facing the health service.

A major challenge currently perceived as facing the NHS is that the money made available by the government for health services, although fairly constant in real terms, is increasingly stretched in the face of growing demands for its use, with a major factor contributing to these increasing demands being the development of new high cost technology. As Chapter 6 showed, the dominant approach to this problem is to attempt to deploy resources more efficiently and effectively, so as to achieve a greater return for a given outlay. Emphasis is also given to diverting costs from the NHS, through increasing direct costs to the consumer in higher prescription charges and enabling the private health care sector to develop. These trends suggest that social scientists will increasingly be asked to conduct evaluational studies to assist in the choice of policy options. This may include assessing the cost and benefits of different types of treatment, including the evaluation of developments in high technology medicine and possibly of alternative treatments, such as acupuncture and homoeopathy; the assessment of the costs and benefits of different forms of care, especially for dependency groups, and the assessment of the implications of possible changes in management, such as the introduction of a greater control of budgets by consultants and general practitioners, and of more formal medical review procedures. The impact of privately, compared with publicly, financed schemes is also likely to become a major topic for study, as will experiments in joint funding between the public and private sector. An example of such joint funding which may pave the way for further collaboration is the agreement to share between the NHS and a private health insurance company the costs of a lithotripter to treat patients with kidney stones.

Evaluational studies have mostly been the preserve of epidemiologists and economists. The increasing consideration given to social costs and benefits, and to patient satisfaction, as well as to the social and psychological components of health and well-being, is however likely to result in the increasing participation of sociologists and psychologists in these types of studies. In addition, this work is in itself likely to open up new areas of enquiry. For example, the development of measures of outcome to be used in assessing interventions for chronic disease may encourage further research to understand more clearly the socio-psychological effects and meanings of these conditions, and of the treatment process, to patients. The evaluation of procedures for treating acute conditions may also stimulate research examining the patterns of organisation and decision-making in acute specialities, which have so far received relatively little attention. Similarly, hospital costing studies may lead to further research into professional relationships, with a view to promoting organisational change and hence to increasing the efficiency and effectiveness of resource use*.

A second area which is likely to receive increased attention, in view of the current emphasis on personal prevention and responsibility, is the promotion of healthy life styles. Smoking has traditionally received the bulk of attention. Other areas which may become objects of expanded interest are dietary patterns, exercise, the management of stress and the use of preventive health services. This will give rise to research concerned to identify more precisely the health effects of dietary patterns and of the impact of different types of stressors, and to examine the influence of the individual's immediate family, and of wider social pressures and resources, on consumption patterns and modes of responding to stress. Attempts to change individual behaviour through increasing knowledge in turn pose questions of the effectiveness of different types of intervention, such as community based programmes or programmes aimed at high risk groups, and of the appropriate setting and personnel for putting the message across.

Thirdly, there is likely to be shift in concern from regional inequalities in health service provision as these inequalities become gradually reduced through the RAWP formula (see Chapter 6), to the district level. This will involve identifying small areas and groups characterised by multiple deprivation, assessing their needs and designing and monitoring interventions. Looking beyond the health care system, the increasing emphasis on the social and environmental determinants of health is likely to result in greater attention being paid to the effects of working and living conditions on health. This may involve attempts to reduce needs for health care through improving housing conditions and encouraging supportive networks, and may lead to experiments to substitute for, and monitor the effects of, schemes to promote or strengthen the individual's social ties.

In addition to developments in the planning and provision of services are concerns regarding the aetiology and cause of disease.

---

* The examples given are merely illustrative rather than intended as a comprehensive list.

Whereas attention has traditionally concentrated on those illnesses, such as psychiatric disturbances, in which the possibility of a wholly biological aetiology is most questionable, recent evidence concerning the differential distribution among social groups of diseases such as asthma, bronchitis and cardiovascular disease suggests that greater attention will be paid to examining the role of social factors in establishing susceptibility of triggering their onset, as well as to the social nature of disease labels and factors influencing the diagnostic process. This in turn will link with, and complement, the growing historical research examining the emergence of specific disease categories (see Chapter 1).

Whereas doctors and policy makers are particularly influential in determining the perception of problems in the health field, research is also likely to respond increasingly to the interests and concerns of other groups as these become more strongly voiced. For example, nurses, health visitors, pharmacists and other groups of health service staff are likely to continue to develop new training programmes and seek new roles in attempts to enhance their professional status, and may thus become more active in sponsoring research to assist in these endeavours. Ethnic minorities may also increasingly draw attention to their particular needs and problems experienced as patients, while health service workers and community health councils may become more active in attempts to preserve jobs and resist cut-backs in resources, and thus contribute to the definition of problems for research. A notable example of the way in which pressure groups may stimulate research is provided by the women's movement, which has given rise to research examining the experience of women as patients and health service workers, patterns of morbidity among women and issues relating to pregnancy and childbirth. The recent emergence of this area of study is clearly illustrated by a comparison of research projects listed in the 1978 and 1982 Registers of Research in Medical Sociology in Britain. The four areas which increased their share of reported research over this period were pregnancy and childbirth (from 4.5 per cent to 9.8 per cent of total), nursing and related occupations (from 5.5 per cent to 9.8 per cent), women and health (no previous category to 4.7 per cent), and historical studies (no previous category to 4 per cent) (Field and Clarke, 1982). The pressures exerted by interest groups are important in directing attention to areas previously ignored and in serving to question general assumptions and social arrangements. Nevertheless, it is important that sociology does not become exclusively aligned with particular interest groups but instead uses its diverse interests and perspectives to increase the understanding of all participants in the health service.

The political and economic climate in the United States, together with concerns over the increasing costs of health services, suggests that future priorities for research will closely parallel those in Britain. However, there are likely to be differences in emphasis, reflecting the characteristics of the health care systems of the two countries. Issues which may receive greater attention in the United States include those concerning patient involvement in decisions regarding treatment when difficult choices need to be made and the cost implications may be considerable, as well as the broad field of medicine, ethics and the law. In other countries, research will similarly continue to reflect their particular circumstances and perceived problems, and will be influenced by the extent to which the specialism is linked to medicine or to sociology (Claus, 1982). For example, in Germany, as in Britain, the sociological study of health and medicine has traditionally had close links with the medical profession. In contrast, in France medical sociology developed largely outside medical institutions, and closely mirrors the general development of sociology in that country, with work on illness and disease (especially mental illness) being embedded in broader philosophical, psychological and socio-historical approaches. This influence of the social and economic context on the nature and direction of research, and hence of the development of the specialism, is not unique to sociology but also characterises the so called 'hard' or pure sciences, such as physics and chemistry. However, sociology is by its very nature more aware of the forces shaping knowledge. The relationship between ways of seeing the world and the strategies and techniques of research is thus of particular concern to its practitioners. As we have seen, the forces shaping medical knowledge and the dominant approach to health have formed a major area of research for medical sociologists (see Chapter 1).

Research with a more theoretical orientation often reflects, and is informed by, general sociological concerns, with examples being provided by much of the work on the medical profession (see Chapter 4), and on the hospital as a form of social organisation (see Chapter 5). However, research activity originally stimulated by policy questions also often gives rise to questions of a more theoretical nature. For example, the ageing of the population not only led to research describing the health needs, dependency levels, sources of support and social isolation of elderly people, but also to questions of a more theoretical nature, such as why elderly people are set apart in society and what are the social forces which create and reinforce their dependency. In other words, although largely becoming established as an area of research as a result of the policy implications of the increased proportion of elderly people, this research activity has in turn given rise to more fundamental questions. In this way, the issues currently identified as being of particular concern to policy makers are also likely to stimulate more theoretical analyses.

To a large extent the distinction between policy oriented and theoretical research is one which is promoted by funding bodies. This distinction can, however, be viewed as based on a mistaken assumption of the nature of the relationship between social science research and policy. This relationship is often seen in terms of an engineering approach or stimulus-response model, which views applied researchers as providing empirical data and offering prescriptive recommendations to solve specific problems. In contrast, the policy making process, although often viewed as characterised by a neat model of rational planning, is in reality generally based on bargaining and incrementalism, and influenced by the competing interests of the different groups involved in formulating and implementing policy decisions. Research thus generally forms only one input into a complex process, which limits its direct influence on resultant policies. Furthermore, rather than providing definitive answers to discrete problems, in practice the main contribution of social science research is often to increase our understanding and knowledge of issues, processes and relationships, and to clarify the implications of policy options. The impact of research thus generally corresponds to Weiss' (1971) enlightenment model, in which social science research permeates the policy making process not by specific projects but by its 'generalisations and orientations percolating through informed publics', so shaping the way in which people think about social issues. This enlightenment function is served not only by policy oriented research, but also by more theoretically oriented work. Furthermore, it does not depend on value consensus, with social criticism often forming a powerful force in serving to reorder goals and priorities. Although it is possible to identify examples of sociological research which conform to the stimulus-response model, such as the development of measures of health based on self care capacities and work identifying the characteristics of low users of preventive health services, in general the major contribution of research has been in terms of its enlightenment function. Notable examples of the impact of research on general thinking, and hence on shaping policies and practice, include work on stigmatising illness (see Chapter 2), on the effects of institutional organisation on patients (see Chapter 5) and on the social costs of family based care (see Chapter 8).

There appears to be some acceptance of the enlightenment model of social science research within government circles (Kogan and Henkel, 1983, p. 141). However, there is little to suggest that this view will become more widely accepted. This is turn is likely to have implications for the funding of research, for the problems of identifying the direct effects of research on policy lead to a questioning of its contribution, and difficulties of justifying expenditure on this activity in a period of economic stringency. Furthermore, with a few exceptions, the direct involvement of sociologists in policy development has been, and is likely to continue to be, fairly limited. This reflects both a lack of credibility of the discipline among many of those in positions of power, and more importantly, the preferences and perceived roles of many sociologists. The decision to stay out of the political arena is often associated with a belief in the importance of maintaining a 'value-free' academic stance, and thus of not being involved in choosing between policy options, or alternatively arises from a desire by those who favour a more critical approach not to be involved in promoting reformist measures (Marsland, 1983).

As far as general perspectives and research methods are concerned, it is likely that the field will continue to display its present diversity. One development may be a greater use of interpretive approaches to complement quantitative approaches to applied research. An increasingly favourable climate for small-scale, interpretive studies, despite the problems of generalising from small samples, is being provided by the recognition of the limitation of positivist, quantitative studies in contributing to our knowledge of the factors associated with low rates of take-up of preventive health services, and hence of the appropriate interventions. Research focusing on patients' beliefs and points of view is thus likely to be increasingly complemented by the application of an interpretive approach to the study of the decision making, attitudes and concerns of doctors and other health service staff.

Marxist and feminist theories have made a significant contribution to the health field over the past few years, and are likely to develop as more coherent perspectives as these approaches to health and medicine continue to expand. Although at variance with the dominant medical priorities and assumptions, they will continue to perform a powerful enlightenment function, and to provide a critique of moves towards greater private financing and privatisation of health services and of interventionist approaches to health. This question of the role of curative medicine, and of individualistic approaches more generally to improving the health of the population, is one which will be increasingly seen as a central issue facing both modern industrial countries and those of the Third World, and will result in greater attention being paid to the relationship between the socio-economic structure, health and health services.

Predicting new developments in sociological theory, which will in time filter down to work in the specialism, is difficult and clearly beyond the scope of this book. However, one general possibility is a move towards unifying what are now distinct perspectives. While some sociologists have tried to bridge differences and find underlying links between perspectives, it does not appear that a breakthrough to a single paradigm or perspective is likely or imminent. Instead, individual sociologists may become less closely identified with a single perspective, and perhaps increasingly employ both quantitative and interpretive approaches to study particular issues. There may also be attempts to integrate these approaches, following the work of Brown and Harris (see Chapter 8). A second general possibility is suggested by the observation that sociological concerns tend to be determined by prior social and political movements. Thus, the quiescent politics of the 1940s and 1950s saw the full flowering of functionalism with emphasis on consensus and stability, whereas the activist politics of the 1960s and 1970s has been accompanied by the entry of more radical and subjective elements into sociological theory. On this argument, a new realism may appear within the sociological theory of the 1980s and 1990s to accompany the tougher and more conservative mood of today, and may be accompanied by a decline in the influence of critical theories.

After the rapid expansion of the sociology of health and medicine in Britain over the last fifteen years and its establishment in both social science and medical departments, it is likely that, in view of the general retrenchment, the next decade will see a consolidation centred around established posts and institutions. This may also be a period characterised by increased tensions, as the specialism (or at least a segment of it) becomes more closely integrated into mainstream sociology, while at the same time funding bodies attempt to mould research more closely to their needs. This may pose particular problems for sociologists engaged in applied research. On the one hand they are required to maintain a close relationship with health professionals and contribute to health policy or clinical practice, and on the other hand to maintain a sociological perspective and approach to problems in the health field, which often involves uncovering and questioning unspoken assumptions. Furthermore, sociologists may increasingly form part of multi-disciplinary teams involved in evaluational studies and other work, which will lead to a greater emphasis on identifying the distinct contributions and roles of sociology, psychology and health economics. The broader task of bringing together the various social science disciplines to further our understanding of health, illness and medicine is one which so far has received relatively little attention, probably reflecting the concern of each discipline with its own development. However, both their increasing collaboration on applied research and greater maturity may lead to greater integration at a theoretical level.

Major challenges for the future reflect the dual emphasis of the sociology of health and medicine. Thus, there is a need to develop rigorous, theoretically based analyses of issues in the field of health and medicine, and contribute both to areas of general sociology, such as the sociology of organisations, the professions and the family, as well as responding more directly to the issues and concerns of health professionals and policy makers and collaborating with other social science disciplines in these endeavours. Perceptions of the value of sociology in the health field can also be increased by communicating more clearly to a wider audience the contributions of different sociological perspectives and methods of research, and by showing how the understandings and insights of sociology can assist in decisions concerning the organisation and delivery of health care, and more generally to the promotion of health and relief of suffering.

References

Claus, L. (1982) *The Growth of a Sociological Discipline*, vol. II: *Case Studies*: Sociological Research Institute, Leuven, Belgium

Field, D. and Clarke, B. (1982) *Medical Sociology in Britain: A Register of Research and Teaching*, The Camelot Press Ltd, Southampton

Kogan, M. and Henkel, M. (1983) *Government and Research: The Rothschild Experiment in a Government Department*, Heinemann Educational Books, London

Marsland, D. (1983) 'Sociologists and social policy', *Social Policy and Administration*, *17*, 4-15

Rothschild, Lord (1971) 'The organisation and management of government R and D', in *A Framework for Government Research and Development*, Cmnd 4184, HMSO, London

Weiss, C. (1981) *Using Social Research in Public Policy Making*, D.C. Heath, Lexington, Mass.

INDEX

Abel-Smith, B. 30
accident and emergency departments 87, 125-6
Acheson Report (Health Care, Inner London, 1981) 185
Ackerknecht, E.H. 30
Activities of Daily Living Index (ADL) 38
Age Concern 193
Akpom, C. 38
Alaszewski, A. 180
Albrow, M. 142
alcohol 18-19, 220, 228-9
alcoholism 22, 49, 60-1, 127, 271-2
Allsop, J. 195, 201
Alma Alta, Declaration of 204-5
alternative medicine 14, 280
Anderson, B. 11
Anderson, M. 248
Anderson, R. 60, 136
Anspach, R. 69
apothecaries 113-14
Arluke, A. 50
Armstrong, D. 29-33, 103-4, 119, 121
Artisans' Dwellings Act (1875) 173
asylums 152-5, 172
    see also psychiatric hospitals
Atkinson, P. 127
Ausubel, D. 26
authority in hospitals 142-4
    see also power
autonomy of medical profession 109-12, 176
    threats to 120-2
Ayurvedic medicine 12

Bales, R. 252
Balint, M. 32
Barber, B. 108
Barton, R. 158-9
Baruch, G. 146, 155
Bateman, J.F. 155
Baumann, B. 49
Becker, M.H. 81-2, 88
behaviour *see* deviance, illness behaviour
Belknap, I. 155

Bender, E.I. 267-9
Beral, V. 214
Bergner, M. 39
Berkman, L. 257
Bevan, A. 183, 193
Binney, V. 255
biomedicine 15-37
    effectiveness of 15-20
    harmful effects 20
Birley, J. 255-6
Bittner, E. 63, 150
Black, Sir D. 208
Black Report (Health Inequalities, 1980) 208, 216-17, 232-3
Blaney, H. 77
Blaxter, M. 28, 61, 91-2, 95-6, 219, 223, 225
blindness 58-9, 64
Bloor, M.J. 51, 124, 129, 131, 165
Boler, D. 264
Bonnerjea, L. 252
Booth, M. 214
Bowling, A. 118
Brenner, H. 228-30
British Medical Association (BMA) 179-80
Brotherston, J. 231
Brown, G.W. 148-9, 159, 222, 239, 255-6, 260-3, 286
Bucher, R. 143, 145, 150
Buffalo, M.D. 69
bureaucracy, hospital as 141-4
Butterfield, W. 77

Calnan, M. 83, 86-8, 96-7, 102, 126, 134, 137
cancer 54, 97
    breast 78, 96
    communication of diagnosis 130-1
    and occupation 221
    and stigma 56-7
capitalism
    and biomedicine 19, 34-7
    and health 227-9
    and the medical profession 112
    and mortality 228-30
    and poverty 226-7
    and state involvement in health

289